THEATRE COMES TO AUSTRALIA

Theatre
Comes to Australia

by

Eric Irvin

University of Queensland Press

ALSO BY ERIC IRVIN

A Soldier's Miscellany

Place of Many Crows, A Brief History of the Foundation of Wagga Wagga

Letters from the River

Early Inland Agriculture

A Suit for Everyman

© University of Queensland Press, St. Lucia, Queensland, 1971

Text set in Imprint 11/13 and printed on 100gsm Unglazed Woodfree

Printed and bound by Dai Nippon Printing Co. (International) Ltd., Hong Kong

National Library of Australia card number and ISBN 0 7022 0607 5

Designed by Cyrelle

Distributed by International Scholarly Book Services, Inc., Great Britain – Europe – North America

PREFACE

Since F.C. Brewer published his *The Drama and Music in New South Wales* in 1892 there have been several books published dealing with the history, or aspects of the history of the Australian theatre, which was first established in Sydney. Apart from their many inaccuracies, these books are not histories of the *theatre*. They are little more than lists of facts, dates, the names of theatres and of stage performers or "stars" of the day.

The theatre is a complex or organic whole. Its essence is participation. The theatre building; the auditorium; the stage and its mechanical aids; the stage-designers and scenepainters; the costumiers; the orchestra and its musicians; the performers, stagehands, machinists; the plays presented; the audience; the critics and their reactions — all these are *theatre*.

A historian writing on the Elizabethan period in English history would be foolhardy to ignore the Continental background to that period. The writer on the theatre in Australia who ignores the history of the English theatre is equally foolhardy. To write a history of the Australian theatre is, in this sense, to put the cart before the horse. Whether we have ever had an Australian theatre in the exact meaning of that phrase is doubtful, but there is not the slightest doubt that for one hundred years or more what we did have was the English theatre in Australia.

The Georgian was a long and distinctive period in English theatrical history. It may be said to lie between the years 1737 —

the year in which dramatic presentations were restricted to the "patent" theatres — and 1843, when the monopoly of the "patents" was abolished and all theatres were permitted to present plays. It was followed by the equally interesting but theatrically more adventurous period we know today as the Victorian. This Georgian theatre was brought to Australia in its entirety by convicted and free Englishmen. Its architecture, its stage equipment, its plays, acting styles, lack of organization and discipline, the irresponsibility of its actors, the peculiarities of its audiences — all were reproduced in Sydney down to the smallest detail. Allardyce Nicoll, in *Early Victorian England,* writes of the English theatre before Victoria came to the throne that

> it was difficult for a self-respecting, moral London middle-class citizen to take his family to the theatre. Quite apart from the physical inconvenience attendant on the unruly manners of the crowd, he would find the playhouse filled almost entirely by the young bloods and riff-raff of the lower middle-class society. Prostitutes walked the lobbies and spectators were liable to insult or abuse from uncontrollable drunkards

and he could have been describing Sydney during the brief but hectic reign of the first Theatre Royal, and the first five years of its successor, the Victoria.

The first play presented in Australia, "in a hut fitted up for the occasion" by convicts for one performance in 1789, was that most Georgian of comedies, Farquhar's *The Recruiting Officer.* Next came Sidaway's theatrical venture between 1796–1800, "in a miniature resemblance of a country theatre at home"; then the convict theatre at Emu Plains (ca. 1825–30) with its "tolerable fit-up of pit and boxes"; Barnett Levey's Theatre Royal (1832–38), and finally the first five years of the Royal Victoria's long reign as Sydney's principal theatre (1838–80).

While the history of the Georgian theatre in Sydney can be based on a great deal of factual evidence, some of it must of necessity be conjectural, and some a matter of logical assumption.

For instance, when we know that the general architectural plan for the smaller Georgian theatre — literally from one end of England to the other, in Scotland, Wales, Ireland, and even America — was that of a long rectangle, with the stage occupying about one half of the floor space and the auditorium the other; and that there was a pit (today's "stalls") with benches, and three sides of the auditorium were taken up by boxes in a construction very like the verandas which surround an inn courtyard, it is logical to assume that this was the kind of theatre built for Sidaway and for Levey, who were imitators, not innovators. In Sidaway's case, support for this assumption lies in the quotation above, "in a miniature resemblance of a country theatre at home". In Levey's, it lies in the dimensions and layout of the warehouse or building in which Greenway and Verge had a hand in designing and re-designing the theatre, and, as it will be seen, in further details gained from printed records, chiefly newspapers.

Of the stagestruck Barnett Levey, the prime figure in the establishment of the permanent theatre in Australia, and therefore "the father of the Australian theatre", we can assume from the existing evidence that in his youth in London he frequented the major theatres, Covent Garden and Drury Lane, as well as the lesser Coburg (later the Victoria, and then the "Old Vic."), Sadler's Wells, Lyceum, Surrey, and others. Here he no doubt first saw many of the plays later produced in his own theatre. There is every reason to believe, too, that in 1818, three years before he came to Australia as an emigrant, he saw Charles Mathews the Elder at the Lyceum in some of his famous "At Home" sketches, which Levey was later to imitate or plagiarize in his own "At Home" series first given in 1829, and again in 1832. Perhaps he even took part in some of London's theatrical activities as one of the minor backstage or front-of-house employees; or he may have played as an unpaid or paid amateur at one of the many English provincial theatres which thus encouraged the stagestruck. Certainly he knew a lot about the theatre of his time, and about the tribulations of a theatre manager, not all of which could have been gained from hearsay or at second hand.

And just as certainly the existing books on the theatre in Australia make no attempt to disentangle his mixed and multifarious business and theatrical undertakings, or to straighten out the muddle created by contemporary references to his theatre and the later misinterpretations to which these have led.

Theatre Comes to Australia covers a subject so far not treated in full — the foundation of the permanent theatre in Australia. From Barnett Levey's pioneering efforts stemmed the first theatres in Melbourne and Adelaide, and all the Sydney theatres which have succeeded his over the years. The story could not have been written if Sydney did not possess such a remarkable collection of Australiana as that housed in the Mitchell Library. I owe to the unfailing courtesy and help of the librarian and staff of this library, of the Dixson Library, and the Public Library of New South Wales, a very great debt. Thanks are also due to the Archives Office of New South Wales, who granted me access to the Colonial Secretary's letters, and to the librarians and staff of the Central Library, Manchester; the Birmingham Public Libraries; the Folger Shakespeare Library, Washington, U.S.A.; and the Harvard College Library, Massachusetts, U.S.A., who patiently replied to my many queries related to the subject of this book. Valuable information has also been gained from the publications of the Society for Theatre Research in London, from the Society's quarterly journal, *Theatre Notebook,* and from the books listed in the bibliography at the end of the present work.

Some of the material in this book has already been published in articles in *Shakespeare Survey 22* (Cambridge University Press), *Theatre Notebook, Opera* (London), and *Quadrant, 20th Century, Australian Literary Studies, Masque,* and *Architecture in Australia.* Acknowledgments are made to the publishers of all these journals.

E.I.
1969

CONTENTS

LIST OF ILLUSTRATIONS

1

A Very Snug Company

On 25 July 1821 the convict ship "John Bull" left the port of Cork in Ireland with a complement of eighty Irish women convicts and twenty-two free passengers, bound for Sydney. The free passengers were loosely described in Surgeon-Superintendent William Elyard's journal as "women and children relatives of convicts". Most of them may have been, but surviving records prove that at least two of them were not—John Lawrie, a soldier, with his wife and five children, and Barnett Levey, late of Whitechapel, London. Surgeon-Superintendent Elyard's slip over the twenty-two "relatives" is perhaps understandable. The convict women were in his sole care, and the crew and free passengers were in the care of the captain, William Corlett. Elyard, knowing he had to deal with some "fly" characters among his charges, gave his attention to them alone, and it is they who figure almost solely in the daily account he kept of the voyage of the "John Bull" from Cork to Sydney.

Elyard obviously expected trouble to develop with the women, and it was not very long before he got it. They were brought on board at Cork on 14 July, and ten days later they complained of the provisions "in a riotus manner". A worrier, Elyard made careful inquiries and found they indeed had cause for complaint, for the cooks had run out of fresh water and had cooked the women's beef ration in sea-water.

As the voyage progressed there was further trouble. The women were allowed on deck each day if it was fine, while their mattresses and quarters were aired. This they saw as a wonderful opportunity for striking up forbidden friendships with members of the ship's crew. Even before the voyage started some of the women had rifled the hold and stolen bread, which they handed out among themselves. They had also to be watched for other reasons. Mary Down, for instance, was detected trying to smuggle to her quarters a piece of smouldering rag with which to keep her short clay pipe alight during the night watches. So it was that first one woman was reprimanded for being found below with the men, and then, about eight days later, no less than three of the women were found below. The three were reprimanded and locked up.

The next disturbance occurred between one of the women and a seaman, who were caught "fighting" on the forecastle. The seaman was punished by the captain, and the woman was confined to the coal-hole "with a collar" for two hours. By this time Captain Corlett and Superintendent Elyard were keyed to a higher pitch than perhaps was warranted. As a result, before the voyage had been completed the steward had been flogged, the second mate, in whose cabin a woman had secreted herself for a whole day, had been thrown into irons, and the chief mate and two seamen had been wounded in a fight on deck, after which they, too, were put in irons. Corlett and Elyard were convinced by all this that mutiny was inevitable, and wore themselves out with anxiety and long hours of watching. One night they sat up, both armed, until 2 A.M., and then again from 4:30 A.M., but the expected trouble did not develop.

Barnett Levey must have watched all this from the sidelines, but if he ever spoke of the voyage and its excitements after arriving in Sydney, no record of this exists. All that is known of this period in his life is that he embarked at Cork for Sydney, where he was to join his brother Solomon, who in his six short years in the colony had already become a very wealthy man. Barnett was then about twenty-two years of age, and Solomon about four

2

years older. Both were short men, of not very attractive physical appearance, two of five sons born to Lion and Deborah Levey in the Jewish East End of London.

When Barnett Levey first stepped on the wharf at Sydney Cove on 21 December 1821 he moved from the old world into a world that was new in more senses than one. He arrived at a time when one of the most notable eras in the Colony of New South Wales was drawing to a close, and an era in which he was to play a public if not very significant part was about to begin. Only a few days before his arrival Governor Lachlan Macquarie had said farewell to the colony which, he said, he had found in a state of rapid deterioration but was leaving with commerce revived, credit restored, good roads and bridges, and the occupants, by comparison, happy and opulent. When Macquarie first came to the colony in 1810 it had a population of about 11,000. During his period of office this grew to nearly 30,000. At his farewell ceremony the commission appointing Sir Thomas Brisbane Governor of the colony in Macquarie's stead had been read.

Macquarie had been recalled largely because of the machinations of an anti-Macquarie party, which did not like his "soft" attitude to the emancipists, and of the unfavourable findings of one Commissioner John Thomas Bigge. With this Commissioner's brother-in-law secretary, that "wine merchant in gaiters", Thomas Hobbes Scott, Levey was to be involved within a few years. But at the moment of being greeted by Solomon, neither the voyage out nor the distant future could have been in his mind, only the pleasure of seeing his brother again after six years.

Apart from the glare, the heat, the bustle, and the colour of the strange colony to which he had come to make his home, in many respects Barnett found this new world to be a miniature London. It was certainly every bit as English as London — less crowded, and with a lower and more open appearance, but the people were England itself and most of them had walked the streets of London at one time or another. The clothes, the accents,

3

the values were much the same, yet in many respects the place was as new as a colony on the moon. The climate, for one thing; and the bush, for another. There was a hot sun in a sky of such intense blueness that it seemed unreal, and round about the town and as far as the eye could see was bush — grey-green, dry, stiff, and forbidding. The Colony of New South Wales was a small civilization fighting a vast wilderness.

The town seemed to lie in a valley between two "cliffs". One of these he was soon to know as the Domain, the other as "The Rocks". He had seen from the deck of the ship that the town was made up of alternate clusters of buildings, open spaces, and bush. In fact the town was hedged in on three sides by what was to him a forest, and on the fourth by the waters of the harbour. In the "valley" of Sydney Cove itself all the buildings were huddled together in a "pack", while in the centre was a small stream which flowed into tanks cut from the sandstone to provide Sydney's water supply. Beyond the cove or wharf area the town opened out into broad, unpaved streets with brick and stone buildings, houses, cottages, and the ramshackle house-substitutes known as skillies. Further out, at odd intervals in the prevailing grey-green, could be seen the gables and chimneys of more substantial private homes. Far in the distance, the boundary to human eyesight, lay the brooding rises of the Blue Mountains.

In his work for his brother at his warehouse at 72 George Street (on the site now occupied by Dymocks Pty. Ltd.) Barnett met and had dealings with all classes of people; with convicts and free emigrants, with civil service and army officials, with currency lads and lasses, emancipists and exclusives. Here, too, he met with visual and vocal evidence of the two main beliefs prominent in the society of the time. One had been expressed by Governor Macquarie, that once a man had paid the legal penalty for his crime or misdemeanour he had also paid his debt to society and was once again a free man. The other was the largely opportunist belief that once a convict always a convict; that he who had erred once merited nothing other than social ostracism and physical

4

slavery. So it was that Levey came to learn that the people of the colony were divided into two sometimes fluid, sometimes distinct parties, the emancipists and the exclusives: those who had erred and earned their freedom, and the "pure Merinos" who had no traffic whatever with convict or ex-convict unless the scales were weighted heavily in their favour. Those who had not erred (i.e. had not been "sent" to the colony) must, it was reasoned, be the superiors of those who had, and therefore all those who had been or were in process of being punished should recognize this superiority. The emancipists, freed men who had helped to build the colony, had quite different ideas. Nor was it long before Barnett discovered that while the arbitrary division which split the colony down the centre seemed clear enough, in daily life it was not always possible or practical to offer rigid support to one side only. There were losses of one kind or another no matter which side one favoured. A free man who sympathized wholly with those who had been freed or were still in bond had to do some re-thinking when one or other "lifted" his personal property. His only recourse then was an appeal to the exclusives, representing the machinery of the law, for protection or retribution. Daily intercourse under these conditions was only possible if one had, as Barnett had, the ability alternately to help and to use both sides, to play one against the other so as to achieve a desired end.

It was a close-knit, homogeneous society, constantly at the boil, today's friend tomorrow's enemy, but the significant point was that friend and foe knew all that was to be known about each other. As in the country town today, any man's move away from the usual or the accepted was immediately known to everybody. When Sydney's newspapers, the *Gazette,* or *Monitor,* or *Australian* wrote about Levey and his activities it was not from the magisterial heights of the modern metropolitan press that they set their sights, but eye to eye with Levey himself, whom their editors and proprietors knew personally as a customer and fellow colonial.

Barnett worked for his brother for about four years. Whether this was the purpose for which he had come to Sydney, whether he came merely to gain enough experience to branch out on his own, or whether Solomon had hoped to find in him the partner he needed cannot be determined from existing records. But whatever real or tacit arrangement may have existed between them, whatever hopes Solomon may have had of his brother's business ability, it was Daniel Cooper, not Barnett, whom Solomon later took into partnership. But he seems at the same time to have made adequate financial provision for Barnett so as to help him on to his feet. Perhaps the true story is that Barnett really intended to strike out on his own and not as an employee or partner of his brother's. But whatever his original plan may have been, it obviously included his brother's monetary assistance.

Barnett did not lack success in these early years. His first six years in the colony were, financially and socially, the most successful and certainly the quietest of his career. In the 1822 Muster he described himself as a merchant, which he was intermittently or by what could better be described as fits and starts. At the same time he was making other moves, playing other parts that were to prove, in the long run, of more significance though not necessarily of more benefit to him and his future.

His rise to wealth and prominence was so sudden as to indicate that Solomon's hand was behind it, and it proved too sudden for his good. For Barnett's was not a mercantile mind. He could, and he did, go through all the motions, and perhaps if he had had his opportunities at some other time than that in which they fell to him he might have got away with his flitting from one project to another, his plans for bigger this and better that, which all seemed wonderful in prospect but were somehow burnt to ashes in the fire of his misapplied energy. Barnett seems to have been a man desperately trying to fill a role similar to that of his elder brother, because he believed it would bring him power and money and was expected of him, but secretly dedicated to another kind of life; privately, when he was able to be, another kind of person entirely.

For Barnett was a theatre lover, and saw himself as the Charles

6

Mathews of the new colony. Theatre was a passion with him,
and with this passion went its usual accompaniments: a convivial
and engaging surface personality, an over-optimistic view of what
was possible, grandiose conceptions so far removed from the
requirements of reality that the few possible of realization had
to be pared down until they were almost unrecognizable, and a
facility in making both friends and enemies. He had a natural
ability as a mimic or impersonator, restricted to caricatures of
easily-mocked national idiosyncracies such as a Frenchman's
mannered politeness and ludicrous attempts to speak English; a
Jew's lisping, guttural mispronunciations; a Cockney's chirpy
cheekiness; a farmer's slow, inarticulate drawl, and the parsimony
and "strange" accent of a Scotsman — theatrical and literary
clichés with which to amuse simple minds. With this and his
ability to sing comic songs suitable to polite and not so polite
society, "little Barnett Levey" was soon a welcome guest at all
kinds of male gatherings where the grog was unlimited, the
society nostalgic for former times, and the entertainer was
momentarily king.

Following one of these "good fellow" gatherings, towards the
end of 1824, a letter was sent to the *Australian* which caused the
editor to acknowledge its receipt without actually publishing it.
The letter advocated the immediate establishment of a theatre
in Sydney, and suggested a means of financing the venture. Both
the style in which this letter is written, and the share system it
suggests, point indisputably to Barnett Levey as its author.

The *Australian* said in extenuation of its refusal to publish the
letter that its "orthographical arrangement. . . is so perfectly at
variance with common usage, that we are compelled to forego
the opportunity of letting it speak for itself". In the face of this
excessively polite way of saying that the letter was misspelled and
ungrammatical, Barnett Levey did the next best thing. He got
somebody else to write another letter in his name, or rather pen-
name, with a better (though not much) "orthographical arrangement". There were to be many occasions in the future when he

7

would have to call on someone else to pen his chaotic thoughts for him, and one of his chief penmen was to be his lawyer, William Charles Wentworth.

This time the *Australian* played the game and printed both the second and the first letter. But even the second letter bears the unmistakable Levey stamp, despite its more orthographical arrangement.

Sir: Your non-insertion of my letter, in consequence of the orthographical arrangements, must be considered as lame excuse. The brightest ornament in a community is a Free Press, and its Editor, who will give fair publicity to argumentation. If you, Sir, as an editor, receive a letter from a correspondent, wherein a few words in spelling do not exactly suit your common usage, prudence at least might induce you to correct them. We are not all of a College. In number there are six; namely, Eaton, Oxford, Cambridge, to country gaol, the stock, and the gallows. I am not a member of any. I therefore did not receive a collegian education. In your animadversion upon my letter, last week, you do me an act of injustice; namely, I therein said that I had been in company with ten or twelve gentlemen, eight of whom offered to be their one hundred pounds as shares; but you, Mr. Editor, endeavoured to make it appear that only eight hundred pounds could be collected; and that the sum would go but very little way. But might you not as well have said, that if eight hundred pounds could be collected among twelve gentlemen, what might be expected from a respectable body of gentlemen and inhabitants, in shares of fifty pounds and one hundred pounds.
I do not wish to be angry with so valuable a member in society, as the Editor of the *Australian*. I trust, sir, that you will give publicity to the letter sent you last week; and hope, at the same time, that if you find a few words not rightly spelled (it being so very grievous to you), you will be kind enough to correct them. Pray, for the future, Mr. Editor, do not criticise on us poor scrawls. I am neither poet, lawyer, nor schoolmaster; but, by giving publicity to this, and my letter last week, will greatly oblige a friend to Australia. *An Amateur.*

8

Beneath this the *Australian* published Levey's first letter.

Sir: If worth a place in your valuable Paper, I beg leave to recommend to some abler writer than myself a proposal for the erection of a theatre. Tis not long since, that I were in company with ten gentlemen; a question arose conserning a place of amusement; eight gentlemen, then in company, offered to be one hundred pounds each, if a place of that sort was establisht in shears. I have not the least dought that, if you, Mr. Editor, was to propose anything of the kind, that it would meat with a very liberal incouragement. We want a little intertainment — our currency lasses would be very much joyed at such an establishment. A very snug company might be procured even in this part of the world, by a little existance of a few amatures, who are only waiting for an opportunity. — Publicity to this will greatly oblidge a friend to Australia. *Amature.*

This letter was followed by an editorial footnote asking the letter writer's pardon for the fact that the editor had not taken the liberties suggested with the misspelled words. "In the next communication he sends us, if necessary, we will attempt to make it 'suit our common usage'", the note concluded. Levey did not write on this particular subject again, but examples of his twisted syntax, with most of the spelling errors corrected, were for some years afterwards to be seen in all Sydney newspapers, and by way of "puffs" and play and other advertisements, even on its posts and buildings.

His letters were straws in the wind. Levey knew the Sydney people lacked, and many of them felt the need for, public entertainment of some kind at night. He had also found out at some of his convivial gatherings that although Sydney lacked a theatre it did not lack "amatures" — capable actors and singers who were eager and willing to supply Sydney's theatrical needs. All that was required was enough money to set the whole thing going, and hence the suggestion in his letters that if Sydney wanted a theatre badly enough the money with which to build it could be raised by means of fifty and one hundred pound shares. Yet there were no takers. The enthusiasm of the eight gentlemen who had offered to "be one hundred pounds each" did not survive the last glass of grog. The *Australian* did not refer to the matter again, and there was no further correspondence. If the establishment of a theatre in Sydney *was* discussed, it was discussed privately. But that Levey's letters were read with interest in at least two quarters became evident first in May 1825, and then in the following August.

In 1819, faced with a bigger convict population than could be used or adequately controlled in Sydney, the Governor decided to establish a government farm of about 2,000 acres at Emu Plains, about 36 miles from Sydney. In this way, it was hoped, work could be found for the surplus convicts in an area where they would be out of touch with the many temptations offered by Sydney. Some of these convicts were from time to time assigned to, or farmed out for daily work on the "Regentville" estate of the pleasure and entertainment loving Sir John Jamison, across the river from the Emu Plains farm. Sir John loved nothing better than to play host to his Sydney and local friends, for whose entertainment he gave dinner parties and plain and fancy-dress balls whenever occasion offered. To help to entertain his guests he was not above calling upon whatever talent was available among his large body of servants, or the convicts at Emu Plains. That some of them not only had talent but were determined to exploit it was made apparent before long, when, with the permission of the Governor of the time, Sir Thomas Brisbane, the convicts built and equipped a theatre.

The theatre was opened on 16 May 1825 with a "triple bill" — *The Mock Doctor; or, The Dumb Lady Cured* (1732); *Barissa; or, The Hermit Robber* (possibly *The London Hermit,* 1793), and *Bombastes Furioso* (1810).* The Governor attended at least one of these performances.

Ten days passed before news of this theatre appeared in the Sydney press, and then the *Australian* announced that there

*Year (in brackets) of first London performance.

10

appeared to be a greater variety of pleasure and entertainment in the bush than Sydney residents dreamed of. The "good people" of Emu Plains had a theatre with its decorations, actors, and very respectable "toll-lollish" performances. "To say that we hope the good example set at Emu Plains will be imitated in Sydney, would be downright affectation", the *Australian* concluded, "for we have indeed no hopes of any such thing."

The Emu Plains theatre was no more than a rough hut transformed by the settlement's enthusiasts into a theatre. It was largely the result of the ability and ingenuity of one man. The hut was made of the usual timber slabs with a bark roof, the interstices between the slabs being filled with mud to keep out the weather. The interior was whitewashed with pipe-clay, and, like the theatres at home, divided into boxes and pit, each with its rude wooden benches.

Canvas for the scenes and the front curtain came from bags, clothes, bed-ticking, and anything else available. Costumes were made up from oddments of cast-off clothes given by farm officials, military men, and the wives of settlers and others outside the farm. Scenery and curtain were painted with pipe-clay, charcoal, and coloured earths. One convict, a versatile tinsmith, made the lamps and candlesticks, while oil and candles were obtained from the rations issued to officials of the establishment. The same tinsmith ingeniously fashioned most of the properties, jewellery and decorations, arms, and even the instruments of the four-piece orchestra — a fife, drum, tambourine, and fiddle — all made of tin. The full lighting for the performance was from four small lamps and twelve mould candles. "Seen at night, and from a distance, they appeared in the eyes of most of the beholders to be quite faultless."*

At the performance on 11 July at Emu Plains the convicts presented *The Lying Valet* (1741) and a play they called *The Welder's Wedge-Box; or, Vulcan Disappointed*. This last was possibly Charles Dibdin's *Poor Vulcan* (1788), renamed by the

Ralph Rashleigh (see Bibliography) chap. xii, pp. 92–96.

players for some reason of their own. Neither the titles nor the plots of plays were considered sacrosanct in the eighteenth and early nineteenth centuries. In the audience this night were Sir John Jamison, Thomas Jamison, John Blaxland, Henry Cox, and other people well known in Sydney. Sir John, indeed, found these performances so pleasurable that at the conclusion of the July performance he sent the convict actors a ten dollar note, and on several occasions provided them with wine with which to ease their parched throats before, during, and after a performance. The Chief Justice, Mr. Francis Forbes, also made a point of making monetary and other gifts to the convict actors whenever he visited the theatre as Sir John's guest.

Press reports and letters dealing with the Emu Plains theatre continued to cause a spate of comment in Sydney on the good fortune of the people living in the neighbourhood of Emu Plains, and on the backwardness of Sydney. Why was not something being done about establishing a theatre in Sydney, everybody asked. As usual, everybody knew the answer. While all wanted a theatre, or said they did, all were prepared to leave its actual establishment to somebody else.

That "somebody" in due course came forward. The next month James Underwood, a successful Sydney merchant and distiller, announced that he was about to have a theatre built adjoining the offices of the Sydney *Gazette,* facing George Street. It was expected the building would take about twelve months to complete.

From Barnett Levey there was not a word.

2

The Momus–Faced Favourite

Solomon Levey bought his George Street property for £400 in 1817, two years after he had arrived in Sydney to serve a seven years' sentence for being partner to the alleged theft of a chest of tea — total value £35 8s.8d. Two years after buying the property he was granted a free pardon. In the same year, 1819, he became a shareholder "proprietor" in the Bank of New South Wales, established by Governor Macquarie in the year of Solomon's arrival.

As a merchant and trader in all kinds of stores he soon became a leading member of the group of wealthy emancipists who profited by their earlier mistakes and managed to turn original misfortune into ultimate success and gain. He became a ship-owner and ship-builder, and launched sealing expeditions. He bought and sold wheat, and had a share in a mill which produced flour from his wheat which was later baked into bread and sold at his Brisbane Warehouse. He dealt in real estate, cattle, household, farm, and pastoral stores — in any commodity, in fact, that could be bought or sold. With it all he became a public figure, a fighter for civil rights (including the right of emancipists to serve on a jury), and a public benefactor with frequent generous gifts to all kinds of charities and appeals by religious bodies.

In 1825 Solomon disengaged himself from earlier partners, William Hutchinson and Samuel Terry, and went into permanent partnership with Daniel Cooper to found the firm of Cooper and

Levey, with its headquarters at the Waterloo Stores in Market Street. Each partner brought £30,000 into the enterprise. In 1826 the firm built new stores, a stone building of five floors, each one capable of housing 2,000 to 3,000 bushels of grain.

As each year passed Solomon's wealth and influence grew, a large part of it attributable to his shrewd business sense and his ability to get on with the warring factions in the Sydney of his day. Apparently Barnett, dazzled by his brother's success, tried not only to emulate but also, somewhat foolishly, to outdo him.

The Cooper and Levey partnership was formed in February 1825 when the partners bought the Lachlan and Waterloo Mills for £4,700. The deeds of partnership, made out by W.C. Wentworth, were signed on 6 May 1825. This year was also an important one for Barnett Levey. It is surely something more than coincidence that a little more than a month after this deed of partnership was signed, Barnett should suddenly achieve sufficient wealth to advertise in June that he would open on 4 July his own cheap wholesale and retail warehouse at the premises formerly occupied by his brother at 72 George Street. He was careful to point out that all orders must be addressed to B. Levey, "as otherwise mistakes might arise", and to add that he would take grain, pork, or fat bullocks as payment for goods, at the market price. This advertisement appeared on 23 June, and the next day he opened an account with the Bank of New South Wales, of which he, too, later became a shareholder "proprietor".

On 25 June he further consolidated his position by his marriage to a Miss Wilson, daughter (or step-daughter) of Mr. Josephson of Pitt Street. They were married at St. John's Church, Parramatta, by the Venerable Archdeacon Thomas Hobbes Scott. The following month Levey was granted a licence as an auctioneer and appraiser. Thus, from somewhere or other he suddenly obtained enough money to open his own warehouse, to marry, and to look forward to a successful mercantile and domestic future as the result of his own labours.

The following year Solomon left for England, and Barnett was really on his own. But an indication of a continuing link with Solomon is contained in an advertisement of Barnett's in December 1825, asking for the return of books borrowed from Mr. Solomon Levey, which revealed that a "fresh supply may be had". This advertisement was one of the first to contain that strange touch of humour for which Levey's later advertisements were to become notable. A listing of some of the books out on loan concluded: ". . . Smollet's works, *Ivanhoe, Tales of the Times, Paradise Lost*— so are the books until found by B. Levey".

Barnett's press advertisements, in fact, some of them obviously penned under great stress of emotion or alcohol, are a revelation in themselves. Some, like his letters, were so capably written as to point to the fact that they were written for him. Others, such as the following, bore the unmistakable Levey stamp.

Rupees 2*s*. 6*d*. each. In consequence of some busy body, with no good intent, sending the Bellman about town, on Thursday last, to cry down the Rupees, as only worth 2*s*. 3*d*., the undersigned has deemed it necessary, in issuing Rupee notes, as it must be admitted, from the great quantity that are in circulation, that they are a complete burthen on the public; and as paper is easily conveyed to and from town, and the Bank of New South Wales not taking them as deposits, the undersigned will either take them for goods, or as deposits, and will give notes to the said amount, and will pay the same on Immediate demand. Good tea at £7 12*s*. 6*d*. per chest. — Cash, Rupees at 2*s*. 6*d*. each; all other goods at original prices. Rupees taken at the same rate.

Indian rupees were among the many foreign coins used as currency in colonial Sydney until, in 1825, the British government passed legislation to provide for "sterling" currency, adopted by the Bank of New South Wales in 1826. In this advertisement Levey was telling all and sundry that, again like brother Solomon, he was in the banking business and was prepared to issue his own notes.

In 1826 the pace for Barnett Levey became a little more hectic. In addition to looking after his new commercial interests, and advising unsuccessful publicans who had had a renewal of their

15

licence refused to become dealers by buying the necessary bulk supplies of Madeira and Cape white wines, porter, gin, rum, and brandy from him, early in the year he attended a meeting called to establish a third Sydney bank, and a meeting of the Bank of New South Wales as one of its "proprietors". In March the newspapers carried some advertisements of his, couched in the usual quaint phraseology, calling for 150,000 feet of cedar, 80,000 feet of floorboards, a quantity of bluegum plank and 100,000 bricks. A little more than a month later it was revealed that Barnett was raising a "handsome building of five floors" at the rear of his house in George Street, to be 80 feet long and 28 feet wide. This building, he announced, was to be known as the Colchester Warehouse, named in honour of Lord Colchester. Nevertheless, with this building going forward, and with all his mercantile interests to be watched, Barnett still found time to take his place as one of the foremost supporters of a committee formed to promote concerts for the entertainment of Sydney's music lovers.

The Emu Plains theatre was still active, and a source of envy in Sydney. Construction of Underwood's theatre was delayed by labour shortages, and in the meantime Levey and a few kindred spirits had hit on this concert plan to fill the need for night entertainment. The Sydney Amateur Concert Society was formed, and gave its first concert early in June. Here the works of Mozart, Corelli, Rossini, Weber, and such contemporary composers as William Shield, J. Hook, Henry Bishop, John Stevenson, and Joseph Mazzinghi were performed before an Australian audience for the first time.

The first concert was held in the long room at Hankinson's Freemasons Tavern in George Street, and was bolstered by the addition of instrumentalists from the regimental bands of the Buffs and the 57th, who provided the orchestral items. There were in addition a number of instrumental and vocal solos, all by amateurs. Barnett Levey, apparently, did not take part in this first concert but was active in the remaining seven given during the year.

16

The newspapers gave a mixed reception to Levey's efforts in the second concert, which with subsequent concerts was held in the schoolroom above the Court House in Castlereagh Street. The *Monitor*, adopting the highly moral tone it deemed necessary in dealing with the arts, mentioned at the start of its report that "according to a barbarous but ancient custom, a foolish comic song was introduced", and concluded, "Mr. Levey sung the comic song with great address and real good-nature." The *Australian* reported that a comic song was sung "inimitably, and with a just and natural fund of humour, by an amateur". It added that the cry of "encore" when the song concluded "was universal". Said the *Gazette*: "A comic song, *The Beautiful Boy*, given with the most irresistible drollery by Mr. B. Levey, was applauded to the very echo. . ."

Nor did Levey restrict himself to comic songs, for at one of these concerts he took part in a duet which the newspapers thought to be something beyond his powers, but was nevertheless enjoyed by the audience.

At subsequent concerts his comic songs apparently drew such applause as to earn the disapproval of the *Monitor*, on moral and aesthetic grounds. But the *Gazette* scaled the peaks of acclaim when it described him as "the Momus-faced favourite of Australia". The *Monitor* felt it could not join in the "raptures" created by these comic songs. It thought the Concert Society was not playing fair in allowing "pantomime and farce" to intrude on the concerts. "However, the stream is against us and we cannot stem it. We will not, however, be carried down by it, but edge aside into a neutral bay." And later the *Australian* criticized Levey, not so much for the indelicacy of the songs he sang as for making too much of whatever inferences they allowed. These, it seems, were presented with an expressiveness too marked, too vulgar, and without sufficient humour to compensate.

Levey's song repertoire was not an extensive one, as he sang the same song sometimes at as many as three of the concerts. While these were not always named in the reports, "The Beautiful

Boy", "Caleb Quotem," "The Mail Coach," and a recitative and air, or scena, from *The Wood Demon* are those most frequently mentioned. Regarding the last, one report said that without some kind of aid the audience could not possibly understand the scope of the piece. This is not surprising, as in this song Levey presented for some reason known only to himself a scene from what was a favourite melodrama in England from 1811 onwards, *One O'Clock; or, The Knight and the Wood Demon,* which was practically unknown to the Sydney concert audience. With "The Mail Coach", however, they felt more at home. This had a speaking part in which "a lively portraiture of chubby landlords, bustling waiters, bawling, complaining, contented and discontented travellers, sturdy coach drivers cracking jokes with the girls they passed, and all the hustle and bustle of a coach journey" were painted. Levey was able to present these "portraits" in a manner at once recognizable to his audience, and to their immediate enjoyment.

The first few concerts were attended by army, navy, and civil officers, magistrates, and members of the "most respectable families" in Sydney. As they progressed the Lieutenant Governor, the Sheriff, the Clerk of the Council, and other dignitaries also attended. Towards the last of them Mrs. Darling, "the amiable consort of His Excellency the Governor", Mrs. Macleay, the Misses Macleay, the Misses Blaxland ("the blooming daughters of Australia"), Chief Justice Forbes and others "condescendingly patronised the laudable efforts made by the Amateur Committee".

Intermission during the concerts gave the opportunity for that social concord on which the newspapers said they set such store. The female and the younger members of both sexes in the audience consumed cakes, jellies, and fruit, while the hardier males fortified themselves for the second half of the entertainment with brimming glasses of port wine negus, and foaming bottled porter (perhaps supplied by Barnett Levey).

It seems that one of the main reasons why these concerts were not continued into 1827 was that by the end of 1826 the performers had exhausted their meagre repertoire and were repeating themselves, a fact which the newspapers were not slow to note, and which accounted for the fall in attendances towards the end of 1826.

But the concerts again revived interest in Sydney's lack of night life, and, as the *Monitor* duly reported, resulted in what it called the formation of a social compact among the good folk of Sydney, many of whom started to give balls, suppers, and other convivial entertainments. "Sociability is hostile to malignity, selfishness, and slander," the newspaper hopefully commented, "and therefore we are glad to hear of its extension." Among those who thus entertained their friends were Mr. and Mrs. Barnett Levey, who on 4 July gave a ball and supper to celebrate the christening at St. Philip's Church that afternoon of their first child, a daughter. The gathering was held at the Freemasons Tavern in the room used for the first concert, and forty couples or more formed into two sets "to set the enlivening country dance afloat". After an adjournment to the supper room, dancing was resumed, and "rosy morn peeped o'er the eastern hills ere the joyous group had bade their kind host and hostess good morning".

Three days after this ball the *Monitor* announced that Barnett Levey, in the extensive pile of buildings now under construction, intended to fit up an area of 80 feet "for the purpose of dramatic representation". The newspaper added that the whole of the building, which was expected to be completed in four months, would exceed the Waterloo Stores in height by 30 feet.

This was not a sudden decision on Levey's part, but one which had obviously been with him some time, and it was carried into effect only after it was learnt that Underwood's projected theatre was unlikely to materialize. In digging the foundations for the theatre Underwood's workmen had caused the partial collapse of the *Gazette* warehouse, and he faced a court case for damages as a result.

Those who were in the habit of reading their newspaper carefully, and had a memory for detail, were not at all surprised to read of Levey's intention to include a theatre in his new building. What did surprise them was the *Monitor's* statement that Levey's building was to be 30 feet higher than the Waterloo Stores. They began to put two and two together, and came up with almost every answer but the right one. The Waterloo Stores were five floors high; Levey's building was also to be of five floors. What was going to take up the extra 30 feet?

Only Barnett Levey could have thought of it. Some few days after the *Monitor* report the *Australian* provided the amazing solution to the puzzle. Levey planned to build right on top of his five-floor warehouse a flour mill complete with huge revolving sails, and not even the derision or disbelief of the whole of Sydney would deter him. This was only the first of a series of grandiose schemes which, had they succeeded as planned, would have made Barnett Levey one of the most remarkable men of his period in Sydney.

But there were those who doubted Levey's ability to carry out some of his schemes, let alone their wisdom, and who were not satisfied with the prospect of a Sydney theatre conducted by him. About fourteen or fifteen of them met on 21 August to provide him with his first real sign of opposition. The meeting discussed the possibility of building a theatre in Sydney, and decided tentatively that £5,000 towards the cost might be raised by means of £25 shares. This, they reasoned, would provide enough money to build a theatre to seat 1,500 persons. At a further meeting the following week the group was almost ready to proceed with the launching of its scheme, and even had for consideration plans and drawings of the proposed theatre, when something was suggested which nobody, and certainly not Levey, had thought of. To prevent a possible collapse of their plans it was suggested that the Governor's sanction should be sought first, in the form of a memorial to him "with a score or two of the names and surnames of some of the most monied and otherwise respectable members of the community drawn out in formidable array at the foot of it".

With two rival theatres mooted in a town where formerly there had not even been one, the strait-laced *Monitor* did not know where it stood. It feared that a theatre of some kind was inevitable, and voiced a strange mixture of disapproval and disgruntled approval the following week.

We believe a theatre will finally be erected in Sydney. As Christians we feel it will only be the exchange of the grosser vice of drunkenness for the vanity and froth of false sentiment, and the refinements of voluptuous pleasure. The people will improve in refinement, but continue equally immoral. Still, a mind cultivated, though equally vicious, has a preponderance, in our estimation, over brutal ignorance.

This paragraph, and an article published in the *Gazette* on 13 September, seem to have been sufficient to force the rival group to reconsider their decision, for nothing more was heard of their proposed memorial to the Governor, his reaction to it if it was sent, or their theatre. The *Gazette* next published the text of two talks on the moral tendency of the stage, delivered at Newcastle-on-Tyne, it said, by the Reverend J. Bromley, on 5 and 12 March 1823. The talks dealt with the "profane and scandalous" play *Tom and Jerry* (1821), and concluded: "If the stage cannot be maintained without lewdness and impiety; if the failing fortunes of the theatre are to be redeemed by a piece so low, so obscene, so impious, so detestable, even let it sink and die." The *Gazette* thus obliquely announced that there were forces gathering their strength to fight a bitter though one-sided battle against the establishment of a theatre in Sydney.

Strangely enough, the hitherto prim and staid *Monitor* was the first to see the uses to which the *Gazette* was being put, with its publication of "very inopportune" objections to theatrical entertainments

wherein under the artful cover of a *set speech* from one "Reverend J. Bromley" of Liverpool ... the said *Gazette* has strongly confirmed the convictions of many of His Majesty's pious and moral subjects in the town, as to the impropriety and inexpediency, after all, of the said theatrical exhibitions.

As the semi-official "government organ" the *Gazette* was

21

able to perform the seemingly impossible: to sit on the fence and keep its ear to the ground. All, and particularly Barnett Levey, had been warned. And Barnett Levey, particularly, ignored the warning. It was no news to him that the church and its clergy were against theatricals. He had, it seems, still more irons in the fire. On 10 October he signed an indenture between himself and one William Foreman of Sydney which, on payment of £130, made him sole owner of 60 acres of land on the South Head Road. The area commenced at the 4 mile stone on the South Head Road (at the junction of the Victoria Road and Old South Head Road of today), west 42 chains south of road west 20 chains at 10 chains across a road, two to left of old hut and north 25 chains to South Head Road. From this purchase stemmed the present-day suburb of Waverley. Again, it is not without significance that Solomon Levey owned several small allotments on the Woollahra and Rose Bay side of Old South Head Road, and had a consolidated grant of 1,100 acres extending from Jersey Road, Paddington, to Fernleigh Avenue, Rose Bay.

Levey's theatrical rival, James Underwood, was disposed of by due process of law when the court awarded a verdict of £65 and costs against him for damage done to the foundations of the *Gazette* building. Only the walls of the theatre had been built, and these remained standing until September 1828, when Underwood sold the land for £1,300. The day after the court verdict was published a triumphant Barnett Levey had an item "from a correspondent" published in the *Gazette* which stated that lovers of the drama would soon have the opportunity to exercise their patronage of this most rational and delightful of all amusements "by the opening of Mr. B. Levey's new theatre, in George Street, which, it is confidently anticipated, will be ready for commencing operations in three or four months, at furthest".

For Levey was a lineal descendant of the opportunist Puff, in R.B. Sheridan's play *The Critic; or, A Tragedy Rehearsed* (1737). It was Puff who laid down for future generations, in his carefully graded list, the "science" of self-advertisement.

Yes, Sir — PUFFING is of various sorts — the principal
are, the PUFF DIRECT — the PUFF PRELIMINARY —
the *puff collateral* — the Puff COLLUSIVE, and the PUFF
OBLIQUE, or PUFF BY IMPLICATION. — These all
assume as circumstances require, the various forms of
LETTER TO THE EDITOR — OCCASIONAL ANEC-
DOTE — IMPARTIAL CRITIQUE — OBSERVATION
FROM CORRESPONDENT — or ADVERTISEMENT
FROM THE PARTY.

Ever the supreme optimist, Levey, on the basis of a few primi-
tive experiments made by a Sydney chemist that year, also announced that his theatre would be lit by gas. He would have seen
gas in use in London's theatres before he left that city. Gas was
first used on the stage of the Lyceum on 6 August 1817, and first
used on stage and in the auditorium at Drury Lane on 6 September
the same year. With Levey, to decide that gaslight was best for
his theatre was to decide that gas would be used. But, as with
so many of his plans, this one failed to materialize. Levey's theatre
for the full period of its life was, like the earlier Georgian provincial
theatres in England, and the Sydney concerts in which he had
taken such a lively part, lit only by lamps and candles.

3

Of the Lowest Class

During 1826 Barnett Levey and other Sydney merchants had had difficulty in collecting payment for both small and large outstanding debts. People had become, as Levey said in one of his advertisements, "bad pays". On the face of it, this was a boom year for the colony. The Australian Agricultural Company, formed in England with a capital of £1 million sterling, began its operations, and the results were felt to some degree in every commercial sector of the colony. There was a strong feeling of optimism about the future. Stores and warehouses were overflowing with English merchandise. There was much wise and unwise speculation in land and foodstuffs. Sheep, cattle, and wheat prices, and the cost of manual labour were all affected. Expert tradesmen, scarce enough at all times, could now more or less name their own wage. The English view of the Australian workman of the period, compared with his fellow-worker in England, was of a man able to earn wages enough in three days to enable him to loaf for the other four.

Throughout the year Levey threatened to take legal action against those who had not paid their accounts, and insisted on cash payment for current sales. By the end of the year he had taken many debtors to court and obtained verdicts against them. Whether they then lost their worldly possessions, under distraint by a bailiff for future sale to meet their debts, as was then the practice, is not recorded. By June, for instance, there were eighteen people in gaol for debt. There is no reason to believe that Levey was any more lenient to his debtors than he was to the servants who worked for him and stole from him with such monotonous regularity. During the year he delivered to justice a male convict servant for the theft of a teaspoon (sentenced to work in irons for six months), and a female convict servant who had stolen a gold chain, coral beads, and other small articles (sentenced to twelve months in the house of correction, the Female Factory). Yet the same Levey was one of the first in Sydney to subscribe money to a fund to help a poor debtor who had no possessions and was in bad health. He was also among the first to give money towards the establishment of the Sydney Dispensary, and to the Sydney Benevolent Society and other public charities.

The truth is that the incidence of petty pilfering, forgery, and fraud among convict and free servants was so high that employers were thinking of asking for increased court penalties for offenders. There was hardly an employer who had not been victimized in one way or another, and it was neither feasible nor good sense to allow all the guilty to go unpunished. Nor could a convict servant be "returned" without good and sufficient reason being given for his return.

The year's work, with its competition and excitement of all kinds, put a great strain on Barnett Levey and the first signs of a streak of arrogant belligerency in his nature began to appear. In June he summonsed a Mr. Joseph Raphael on a charge of having assaulted him in a public saleroom. The Police Court was told that both were at a sale when Levey, seeing Raphael inspecting some of the goods, said in the hearing of several people that the goods were for ready cash sale only. Raphael objected abusively to this slur on his ability to pay cash and later, according to Levey, threw an orange at him. The Bench decided the complaint was not established by the evidence, and dismissed the case. But Levey, who could not hold his tongue and was not merely vocal but vociferous in his claims and charges, was aggrieved by this verdict and carried on a slanging match with the accused in the courtroom. As a result the Bench "deemed it conducive to the public peace" to order each party to be bound over to the other for twelve months.

Outraged by what he considered to be an affront by the Bench, Levey sent good money after bad by taking the case to a higher court. The only thing established beyond doubt at the subsequent Quarter Sessions hearing was that each side had an even score in the matter of hurling abusive words, but that the alleged assault, or orange-throwing, had not taken place. The jury returned a verdict of not guilty.

But if Levey had worries in 1826 they were to be multiplied the following year. Wheat; his famous windmill; plans for new buildings; the first faint tremors of an approaching economic depression that was to reach its peak by 1829; the start of what was to be an almost three years' drought; the presence of the hated Australian Agricultural Company, and his own uncontrollable, ebullient, drink-heated nature served to bring on a period of sickness which towards the end of the year was given as the explanation for the delay in opening his theatre.

Levey's brush with the Australian Agricultural Company occurred when some of their agents poached on his employees. Experienced mechanics, or tradesmen, especially in the building industry, were hard to come by, and the agents managed to "buy" two sawyers while they were actually in Levey's employ. Being successful in this, the agents a few days later also induced a carpenter to leave his employ. This loss of three trained, experienced men was serious, and Levey very quickly advised "the Honourable Company" through his favourite medium, the paid newspaper advertisement, that if it happened again he would take the matter to the courts. Not that the loss seems to have made very much difference to his plans. Work continued on his Colchester Warehouse, and while the theatre may have been for the time ignored the storerooms were not, for on 27 January Levey announced his first essay in wheat speculation on a large scale. In an advertisement containing a "pledge" he advised wheat-growers and others that because of the fluctuating price of grain

26

and the uncertainty of its sale in the Sydney market, he had built a store "fit for the reception of 20,000 bushels". This could again be construed as an attempt to outdo Solomon, whose stores were said to hold 15,000 bushels at most.

Barnett's stores, it was said, were to be ready in two months, and in the meantime he pledged, for two years at least, to prevent settlers from being discouraged by the present low grain prices, that he would pay seven shillings a bushel for wheat of 58 pounds to the bushel. He assured cultivators that by this opportunity they could put their seed in the ground sure of a sale at seven shillings a bushel. "Go till the ground," his advertisement concluded, "put good seed therein, from good comes good, from bad seed comes bad. Remember 58 lbs to the bushel."

Levey was undoubtedly working, either consciously or unconsciously, towards the goal achieved by Solomon as a speculator in wheat, and as a mill owner. His mill was to be his money-spinner.

At about this time, however, Levey received a letter from the Acting Attorney-General, W.H. Moore, telling him that work on the construction of a windmill "on land to which he had no claim" must cease immediately, as the mill was considered likely to be a danger to the public. Levey, thoughtlessly inclined to "take on" anybody who questioned his actions, regardless of his size or importance, said in his reply that he would not furnish any particulars regarding his claim to the land, and just as certainly would not stop building his windmill. The letter was signed by him, but was written by W. C. Wentworth, and so incensed the Governor, Lieutenant General Ralph Darling, who took office on 19 December 1825, that he included it in his despatches home, with a covering letter in which he described Wentworth as "appearing desirous to lead the public and degrade the government on all occasions". Levey he described contemptuously as "a person of the name of Levey. . . who is of the lowest class".

Levey's reply to the Acting Attorney-General, dated 30 January 1827, read:

Sir: It is not true that I have ever had any notice to dis-
continue the building of the mill on my premises although
it has been notorious to the government and the whole
colony that this building has now been in progress for upwards
of nine months.

The enclosed certificate from my neighbours, who are
most interested in the abatement of this nuisance if it be
one, will shew that they do not view it in this light, and I
can only say that if it be a nuisance the government windmill
is an equal nuisance and I will take care shall meet with the
same fate as mine. I decline furnishing you with the particulars of my title to the yard upon which that building is
being erected.

I believe it to be as good a title as any in the town; and
I will take care to defend it if it be sought to be impugned.

If this notice had been given me in due time, I might
have desisted. To desist now would be next to ruin; and if
the government are really so anxious about the lives of His
Majesty's subjects as is pretended, let them pay me for their
default in not giving me notice sooner and I will then leave
off. I am, sir, your obedient servant, B. Levey.

Did Levey grin to himself as he signed his name beneath that
customary "your obedient servant"? Obedient he was determined
not to be, and furthermore, when it came to a question about his
right to build on the land he occupied, he would still show them
a thing or two. Levey's right to that land was inalienable.

He could not have known that a copy of his letter would be
sent by Darling to England, but he must have known that it
would automatically be drawn to the attention of the Governor,
and that it was the kind of letter to make that proud if not haughty
martinet his enemy. It was not the wisest letter he could have
written, and it seems that here the wily Wentworth took advantage
of Levey's immediate desire to "score off" the Acting Attorney-
General by so phrasing it that he, too, was able to get at a Governor
and a government for which he had little liking. In any case, the
Governor showed in this and other instances where his authority
was either questioned or criticized that he had a very long memory.

This time it was the *Australian* and not the *Gazette* which seems to have had its ear to the ground. Levey's letter to the Acting Attorney-General was dated 30 January, and had presumably been delivered to that official by the next day. On 3 February the *Australian* published a brief article in which it expressed its doubts whether Levey's windmill would be built. "The government, we understand, have interfered, either by way of remonstrance or prohibition, and have either suggested the propriety of forebearing to place a windmill on the summit of the pile, or peremptorily interposed 'authority'." The newspaper added that between fears about the public safety, and fears about disappointment to an adventurous speculator, the matter must for the present rest. It added a rider to the effect that it believed the height of "this stupendous building" was out of proportion with the thickness of the walls and the width of the basement.

The *Gazette,* in a reversal of its usual role, countered this on 9 February by saying that Levey's new building, despite "omens dire", was progressing favourably, and that no danger could reasonably be apprehended from the mill. The mill, it said, would have eighty sails instead of the usual four, twenty on each arm, and each sail 18 inches long. Presenting the appearance of a fan, the sails would have the power by internal machinery of slackening themselves according to the strength of the wind, and again expanding as it dropped. As to the mill being a danger to the public, or frightening horses in the street below, the *Gazette* saw in these claims nothing but a welcome excuse to exercise its sense of humour. As well say the mill would frighten the fish as the horses, and that as a result the Sydney people would not have whiting for breakfast, it said. Besides

... it should be borne in mind that, as the mill will most probably be seen from New Zealand, it may be, happily, instrumental in turning some of the benighted and savage inhabitants of that and the neighbouring islands, from the error of their ways, by inducing them, through the spirit of emulation, to grind corn and leave off eating their neighbours.

Barnett's next mercantile venture was to charter, with the

captain, the brig "Bona Vista" for £2,500, with a cargo of American and colonial flour and other colonial produce for sale or barter in Mauritius and the Cape of Good Hope. It was to bring back a cargo of wine, sugar, butter, and other commodities scarce in the colony. The ship left early in March, by which time Levey had announced that he had already contracted with the colony's cultivators for 15,000 bushels of wheat "of the growth of the ensuing season" at seven shillings a bushel.

Meantime, Levey may have forgotten or put out of his mind the brush he had had with the Acting Attorney-General over his mill, but it had not been forgotten in official quarters. Inquiries were put on foot, and as a result on 13 March John Oxley, Surveyor-General, wrote to the Colonial Secretary, Alexander Macleay (obviously in reply to queries by Macleay) that he, Oxley, had suggested to Barnett Levey last December he should seek the approval of the Governor to the erection of his mill. Levey had said he would do so in a few days, and would have done so before but he had been unable to obtain a copy of the plan to send with his letter in explanation. Oxley also told Macleay that the land first occupied by Solomon and then by Barnett Levey had not been alienated by either grant or lease. This was quite true. It was bought outright by Solomon.

But Levey, it appears, was preoccupied with his dreams of bigger and better buildings. Once again it fell to the *Gazette* to announce in May that the following month Levey would lay the stone of a new building on his property in George Street. This time the building would exceed the dimensions of the Waterloo Stores on all points. Perhaps this wild desire to outdo the Waterloo Stores was the only thing clear in Levey's mind about the proposed building, for in describing the stone-laying ceremony the newspapers referred variously to the building as "Mr. Barnett Levey's intended mansion", "Mr. Barnett Levey's edifice", and "Mr. B. Levey's intended house". But whatever the building's intended style or purpose, there was nothing ambiguous about the ceremony of laying the foundation stone. This was done with full Masonic honours, and was turned by Levey into a public occasion in a town in which few excitements existed apart from the occasional hanging or turn-out by the military. A procession of the Masonic brethren of the two lodges, attended by music and banners, marched through the town to 72 George Street, and there formed up together with an admiring and excited crowd to watch the Worshipful Master of Lodge 260 lay the stone with due ceremony. Beneath the stone a square had been hollowed out in which was placed a copper plate with the following details engraved on it for the benefit of posterity.

> The Foundation Stone of This Building Laid, and this Plate Deposited, on Monday, the 25th June A.D. 1827, by the request of Brother Barnett Levey, Esquire, Sole proprietor. This Ceremony was performed by the Worshipful Masters, senior and junior Wardens and Brethren of Lodge No. 260 Samuel Terry, Esquire, W.M. Robert Campbell, Esquire, S.W. Thomas Bolton, Esquire, J.W. F.H. Greenway, Esquire, Architect. Attended by the W.M., S.W., J.W., and Brethren of the Lodge No. 266 together with other Masonic Brethren in this Colony. Lieutenant General Ralph Darling. Br S. Clayton, Sculp. P.S.W.

The stone safely laid, corn, wine, and oil were poured on it, passages were read from Holy Writ, and more music closed the ceremony. Dollars, half-crowns, and dumps were then thrown on the stone by the assembled company as a gift to the workmen, after which the Masonic Brethren repaired to the Colchester Warehouse where refreshments awaited them.

All this time the proposed theatre was neglected. Perhaps Levey had heeded the warnings given earlier in the year, or perhaps he had merely concentrated on building what seemed likely to be the quicker and more certain money-maker, his stores and mill. Apparently by the end of June there was in the lower part of his warehouse an unoccupied apartment said to be capable of holding a stage, pit, and boxes to accommodate about 900 persons. An adjoining building was ready for use as a greenroom. Both continued to be neglected for a little longer, for Levey had still another project in hand to occupy what remained of his energies.

In July work was started on a "cottage" on his South Head Road property, 50 feet by 35 feet, designed as a residence for the Levey family. There was to be attached to this house a garden from which Levey proposed to supply Sydney with vegetables at a third cheaper than the market rates. The cottage itself was on the usual Levey grand scale. It had three large cellars and kitchen in the basement; two parlours, two bedrooms, and a storeroom on the ground floor; large dining room, two bedrooms, and a lobby on the first floor, and a bedroom in the attic. There were stables and other offices, and a well with a plentiful supply of water. Levey named it Waverley House, in honour of Sir Walter Scott.

This new activity brought a gibe from the *Gazette,* which said in its issue of 15 October 1827

> Mr. Barnett Levey, besides the erection of his frightfully lofty temple in town, is also building a handsome dwelling house upon his estate on the South Head Road within a few minutes' walk of "Bellevue." As soon as this house is finished Mr. Levey intends erecting a church near his estate for the benefit of the neighbourhood in that direction.

Levey made his reply to this by means of a paid advertisement, finishing his remarks with the statement: "In this morning's paper you make a great error. As far as your statement goes as to building a house on my little estate is true, but as to building a church is totally wrong. I think a grog shop would find more inside passengers on that road."

Levey then turned his attention to the theatre, calling a public meeting to launch a share scheme to finance its construction. This meeting was followed by another, and another, at which various matters were chewed over. Levey found his greatest difficulty lay in getting the theatre "enthusiasts" to make a definite commitment. However, by the middle of August the *Gazette* was able to report not only that £1,000 in £20 shares had been promised, but also that a respectful letter had been addressed to the governor soliciting his sanction and patronage for the undertaking. The governor was reported to have referred the matter to the magistrates, and they were accordingly petitioned for a licence to institute a theatre on a small scale. The licence was not granted.

As the year progressed, with its threat of an action against him by the Attorney-General for committing a nuisance with his mill, the continuance of the drought, which boded ill for his promised 15,000 bushels of wheat, and the fret and worry consequent upon an incomplete warehouse, mill, theatre, "edifice", and "cottage", Levey faced a future which looked a great deal cloudier than it had at the beginning of the year. Already he must have been feeling regrets about the letter he had sent the Acting Attorney-General, for by now he realized that the success of a great deal on which he had set his heart largely depended on the good will of both the Attorney-General and the Governor. But even this could not dim his optimism.

Towards the end of the year he had a painting executed of his new "edifice" as it was to appear when completed, which he described as the Colchester Warehouse, though it was being built in front of the building which originally bore that name. From this it is evident that Levey planned the whole as one building from the start, building the off-the-street half first, and then the half with its frontage to George Street. Like so many colonial architectural projects, this one was grandiose in conception but meagre in achievement. It was to be, in effect, a striking "palace" with statuary. It materialized, because of financial and other difficulties, as the plain-fronted Royal Hotel of two years later.

The painting, which Levey is said to have sent to England, showed a grand colonnade of the Corinthian order on the front of the building. On two wings were figures representing Comedy and Tragedy. Over the front was Apollo surrounded by the Muses, and surmounting the whole on a pedestal was the Genius of Australia supported on the right by the Genius of the Arts and on the left by Commerce.

It seems logical to assume that this building was designed for Levey by Francis Greenway, and that the painting was done by the English artist, Augustus Earle, who had painted somewhat similar figures to decorate the concert room for the series of amateur concerts in 1826. It was Earle who prepared the necessary drawings for the panorama, "View of the Town of Sydney", which was exhibited at Burford's Leicester Square panorama from 1828 onwards. From one of these drawings a very incompetent engraver in England produced the only illustration in existence today of Levey's building and incomplete mill as they must have appeared in 1827–28. By this time Levey had moved the mill from the original Colchester Warehouse at the back up to the front of his new building, and overlooking George Street.

But three more happy events remained for Levey before the year ended. His ship, the "Bona Vista," returned from the Cape in November complete with the hoped-for cargo of wine and sundries. In the same month his first son was born, and on Christmas Day his fabulous and contentious mill was set in motion for the first time.

By now it was obvious to many, if not to Levey, that he had over-extended himself financially and physically. His commercial transactions, his building projects, his speculations of all kinds, had involved the expenditure of large sums of money, and he had not shown himself to be the most canny or cautious merchant in the town. In his personal relations he had proved to be irascible, impolitic, ruthless, and arrogant in turn. These were not qualities with which to build either personal or business relationships, and perhaps he had been made to realize this, for he left Sydney for a short while and lived on his 320 acre farm at Lapstone Hill, possibly to recuperate from his illness, but also to plan his activities for the coming year away from the distractions of Sydney.

The land at Lapstone Hill had been given to him by Sir Thomas Brisbane. Levey had built on it a four-roomed weatherboard house, outhouses, piggery, and stables. A great deal of the land had been fenced, 15 acres of it had been cleared by convict labour, and 10 were under cultivation.

4

Little Vivacious Colonist

Licence or not, Levey determined early in 1828 to proceed with the completion of his theatre in the original Colchester Warehouse. Canvas was bought for the stage, and an amateur artist was engaged to paint the scenes. But there was more to this sudden theatrical activity than mere stubbornness. He now believed that in the theatre remained his one chance of making enough money to keep himself afloat. Money was tighter than it had ever been before, and his schemes were not prospering as he had hoped they would.

He also looked to his mill as a potential money-maker, announcing on 11 January that it would be ready for grinding on 17 January. His stores and granary, he advised the public, were now open for the reception of grain and any goods requiring storage, at the rate of one halfpenny a pound a month for wool, threepence a bushel for grain, and five shillings a ton for other stores. Grain would be smutted, ground, and dressed at fifteen pence the bushel. But agricultural and financial conditions in the colony being what they were, there was no great rush to pack his stores or overload his mill with grain, so it was that ten days after his mill had opened he again advertised for intending shareholders in his theatre to attend a meeting on 29 January finally to settle matters for the approaching winter. A holder of five £5 shares was to be admitted to the theatre free, his advertisement announced. It was also said that the meeting would form a management committee.

Three days after this meeting, which again produced little in the way of real encouragement, he launched another attempt to raise money. At the same time he instigated the delivery of two letters which appeared in two of the newspapers, praising his mill and the pioneering work he had done "for Australia". These letters were also a pathetic attempt to make friends with the many with whom in his more affluent days he had made enemies, and to call bygones bygones. Enemies as well as business, he had found, could be unprofitable.

The attempted money-making scheme involved the sale of some of his land on the South Head Road. Levey proposed the sale of 63 allotments, each with a 30 feet frontage and a depth of 300 feet. Each purchaser was to be required to build a cottage, "the whole to be erected under a joint continuation of verandah". At one end of the resulting terrace was to be a school, and at the other an inn or boarding-house, with a lawn to front the terrace and a fountain in the centre. The completed project was to be named Waverley Crescent. The idea, like so many of his ideas, was excellent and farseeing, but the timing proved to be unpropitious.

Meantime, to keep the name of Levey before the public and to foster his plans for the mill, the theatre, and the crescent, the following "puff" was published in two of Sydney's newspapers.

Sir: I have been to see Mr. Levey's new mill at work, and also have had some wheat ground by it. The machinery is on an improved plan, and of the very safest description. The wheat which I sent was very smutty; but, to my astonishment, the flour I received in return was of the best quality I have ever seen since I have been in the colony.

Mr. Levey's prices are very reasonable; added to which is the great saving of trouble in having such a convenience as the Colchester mill in town. I can now go to the market, buy a bag of wheat, send it to Mr. Levey's, and have it ground all upon the spot, as one may say, and above all, I am sure that I got back my full proceeds. I am sure, sir, you will be glad to notice so great an advantage; and I beg to subscribe myself, your obedient servant, *Pro Bono Publico*.

It is difficult to gauge what effect, if any, this letter had on Levey's fortunes. All that is known is that three days after it appeared the same newspapers were favoured with another attempt to "drum up trade" for Levey's mill. The second letter also had the persuasive Levey touch, especially in the "good fellow" promise of a dinner.

Sir: It is with the greatest pleasure, for the last two or three days I see Mr. Levey's mill at work. I have such interest in the well being of this Colony, that I never forget to look for his mill before breakfast, as much the same as I do for a newspaper. I like to see it going. It must be well known to all parties that Mr. Levey has been at a very great expense in fitting up such an immense building; and as to myself I sincerely believe he has done it more with a view to benefit the Colony than of himself and family. If others think with me, we have a right undoubtedly to expect the public support — and I hope they will truly give it him; and if at any previous time they may have had an altercation with Mr. Levey, not allow that altercation to have anything to do with the mill, but be manly — and let the mill go.

And if it goes until the first day of January next, 1829, which I am not at all afraid it will, and if I am living, I shall feel the pleasure in giving Mr. Levey, and any friends to the number of forty, that he may think proper to invite, the best dinner, wine, &c., &c., which can be got in New South Wales. I am, sir, *An Emigrant of About Five Years Standing*.

A few days later Levey advertised that unpaid debts would be handed over to his solicitor. Some of these, he claimed, had been outstanding one, two, and three years. And again he held a meeting of "friends of the theatre", which was poorly attended and closed without any definite arrangement about finance, despite Levey's assurance that he would be ready to open the theatre in six weeks "if folks would only come down with their dumps".

Throughout March he constantly kept the shareholder plan before the public, with meetings and advertisements, and apparently by the end of that month had received sufficient promises for him to announce that all the £5 shares (200) had been taken up. The *South-Asian Register* then joined the chorus in his praise. "Mr. Barnett Levey, our little vivacious colonist, has erected a pile of buildings which will cost him about £15,000, and the front part he intends for a theatre, or the*aitre*, as he calls it", the journal announced, making at the same time one of the many journalistic mistakes which have helped to add confusion to past accounts of Levey's activities. The theatre was not in the front of the building, not at this stage, at least, even though the same journal repeated at the end of its report that "to build a theatre for the public benefit, like what he has built, and a warehouse behind it, four storeys high, with a handsome, lofty windmill, surmounting the roof, is not a common performance in England".

Levey's theatre never had a street frontage or facade. The illustration used in C.H. Bertie's *The Story of the Royal Hotel,* and in Paul McGuire's *The Australian Theatre* as Levey's Theatre Royal is in reality the architect's first grand conception (an almost direct "pinch" from the design of one of the larger English provincial theatres) of its successor, Wyatt's Victoria Theatre in Pitt Street. This engraving, bearing the title "The new Theatre Royal", first appeared in James Maclehose's *The Picture of Sydney; and Stranger's Guide in New South Wales, for 1838.* Although the word "new" should have proved insurmountable, and the date shown on the building is plainly 1838, writers ever since have nevertheless assumed this drawing or engraving to be an illustration of Levey's 1833 theatre. Apart from the fact that Levey's Theatre Royal had no street frontage, when the Victoria Theatre opened in 1838 it was the architectural "wonder" of the year, and Maclehose naturally featured it in his almanac. The index to this simply described the illustration as "the Theatre Royal" (which the Victoria was originally to have been called). For positive identification it is necessary to turn to an advertisement for Maclehose's forthcoming book in the *Colonist* for 21 December 1837, where will be found among the illustrations listed as being in the book, "New Theatre, Pitt Street". If still further confirmation is required it is only necessary to turn to Joseph Fowles's *Sydney in 1848,* where the same facade is to be seen, pared down considerably by economic necessity when building actually started, but still recognizable.

Early in April Levey discovered, after calling a meeting of shareholders who had apparently never subscribed any money, how valuable were the earlier promises. No matter how good the intentions of these prospective shareholders may have been, they either could not or would not "come down with their dumps" when the need arrived. Levey did the next best thing, if not the only thing left for him to do: he announced that he would "get up" the theatre solely from his own resources.

It was now the turn of the *Gazette* to comment, probably using inside information. Levey had defied the Colonial Secretary and the Governor over his mill. He had continued to pursue his dream of a theatre despite the "official" attitude made clear in the *Gazette's* publication of anti-theatrical matter, and its dire warnings about the necessity for official approval of any theatrical scheme. The newspaper now came out with a wordy leading article. Though it had no ulterior motives of any kind, the *Gazette* said, it doubted whether colonial society was yet ready for theatrical exhibitions. With a hypocritical, tongue-in-cheek attitude it said that until it had been assured of the fact only a few days ago it had given no credit to the report that anything in the shape of the theatre was really in progress. But it had now been given to understand, the journal claimed, that some hundreds of pounds had been expended in the mere preparation of scenery, and for the sake of all concerned it felt it necessary to ask the pertinent question whether a theatre would be allowed.

Levey again defied the warning inherent in the *Gazette* article. Neither his mill nor his Waverley Crescent plans had provided the expected financial return, and now, obviously struggling to get enough money to complete his theatre — which he still obstinately believed would provide him with a satisfactory living —

he advertised for a partner willing to bring a capital of at least £10,000 into his enterprises. No such partner was obtainable.

Still Levey persisted, perhaps because he had no choice. He must have known that even if he thought it necessary to apply for a licence for his theatre it would not be granted, for he next announced that he had no intention of applying for a licence because his was to be a "private" theatre. The "official" reply again appeared in the *Gazette*, cloaked in the usual "mind you, we don't *know*, but still we believe" ambiguity.

> We certainly are not inimical to the exertions of Mr. Levey, or any other colonist in prosecuting any undertaking that may be considered laudable; but still we are not without our reason for concluding, should Mr. Levey be disappointed in procuring a licence, if thought worthy of solicitude, that no private theatre will assuredly be allowed to be set on foot. After all we may be mistaken.

Levey countered this advice with a public call to those ladies and gentlemen who had applied from time to time for theatrical engagements to make fresh applications, as he was now ready to receive them. At the same time he thanked the many friends of the theatre who had already stepped forward to engage boxes, and those who had sent play and music books to and for the use of the theatre. For Levey did have the backing of the majority of the public in his attempts to establish a theatre, even if some of them, possessed of an "American republican spirit", were merely egging him on in his so far successful attempts to best or thwart officialdom and the "moralistic and saintly" among the population. Both he and they knew that once his theatre was opened with a programme of the plays and farces common to the time it would not lack patronage. Officialdom also knew this, and feared it. The newspapers, even the *Gazette* in its odd, inverted way admired his pluck or foolhardiness, and supported him whenever the opportunity offered. Levey, it must also be said, supported them, for his annual advertising costs must have been very high.

In May a new monthly with the strange title of *The Blossom* came to Levey's support. It brought the real struggle out into the open, which the Press had not done so far. It stated quite openly that the strongest opposition to the theatre came from Governor Darling himself, for whom *The Blossom,* apparently, felt the necessary respect but no admiration whatever.

> Governor Darling, it would appear, has determined to set his face against the introduction of all British feeling and British privilege in the Colony — we lament to record, that the Governor's beck is so particularly attended to — to that degree of humiliating debasement... What is there in Governor Darling to cause such alarm? We have seen him, and care no more about him than any ordinary individual, in the direction of our feelings — we respect him, because he is our Governor, but that is all — and all that is ever required. Oh! Australians and British colonists, divest yourselves of this degrading feature — lest too late you find your country in a state of abject vassalage.

Levey continued to keep his theatrical proposals before the public. He told the *Monitor* he would present plays only after he had used the pruning knife to see that nothing remained in them which could cause the slightest offence. "And we know that, in one of the intended exhibitions, one character, who by the author of the play is made to represent a libertine, will be omitted altogether", the newspaper reported. The *Gazette* suggested in reply to this that it might be better to choose those plays which did not require docking. It said Levey's announcement reminded it of a bill of fare at a country theatre in which it was said that *Hamlet* would be presented, but omitting the parts of the King and Queen as "too immoral for any stage".

By this time officialdom had decided to drop the kid gloves with which they seem to have been handling Levey, and to rely no further on the hints and innuendos pointed his way in the *Gazette*. Alexander Macleay, the Colonial Secretary, finally decided that as Levey was "playing possum" — building his theatre with the intention of opening it without applying for a licence, and thereby saving himself from making an open break with the law — the time had come to bring him up short. Levey had built and opened his mill against the directions of authority, on the slim pretext that he had not been told in time that he was required first to get the Governor's permission. This time there would be no chance of such a pretext. "I am directed distinctly to apprise you, that the Governor will not license a theatre", Macleay wrote to Levey in a letter dated 4 July 1828, "and further that His Excellency is fully determined to resort to every means within his power, to put a stop to your unauthorised proceedings in this and other respects".

Levey was now a man still full of fight but with his ammunition spent. His dream of wealth through a lien on wheat at seven shillings a bushel had been evaporated by the drought. Wheat was still available, but as most of it was imported it was very costly, and very few of those who did buy it called on Levey's mill to grind it. On 10 June 1828 wheat was 16s. 6d a bushel in Sydney, with some grain reaching 18s. His new building in George Street was just about completed, at a cost said to have exceeded £10,000. Too much was going out and not enough coming in. How was the situation to be remedied? There was still one hope. Perhaps if he let his mill and stores the lessee would be able to gain the business which had so far evaded him? So it was that "in consequence of the proprietor's continued bad state of health" an offer was made to let the mill and stores for twelve months, or the mill alone, even though the stores, Levey's advertisment claimed, were large enough to contain 50,000 bushels of grain. The fact that no one applied to become lessee at least proves that nobody in Sydney felt he could succeed where Levey had failed.

So Levey took the only step left to him. He raised a private mortgage on his uncompleted South Head Road "cottage", Waverley House, including ten acres of land and the few cottages that were then being built in his Waverley Crescent. The mortgage was for £1,085, and the mortgagor undertook to complete Waverley

House and the cottages within six months from the date of the deed, 1 August. This was the month in which the *Monitor* admitted that trade in Sydney was at its lowest ebb, and pecuniary embarrassment daily increasing.

Now Levey had the money he needed, and the devil take gubernatorial warnings and admonitions. Rehearsals were fixed for three days a week during August, and on 1 September Levey signed a Press advertisement announcing that because of the demand for boxes at his theatre he had had six more constructed. He added a warning that those who did not pay for their boxes by 12 September would lose them. This advertisement appeared in the *Gazette* of 3 September, and by one of those ironies of fate which occasionally dogged Levey, in the same issue appeared another advertisement, also dated 1 September, which put a sudden end to his theatrical plans. The advertisement was a government notice of an act hurried through the Legislative Council "for regulating places of public exhibition and entertainment". The framers of this act borrowed liberally from a similar English act of 1737.

Because of the "evil consequences which the unrestricted power of opening places of public exhibition and entertainment, in the present circumstances of this Colony, must necessarily produce", this act virtually banned any kind of stage performance given without a licence. It not only penalized the producer and those connected with any such unlicensed performance, but also the owner of the premises in which it was given and the audience which watched it. Furthermore, it laid down that every building in which unlicensed performances were given should be deemed a disorderly house, and that every person found therein "shall be deemed a rogue and a vagabond" and subject to the penalties laid down for such persons.

Governor Darling had effectively covered every bolt-hole, and brought Levey's world down about his ears. Nor could that weathercock, the *Gazette,* forego this opportunity to crow over his fall.

43

Some months ago we delicately suggested the propriety of feeling the pulse of the government on this important subject — so far important as thousands are dissipated by building castles in the air. But it would appear, as ought not to have been the case, that our hints were not regarded with that attention to which it will now prove they had claim.

It was now the turn of the moralists to move in, lest, even in the face of this all-embracing act, Levey should be granted a licence. Following the Governor's lead, the "better class" of colonial society adopted a thin-lipped, contemptuous, and determined opposition to the establishment of a theatre. The clergy preached against the vice and abominations of theatrical exhibitions from their pulpits, and extended their strictures even to concerts. A gentleman who signed himself "Amicus" wrote to the *Gazette* giving thanks that "Divine Providence" had, for the present, "through the wisdom of our rulers, delivered us from one moral evil with which we were threatened". It was the writer's belief that parents of moral habits were aware of the serious moral evil from which they and their children had been delivered, and he would not believe otherwise until he saw them preparing their children for the stage as an honourable profession. Just the same, he hinted darkly, there were some husbands and parents who were not so aware.

Nevertheless, despite the new act and the obvious opposition to Levey's theatre, the *Australian* with what could have been either optimism or bravado announced on 19 September that "the folks here who love to have a little rational recreation at times, will be glad to know that it is fully anticipated the government will make no opposition to granting to Mr. Levey a licence for the opening of his theatre".

Now followed a tussle which was looked on by one party as good contending against evil, and by the other as a group of government-backed moralists and hypocrites fighting the "evils" of the theatre while condoning the horse-racing, gambling, cockfighting, drunkenness, and other evil habits to which the "higher classes" of the colony's society were prone.

The *Monitor's* reaction to the anti-theatrical act was immediate and diffuse. In a leading article several columns in length it expressed amazement at the hypocrisy of the whole unsavoury business. At a recent "junketing" at Parramatta, the newspaper claimed, the people had seen the first men in the Colony, persons renowned for religion, parading the racecourse; proposing toasts at the "great Agricultural Dinner" in the presence of clergymen, that were so lewd a London coal-heaver would have blushed to hear them; attending prizefights at which constables cleared the ring and magistrates kept the time; gambling at the *rouge et noir* table; shutting themselves up all day Sunday so that they could gamble undisturbed, and paying a dollar each to witness a cock-fight. The newspaper suggested the real reason for the act was that the government disliked windmills more than it did theatres, and that government supporters, unable to petition against the mill, attacked it with a side-wind — a petition against a theatre. It expressed the conviction that the act was not the work of Governor Darling, but came into being through the unconstitutional and unscriptural influence of the clergy. Why not give Levey a *trial* for a season, the newspaper urged. Applicants for a licence to sell spirits were given a trial, and if they failed to conform to the law were deprived of their licence. "The theatre being now built, and all the expenses incurred, why not treat Levey with equal justice?"

Petitions and counter-petitions were hawked about Sydney. Not even Thomas Livingstone Mitchell could escape them, as he wrote to his brother in Scotland on 3 October 1828:

> . . . I have just been called on by the two clergymen to sign a petition *against a theatre* which has been erected, on the plea that the people are too bad, and that the theatre will make them worse!! Who would live in such a country! Yet *I* must, for I can't afford to come back. . .

It is to be feared that the efficient Mitchell signed the petition, for he would not have risked official disapproval by doing otherwise. One Major John J. Jackson, with his head more in the clouds than Mitchell's, did sign a petition, the wrong one, and later got a severe rap on the knuckles for his pains.

Levey was not such a fool that he did not know when he was beaten, or when he was about to be beaten. Since he could not have a theatre of any kind without a licence, why, then, he would apply for a licence. But so as to make it something more than a mere plea from the "suspect" Barnett Levey, and to show that he also had his followers, he would send his application to the Colonial Secretary accompanied by a petition with as many signatures as possible for the establishment of a theatre in Sydney. Thus it was that two groups of door-knockers were to be seen in Sydney's streets urging householders and merchants to sign for or against a theatre.

The clergy were first to the Governor with their petition, because it had fewer signatures. Although the *Monitor* had made a both-ways bet by saying first that the clergy were responsible, and then that Levey's disobedience over the mill was the real reason for the moves against the theatre, at least it made sure of having something on whichever should prove the winner. In this case it was wrong about the clergy but right about the mill. Levey's petition was received and his licence refused some four weeks after the Governor received the clergy's petition, which was sent under cover of a letter from Archdeacon Thomas Hobbes Scott. So much for the optimism expressed by the *Australian* and others.

In the letter he sent on 15 October to the Governor with the petition, the Venerable Archdeacon said that whatever his own opinion might be on the drama generally, he had placed his name to the petition because he felt that in such a community as Sydney then was, a theatre would be the resort of the vile, the vicious, and the debauched. He added that although the number of signatures collected by the two clergymen was small, the Governor would understand that numbers were too easily procured, whereas the names appearing would be found to constitute the most responsible of the inhabitants of Sydney.

Slightly less than a month later Levey received a curt letter from the Colonial Secretary telling him that as he had "long since been informed" no theatre licence would be granted to him, it was only necessary to add that the Governor did not deem it expedient "under present circumstances" to license a theatre in Sydney.

It is certain that many more people signed Levey's petition than signed the clergymen's, which is why Archdeacon Scott made his barbed reference to numbers being "too easily procured". It is equally certain that Governor Darling regarded most of the signatories to Levey's petition as he did Levey himself — as of the lowest class, and therefore hardly worth considering. The people did *not* know what was good for them, or even whether what they wanted was good or bad for them. He knew that a theatre would be "bad" for Sydney.

But while Levey's petition was officially ignored, not all of those who had signed it were. On 14 November the Colonial Secretary wrote to tell Major Jackson that His Excellency the Governor felt surprised and disappointed on seeing that he had attached his name to a petition for the licensing of a theatre in Sydney. Had Major Jackson reflected before he signed he would, the Colonial Secretary felt sure, have realized that such a measure could not fail to disturb the public tranquillity. "I have only to add that His Excellency requests that you will in future . . . not lend your name inadvertently to such applications, especially when they are known to be in opposition to the views of the Government."

Major Jackson replied expressing his qualified regret that by signing the petition he should have met with the Governor's displeasure. He said he had merely wished to support an industrious individual who had spent large sums in improving the town, and by so doing encourage what, under proper regulations, he thought was a rational relaxation. However, Major Jackson assured the Colonial Secretary that he would withdraw all countenance from that or any future attempt of the same sort.

With the colony's legal and religious power ranged against

him, Levey knew that no matter how the *Monitor* and the *Australian* railed and ranted against the cant and hypocrisy among Sydney's leaders they would not succeed in getting him a theatre licence. To the contrary, such friends were at the moment more of an embarrassment than a help, for they, too, had incurred Governor Darling's displeasure because of their outspokenness, and were to be the subject of more of his autocratic pronouncements. Levey must have known by this, if he had not known it all along, that his initial mistake had been made in 1826 when he signed the letter penned for him by W.C. Wentworth about his mill. All the troubles over the establishment of his theatre stemmed from this, and if it ever was to be established some propitiatory gesture was necessary. The mill was obviously not paying its way, and had in no way justified the huge cost of its construction. Levey would capitulate.

Only a few days after receiving the letter rejecting his petition Levey wrote to tell the Colonial Secretary he was prepared to dismantle his mill and re-erect it at some suitable location within or without the town boundaries. But only Levey knew this was a provisional capitulation. If it was necessary for him to make a move indicating repentance, so as to achieve his goal, then he had made that move. Meantime, he continued to pick situations for his mill which were not acceptable to the Governor, and to criticize on every possible ground situations suggested to him. If and when he got what he wanted would be time enough to make a decision about the mill. He again left Sydney for his Lapstone Hill farm to recuperate.

He left behind him a Sydney financially moribund. There were now ninety-one people in gaol for debt. Never had money been so scarce, never had debtors been so hard to bring up to scratch. Those who had money were carefully and cautiously hoarding it, hoping to ride out the storm; those who had none were, like Levey, trying their hardest to think out some means of getting it. There seemed to be no immediate answer to his two most pressing problems, which were really one and the same — how

48

to make enough money to save his tottering empire. In other words, how was he to open his theatre, which seemed to be the only sure money-spinner left in an economy turned topsy-turvy by drought and depression, rabid moralists and a hostile Governor?

By 16 December he was advertising his return to Sydney and the opening of his spacious warehouses, and attempting to bolster his prospects by basking in the light of his brother Solomon's success.

> From the advertiser's general knowledge of the business of a merchant and dealer in the Colony, having had seven years practice in, and the entire management of a house notorious for transacting an unusual proportion of the trade of the Colony, which was conducted with care, correctness, and profit — his patrons will feel sufficiently assured of his capability of doing them justice

Levey wrote of himself. That his claims were not strictly true must have been known to many others besides Barnett Levey, but as Solomon's name was not actually mentioned, what harm was there? The advertisement further announced that Barnett would in the New Year conduct an auction of books, plate, and paintings, by candle-light, and that his new building would be let as a hotel. This auction of valuables by "candle-light" was an attempt by Levey — ever in search of novelties to attract the gambler and the passer-by — to revive the eighteenth century English auction in which the last bid before a candle stump flickered out secured the goods.

49

5

Mistrust Stalks Abroad

Like the results of his thoughtlessness, Levey's mill was inescapable. It towered above the squat Sydney of its day as Macquarie's lighthouse at South Head towered over the "boxes" at its base. It could be seen from every town vantage point, and from its top could be seen the ranges of the Blue Mountains. Here was a gargantuan structure whose like could be found in no other British colony. Few of the world's major cities of the time had buildings as high as the total height of Levey's warehouse and mill, and it was to be many years after it was dismantled and Levey himself had passed into history before Sydney again had a building equal to it in height. No wonder that Mrs. Garling, after she and two friends had been taken on a tour of the mill by Levey, described it with such a sense of wonder in a letter to her friend, Mrs. John Piper: ". . . we went to the very top where the works are and walked outside. The prospect from there was beautiful. We could see the whole of the town and the mountains all round. The people appeared like children walking along. . ." The warehouse with the mill on top was in fact some 90 feet high, and possibly higher.

The mill itself was a building with six floors and a top portion containing the sail shaft and machinery. It was said in 1830 to have cost Levey more than £4,000. The dressed flour, the cleaned wheat, and the mill tackle were received on the first floor. The second floor contained the winnowing, dressing, and smutting machines. On the third floor, which had an external platform, were the miller's room where the flour was received from the stores, and two pairs of patent regulators used to control the mill sails. Burs, spur wheels, hoppers, and other fittings were on the fourth floor. The fifth was a receiving floor, capable of receiving 500 bushels of grain, while the sixth held the brake wheel, the crow wheel, brake, and sack tackle. Above this was the mill top, housing the sail machinery and accessories, which also had a "walk" around it.

Assuming a minimum height of 5 feet 10 inches for each floor, the total height of the mill was 35 feet, to which must be added at least another 6 feet for the mill top.

Levey's Colchester Warehouse, described variously as being of five floors and four floors, did actually have five floors, one of which was partially beneath the ground. These floors were: a wine, spirit, and oil store with a height of 12 feet, the theatre above it with a height of 19 feet, the first granary above the theatre, 10 feet; second granary above this, 10 feet, and an attic floor with a conjectural height of 6 feet. If it is again assumed that the store was completely below ground level, then the total height of the warehouse was 43 feet. If, on the other hand (and this seems to be almost certain), the store was partially above ground another 6 feet must be added to this, which gives a total height of 49 feet. On top of this warehouse was Levey's windmill with an estimated height of 41 feet, making the total height of the building 90 feet. Again we are reminded of one of Levey's earliest boasts — that his Colchester Warehouse would be 30 feet higher than the Waterloo Stores. These stores were of five floors, and if it is assumed that the floors were each 12 feet high a total of 60 feet is arrived at. This may seem at first glance a little too much like making the facts fit the theory, but not so much so when it is realized that Levey's granary floors were only 10 feet high because the extra height they would have had was needed to add the height essential to his theatre.

For at least the first four months of 1829 letters on the proposed removal of Levey's mill from the top of his building to a site outside Sydney circulated between Levey, the Colonial Secretary, and the Surveyor-General. From the beginning of these negotiations the "circle" seems to have been: Levey suggests site to Colonial Secretary; Colonial Secretary refers to Surveyor-General; Surveyor-General refers back to Colonial Secretary objecting, and suggesting another site; Colonial Secretary suggests new site to Levey; Levey rejects new site and suggests yet another to Colonial Secretary; Colonial Secretary refers to Surveyor-General — and back again, full circle. By this means, either deliberately or simply by availing himself of an ideal set of circumstances, Levey delayed the actual removal of his mill while at the same time he was able to present himself to officialdom as a "reformed" character.

For Levey had not, despite the act and the opposition of the "respectable" inhabitants of Sydney, given up hope of opening his theatre. At this stage he thought back to the concerts given in 1826 by the Sydney Amateur Concert Society. The moralists and hypocrites had made no objections then. In fact, the "cream" of Sydney society had attended and shown their enjoyment. Why should they object now if Levey, one of the prime movers in 1826, an active participant in the concerts, and now with a costly empty theatre on his hands, should decide to hold similar concerts in that theatre? Theatre — ? That word could be used as a weapon against him in his new efforts, so the concerts would have to be held in the theatre renamed for the purpose the "Royal Assembly Rooms".

But first of all he had to keep the ball rolling with correspondence on the removal of his mill, so that the sprat should catch the necessary mackerel; he had to try to raise money by offering to sell his shop, the original building erected by Solomon Levey on the George Street frontage; and he had to obtain a licence for his new building, in front of but joined to his Colchester Warehouse, which was to blossom forth as the Royal Hotel.

The shop was not sold, but he did gain a licence to conduct

his hotel, which was at least a sure way of earning a living. Good times or bad, grog customers were never entirely lacking.

Early in July he obtained from the Colonial Secretary a licence to conduct public balls and suppers in his Royal Hotel. This was followed a little later by the licence for which he had been angling all along, which permitted him to conduct concerts in his Royal Assembly Rooms. On 14 August Levey advertised that the first vocal and instrumental concert would be held in the Royal Assembly Rooms on the 20th instant. Tickets and bills of particulars were to be had at the Royal Hotel.

From the wide entrance door of the new Royal Hotel in George Street on that historic night there issued a blaze of light to greet and entice those Sydney people who had paid to attend the first concert to be held in the hall renamed the Assembly Rooms, but which almost all of Sydney knew to be Barnett Levey's Theatre Royal. This was a social occasion, and the fact that Levey's controversial theatre was to be seen for the first time added zest to an already unusual night.

Arriving in conveyances of all kinds and on foot along the dimly lighted street, members of this first night audience climbed the short flight of steps to the hotel's lamp-lit portico, and then entered the doorway where they surrendered their tickets. A few steps down the hall and they entered the spacious saloon, or assembly room of the hotel. This, too, was ablaze with light and bright with the promise of later delights, for down its length ran a table spread with "various confections, interspersed with solids and liquids". At one end of the room, taking pride of place, was a portrait of the much-loved and always remembered Governor Lachlan Macquarie. The *Australian* noted:

> Here might be led down the merry dance. But whilst a gloomy spirit of mistrust does stalk abroad, scattering far and wide the seeds of corruption, and helping to loosen every bond that unites human kind, people can never hope to live prosperously, much less feel that confidence, and enjoy that degree of innocent hilarity so essential to the enjoyment of social intercourse.

53

This newspaper had much more to say in the same vein, in support of Levey's efforts to entertain Sydney, and the "vile system of espionage" working against him, before it decided to "drop a curtain upon that pitiable scene".

Levey's first audience passed through the saloon to the doors at the end, which gave on to the side and back (always known as "front", because they faced the stage) boxes. These were not the enclosed "rooms" of Victorian and later times, but small areas divided by sometimes low, sometimes high partitions, with benches installed. A single seat could be booked or a whole box. The audience saw a theatre of "limited dimensions" as yet plainly painted, but illuminated at all points with candles in sconces, candelabras, and chandeliers. The stage curtain was of green baize, the traditional theatre front curtain since Restoration days, and on either side of the proscenium arch were the traditional stage doors, not plain, as was usually the fashion, but painted with representations of the classic muses. Beneath and in front of the footlights was the usual orchestra pit with its shaded oil lamps for the musicians. The fronts of the boxes, particularly those nearest the stage, had devices or emblems painted on them.

The theatre was able to accommodate about 700 people in its pit and two tiers of boxes. The lower tier was the dress boxes, the front boxes of which (those facing the stage) were level with the last or topmost bench in the pit. Next to the stage, on either side, were the private boxes. The rest of the side boxes and the upper tier of boxes completed the theatre's accommodation. All of these boxes were lined or hung with red baize, making a cheerful contrast with the curtain. There was at this time no gallery, nor was the theatre as ornate or finished in its decorations as it was later to be.

At eight o'clock the curtain rose to reveal all the night's entertainers on the stage, assembled in front of the newly-painted drop curtain, in which the scenic artist's "tact in perspective" was said to have been well displayed. It depicted a flight of steps leading to a lofty temple in the distance. Mrs. Garling, when she

54

described her tour of the famous mill, added towards the end of her letter that she had also seen Mr. Levey's theatre. "We saw the drop curtain being painted, besides other scenes, tragedy, comedy, and farce done in high colours." The colours, seen in daylight, were indeed high, but at night under the dim light of lamps and candles they "carried" to the back of the house — which is why they were used.

After the performers had been greeted by the applause of the audience, the orchestra opened the first half of the concert with the "grand overture" to *Lodoiska,* a popular opera of the time "arranged" by Stephen Storace. This concert was, in fact, merely a repetition of one of those held in the schoolroom three years earlier, with most of the same performers appearing. Mr. Levey, of course, obliged with one of his well-known comic songs, "The Beautiful Boy", and was able the next day to read in Sydney's three newspapers that he had lost none of his "inimitable drollery". The three were equally firm in their criticism of what transpired during the interval, when Mr. Levey the theatre-owner and singer of comic songs had the gratification of seeing Mr. Levey the publican doing a roaring trade in refreshments. Instead of the audience retiring to the saloon they "discussed" their edibles and drinks in the theatre boxes and pit. Jellies, custards, oranges, solids of all kinds, porter, brown stout, and *l'eau de vie* were passed from hand to hand, over people's heads and along the seated rows. Some of the gentlemen even smoked their "segars" to show how relaxed they felt in the general jollity of the evening. Nor did the feasting cease with the renewal of the concert, for young Mr. Josephson's excellent performance on the concert flute was in a great measure drowned amid the drawing of corks, tinkling of glasses, nut-cracking, and party-like chattering in pit and boxes.

The success of this concert led Levey to announce that a second would be held in three weeks' time. Ladies and gentlemen engaging boxes were asked to send a servant to occupy them as soon as the theatre opened, to prevent intrusion by "squatters".

Parties taking the dress boxes were also warned that they must attend in full dress, or would otherwise have to take their seats in the upper tier of boxes.

And in between these concerts Levey the publican and caterer continued to hold his profitable public balls and suppers.

The happy swilling that ensued at both his concert and his suppers drew satirical comment from a contributor to the *Gazette*, couched in stanzas "to be set to music" and sung at the opening of the "Opera house". "The dram-a and the dram-o", as this work was entitled, was meant to paint by way of a duologue between the theatre and the hotel, a picture of the supposed enormities Levey was committing.

Quoth dram-a — 'tis strangest presumption to think,
That you who have naught to commend you but drink,
And the fumes of Bengal, and the smoke of Brazil,
And the clanking of pewter, should use me so ill.

In passing, "dram-a" averred that she was grieved to see her stage clad in the symbols of folly and riot run mad, and feared that her pit should lead to the bottomless pit. "Alas", she cried:

That my cornices, pilasters, cupolas, pillars
Should rise to be crowed o'er by windmills and
                    millers,
That my curtain should fall, and my screen form the
                    drop,
And my scenes be the scenes of the tap room and shop.

In reply "dram-o", clapping her dungaree to her rum-shotten eyes, says she is blameless; she keeps accommodation for all, and allows no man to pass should he want a mouthful of grog or a crust. The satirist himself provided the coda.

Long life to our rulers who give us the chance
Of mingling the opera sounds with the dance,
Each heavy-heeled bumpkin with vigour may prance,
And shout "We shall thus our dear country advance".

But Levey was untouched by these shafts aimed at his theatrical, hotel, and milling activities, and his often repeated claim that he had no other wish than to "Advance Australia". His second concert had among the audience the Chief Justice, Mr. Forbes; Mr. Justice Dowling and family; the Attorney-General; Mr. Sydney and Mr. Francis Stephen and their wives; Mr. and Mrs. Keith; Mr. and Mrs. Garling and their daughters; Colonel Dumaresq, and other military as well as civil officers. This time Levey sang a comic song, "Birch the Pastrycook", during the interval, leaving it to his audience either to remain in the theatre and listen, or retire to the saloon for refreshments. During the second half of this concert his song-sketch, "The Mail Coach", was "extracted from him by the loud calls of the audience".

For his third concert, held on 14 October, Levey had a number of minor alterations made to the boxes "to prevent intrusion", and had a new drop curtain painted. Ever planning ahead, and with but a single goal in view, he had noted the popular demand for his sketch and the statements in the press that he should be allowed to use the theatre for the purpose for which it was designed. Once again he determined to try the strength of the government ban on theatricals. Everything was again going well with him, and prospects were brighter than they had been for a long time. In addition, he had become a father again, of a son born on 10 October.

At his third concert Levey sang for the first time the comic song which Grimaldi the clown had made famous at Sadler's Wells in the 1810 pantomime *Bang Up; or, Harlequin Prime*. This was "Tippety-witchet, or Pantomimical Paroxysms", which no doubt Levey had heard Grimaldi sing at that theatre. It was a song very much like "Old Macdonald Had a Farm" in intent, but with human instead of animal noises after each verse.

> This very morning handy
>   My malady was such,
> I in my tea took brandy,
>   And took a drop too much. (Hiccups).
>   *Tol de rol, etc.*

57

Now I'm quite drowsy growing
 For this very morn,
I rose while cock was crowing,
 Excuse me if I yawn. (Yawns).
  Tol de rol, etc.

But stop, I mustn't nag hard,
 My head aches — if you please,
One pinch of Irish blackguard
 I'll take to give me ease. (Sneezes).
  Tol de rol, etc.

I'm not in cue for frolic,
 Can't up my spirits keep,
Love's a windy colic,
 'Tis that makes me weep. (Cries).
  Tol de rol, etc.

I'm not in mood for crying,
 Care's a silly calf,
If to get fat you're trying,
 The only way's to laugh. (Laughs).
  Tol de rol, etc.

In cold print the song seems almost meaningless, but as presented by Grimaldi with a musical accompaniment, and with each verse followed by a studied pause and "business" before the introduction of exaggerated sneezes, hiccups, yawns, and laughs it almost convulsed his audience. Levey's audience was equally delighted.

Although the third concert had to be postponed to 19 October because of unfavourable weather, it was such a success that Levey felt emboldened to announce from the stage that at his next performance he would be "At Home" after the manner of the celebrated Charles Mathews. This entertainment, announced for 4 November, consisted of two halves, the whole being given by Levey alone. The first half was an expanded version of his "Mail Coach", and the second, "A Dab at all Work", detailed the trials and vicissitudes of a provincial theatre manager.

On 2 April 1818 Charles Mathews the elder had given the first of his "At Home" performances at the English Opera House, later to become famous as the Lyceum. An actor who until then had not had much success, Mathews drew large audiences with his gallant and successful attempt to amuse London by his sole efforts. His programme proved so successful it was presented four times a week until 17 June, and was followed by similar one-man entertainments of his for many years afterwards. It was the first of the "quick change" impersonation performances which have ever since been a feature of theatrical fare. For its setting Mathews used no more than a room scene with such properties as a table, lamp, and chair, and the necessary costume accessories. His first entertainment was *Mail Coach Adventures,* and it must have been on this that Levey modelled first his comic sketch, and then his "At Home."

Levey had memorized but a pale shadow of Mathew's performance, and had added a number of simple caricatures of his own. What he was not able to imitate was Mathews' "Lecture on Ventriloquy", in which the actor, playing valet to a supposedly sick man, "threw" the voice of the sick man, the housekeeper, the butler, and a doll "child", and finished by singing a duet with each of these characters in turn.

The people of Sydney proved no different from the people of London when faced with the prospect of seeing a one-man performance. Levey had a full house, and also an unwelcome but surely not unexpected visitor. The "laird" himself, the angry Colonial Secretary, Alexander Macleay, appeared in person backstage and attempted to stop the performance. He had right on his side, for this was to be a theatrical performance not a concert, and Levey had been expressly forbidden to present theatrical performances of any kind. His licence was for balls and concerts only. But once again Levey confronted officialdom with a *fait accompli,* this time a full house. The excitable little Barnett Levey, volubility itself, was placatory and derisory, appealing and abusive in turn while the dour Scot fumed and snorted and looked high disdain at the wily Levey. Did the Honourable Colonial Secretary seriously expect him to give the whole of the audience its money back and send everyone home?

Did he want to see a riot that would end with the destruction of Levey's theatre? The wordy backstage battle was furious, and lasted for some time, with Macleay standing by the law and Levey finally playing his trump card, the waiting audience, for all it was worth. Maybe the government thought the Sydney people were not yet ready for theatrical performances, but the Sydney people themselves thought otherwise, as Mr. Macleay could see for himself. Levey finally won a grudging permission to present his performance for that night only.

Again the night was an unqualified success for Levey, but as it was the first and last of its kind it availed him little. He reverted to his concerts, announcing that a "splendid vocal and instrumental concert" would be given at the Royal Assembly Rooms on 27 November. For this, he said, the saloon would be specially decorated with shrubberies, and would have in the centre an illuminated transparency depicting Science instructing Europe, Africa, and America. Said the *Australian*:

> We hear the great *Censor Morum* — the mighty Mac means to make a stir, and to call his puritanical exertions into play, so that if there not be plenty of bowing and scraping, and all sorts of cringing work, Sydney is to have no more concerts — no — not to hear the shrieking of a wry-necked fife, much less the sonorous bagpipe, unless the laird will it otherwise. . .

The concert was a failure, being poorly attended, and using this fact as an excuse and an example, Levey, a consistent trier, applied to the Colonial Secretary on 12 December for permission to present another "At Home". In the meantime he announced another concert for 31 December, to close the year. This was so poorly attended that he refunded their money to the few who had turned up.

The public wanted no more concerts. Having enjoyed his "At Home" to the full, they showed that they considered concerts a poor substitute in the only way they could — they stayed away. As if this was not misfortune enough with which to have a New

Year ushered in, on the following day Levey received the Colonial Secretary's reply to his letter of 12 December. He was told that he could have no more than a licence similar to his former one, allowing him to hold balls and concerts, and that this would be forfeited by any breach of the condition on which it was granted.

Levey tried once more, on 7 January, only to get another refusal. "Your former application having already been decided on by the Governor in Council, the subject cannot again be brought forward", Macleay wrote in reply.

6

And Levey, Long Live He!

Barnett Levey was now desperate. He could still live on the profits of his hotel, but nothing was available to meet the overdue mortgage on his Waverley estate, or on the large sum of money expended on his buildings. The mill had never paid for itself, and the hotel was little more than a bar and a taproom, with a saloon in which the occasional public ball was held. With concerts no longer popular and "At Homes" forbidden, his most important potential source of income was cut off. Again he made a move which could be interpreted either as an attempt to hand his failures over to someone else (as with the mill), or as a forlorn hope that somebody would be willing to pay for the privilege of proving he could run things better than Barnett Levey. Early in January 1830 he advertised that the proprietor of the Royal Hotel, "being in a very bad state of health, which prevents him paying attention to business", was willing to let the Royal Hotel, with or without stock. The attempt was not successful. Nobody was interested enough to take on the hotel, and on 4 February his Waverley estate was sold up.

Three weeks later he tried again, this time advertising his granary and stores to let. He let a little space, but financially the result was little more than the provision of something where before there had been nothing. Barnett hung on, faced with what he must have known was to be the final collapse of his grandiose dreams. And meanwhile the convict theatre at Emu Plains again opened its doors, presenting *Rob Roy* and *The Village Lawyer* on 8 May to a house "crowded to excess" with not less than 200 present. Among the audience were the Chief Justice and Mrs. Forbes; Sir John Jamison; Mr. Cox, and Mr. Blaxland. The *Gazette* reported that the theatre was a place of private amusement only, but that presents were offered and accepted of materials for dresses and decorations.

What Barnett Levey — deprived of the opportunity to open either a private or public theatre, unable even to present his sketches — must have thought on reading this requires no elaboration. Governor Darling and the Colonial Secretary were anti-theatre, but still they condoned a theatre in a convict settlement attended by people who were not only free but also "respectable". Nor did the anomaly escape the attention of the Sydney people themselves.

But Levey knew there was no redress, and in any event he had other matters on his mind. He had determined on a last desperate bid. If it came off, it would bring him a badly needed £10,000 to keep in his name everything he had worked for. He advertised the disposal of his "valuable and extensive premises" on the plan of a tontine, in 200 shares at £50 each. A tontine, he was careful to explain, was a plan by which a shareholder or tontiner bought one or more shares and nominated as the beneficiary one of his youngest dependents. Each shareholder received an annuity on his shares during his lifetime. On his death the shares passed on and eventually the stage was reached, in theory, when the last survivor enjoyed the whole of the income. This ingenious form of gambling was initiated in France by a Neapolitan banker named Lorenzo Tonti, as a means of raising government loans. Throughout the eighteenth century the tontine was used in England and elsewhere to raise money for building houses, hotels, baths, and other buildings.

Levey's advertisement detailed the extent of his buildings, including the mill, which he had still not dismantled; their value, which he estimated at £16,000, and their prospects as money-earners. The theatre, he advised intending subscribers, would be sure to be licensed at some time in the future, "as the civilisation of the colony advances". Lists for those wishing to subscribe their name to the tontine lay at the Royal Hotel, at two inns in Parramatta, at Mr. Doyle's at Windsor, at Mr. Bodenham's in Sydney, and at the two Sydney banks.

But even such a wide-cast net as this was not large enough to catch the wily capitalist. Tontiners proved as scarce now as theatre shareholders had a few years since, and the tontine scheme simply petered out. This despite the fact that the *Australian* claimed on 9 July that upwards of "130 lives" were nominated and only about a score of shares remained to be sold.

Meantime, to counter the still active Emu Plains theatre, and to bolster his finances, Levey announced a final concert for 31 August. The unpredictable Sydney public crowded it to the doors, which could not have been solely because admission charges were only five shillings for boxes (that is, for seats in the boxes) and three shillings for the pit, as against the previous seven and five shillings. The audience heard a number of amateurs sing, play, and recite, and the "inimitable Barnett Levey" sing "Birch the Pastrycook", "Flow Thou Regal Purple Stream", "The Beautiful Boy", "My Love is Gone to Botany Bay", and his "Miss Manglewurzel", a song in which ridiculously maltreated words were sung in a high falsetto voice. This character song was obviously based on the caricature of Miss De Camp in *Blue Beard*, which Grimaldi introduced into his burlesque of that play at Sadler's Wells. It made fun of the English habit of paying large sums to foreign singers for them to sing something the English couldn't understand. Levey's audience loved it. The newspaper reports were again almost unanimous in their claim that Levey alone should have been allowed to entertain the house. Only the *Australian* found the concert, apart from Levey's contribution, "insufferably tame and insipid".

Delighted with this fresh sign of encouragement, Levey again bounced up like a rubber ball and applied to the Colonial Secretary for permission to present an "At Home", and was again refused.

Soon after this the "theatricals" at Emu Plains, also emboldened by favourable press reports of their performances, were foolhardy enough to advertise for the first time in those newspapers that on 30 November they would present the celebrated national tragedy of *Douglas,* and the farce of *The Padlock,* "by permission". Darling had been lax and certainly unfair in permitting these performances at Emu Plains while withholding permission for a theatre to be opened in Sydney. His reasons can only be guessed at, but now the convicts had very foolishly forced his hand. These advertisements appeared on 6 and 10 November. On 22 November the Superintendent of Convicts at Emu Plains, John Maxwell, received a curt letter from Alexander Macleay informing him, with each word underscored, that any further performance by the convicts was immediately to be discontinued. The performers were to be assigned to private service, he instructed, and others would be sent to Emu Plains to replace them.

Small comfort to Barnett Levey. Every move he had made to establish a theatre in Sydney had been blocked. A special act had even been "invented" to ensure that no public performance could be held without a licence from the government — an act which the Colonial Secretary had himself policed to the extent of hounding Levey in his own theatre. And yet its strength, ineluctable in Sydney, had not been sufficient to carry it a distance of 36 miles or so to Emu Plains. Darling, the Governor with the attitude of a drill sergeant-major, was seen by him as the arch-enemy. This finding was endorsed by the emancipists, the press, and Wentworth and his allies. Macleay, willing tool of the autocrat, was also proscribed. It was a brawling atmosphere in which neither side was able to see the other's good points. There could be no freedom until the colony had freed itself of Darling the incubus, said one side. There could be no progress, no real development, until the emancipists, despite their wealth and parvenu arrogance, learnt to accept their lowly position in a society designed at the outset to provide free convict labour for the exclusive few, said

65

the other. It was deadlock, but only temporary. Darling could not last for ever. The wonder was that he had lasted as long as he had.

At this stage the *Australian* took it on itself to make a remarkable prediction. It said that in eighteen months' time, despite all the "Saints" could do (i.e. the anti-theatrical hypocrites who were against the drama on what they called moral principles) Sydney would add to its public amusements the moral and intellectual drama.

Again, small comfort to Levey. His world was down about his ears. All his buildings in George Street — hotel, theatre, warehouse, windmill — it appeared, were mortgaged to the limit, and now the reckoning had arrived. On 30 November, "by order of the mortgagees", it was announced that "that splendid property No 72 George Street" would be offered for sale without reserve on 17 December at public auction.

Levey's collection of buildings was described in various newspaper references as having cost him from £16,000 to £20,000 to build. It occupied a George Street frontage of 50 feet, of which 17 feet were taken up by the store or shop originally built by Solomon Levey, and later used by Barnett as a store and a home. When Barnett took over he first built his Colchester Warehouse, well back from the street, and later built his Royal Hotel in front of this to the same height. That these two buildings were joined and equal in height is proved by the fact that all the advertisements for the auction sale describe the topmost floor as being a loft, 217 feet long and 33 feet wide.

The George Street frontage of the Royal Hotel in 1830 had a built-up portico 40 feet wide by 10 feet. Beneath this portico was the ground or sub-basement floor of the building which, like the store which comprised the ground floor of the warehouse behind it, was not entirely a basement but was partly above ground: sufficient to provide light and ventilation. Dealing with the hotel building first, in 1830 the ground floor contained a taproom and store; a kitchen 40 feet by 21 feet by 11 feet with two fireplaces,

66

oven and other necessaries; a water tank, over which was a wine storeroom 20 feet by 9 feet; and a store 60 feet by 32 feet by 12 feet. The tank contained an estimated 70 tons of water, and had a pump in the centre.

Walking up the portico steps and across the portico the visitor found first of all a lobby or hallway 40 feet by 9 feet, two parlours 21 feet by 15 feet by 17 feet, a bar 15 feet by 10 feet, a bedroom 15 feet by 10 feet, and the saloon 60 feet by 30 feet by 17 feet, which contained an entrance to the theatre at one end. At the front end of the lobby was a circular staircase which communicated with the lower and upper floors.

The floor above the saloon contained a walk or verandah over the portico, a Masonic room 40 feet by 21 feet, an anteroom 12 feet by 9 feet, and a supper room 60 feet by 32 feet by 12 feet. The next floor had originally been designed to contain bedrooms, but at the time of the sale it was still unfinished, lacking joists and floorboards. Above this again was the 217 feet by 32 feet loft. The warehouse building, which contained the theatre, has already been described.

In the backyard, connected with George Street by a side entrance or laneway (which was also the entrance for the pit audience of the theatre), was a coach-house with kitchen and stables, and bedrooms and a hayloft above. There was also a well, and a spring in the centre of the yard, 4 feet below the surface.

This large, even grand assembly of buildings, which drought, depression, and an unsympathetic governor (to say nothing of the idiosyncracies of its owner) together had rendered useless for the purposes for which it was designed, was sold in four lots. Lot 1 was the Royal Hotel; lot 2 the warehouse and theatre; lot 3 the original shop or store, and lot 4 the yard buildings. The mill, though still *in situ,* was not for sale. It was, according to the advertisements, to be removed to another site.

The mortgagors possibly, and Levey certainly, expected the buildings to go for a total of £10,000 at least. They in fact were sold for £3,595, lot 1 bringing £1,750, lot 2 £1,200, lot 3 £500, and lot 4 £105. The buyers were Cooper and Levey, from which it may be inferred that Barnett's "empire building" was financed all along by Solomon, whose firm now moved in to save what was left of his money and assets.

The first thing the new owners did was to pull down the portico front to the hotel and replace it. They also called tenders from builders, carpenters, and masons for alterations and additions designed to turn the hotel into what it should have been from the start, and what it possibly would have been had Barnett Levey's many schemes succeeded — a modern and comfortable hotel.

Barnett, now entirely on his own, advertised first from a Park Street address that he would conduct a raffle of a diamond-cut set of coral "ornaments" — comb, headpieces, necklace, ear-rings, bracelets — set in fine gold, and with cameos. He said it had cost the proprietor £250 in one of the best manufactories in France. The raffle was to consist of twenty members at £4 each, paid in advance. The ornaments would then be thrown for with the dice, the highest of three throws to be the winner. As with so many of Levey's minor activities, silence covers the result. He also started business as a watchmaker, which in effect meant that he employed someone skilled in that work at his shop, located in George Street at the King's Wharf.

Then in May the newspapers announced further details of the alterations at the Royal Hotel. The Corinthian pillars in front had been replaced by Doric pillars of white freestone; the apartments were being partitioned off, making the whole building "adapted for a first rate inn". As for the theatre, it was to remain untouched "till our political moralists cease to ape the fanatics of former days in other respects besides their vicious fooleries and their hypocritical saintship". Among the improvements was the addition of an "orchestra" to the hotel's elegant saloon. This was no doubt a structure built out from one of the walls (almost certainly over the end wall doorway leading to the theatre) like a balcony or a solitary theatre box, and surmounted by the royal

The original eighteenth century seating in the gallery of the Theatre Royal, Bristol (1766). British Travel Association, 1967

Proscenium and front curtain, the restored Georgian theatre at Richmond, Yorkshire (1788). *Yorkshire Post*, 1965

Auditorium of the restored Georgian theatre at Richmond, Yorkshire (1788). *Yorkshire Post*, 1965

Barnett Levey's George Street building with the incomplete mill on top (numbered 14). Robert Burford, *Description of a View of the Town of Sydney, N.S.W.* (London, 1829)

coat of arms. Here a band or an orchestra could provide music without impeding the free flow of the people in the saloon.

In August Levey, who had retained his auctioneer's licence, was auctioning property at Windsor during race week. He would have made an entertaining and amusing auctioneer, his "theatrical" personality having a great deal to do with the success of his sales.

The Royal Hotel was reopened in October by Mr. G. Sippe, late bandmaster of the 57th Regiment, and a personal friend of Barnett's. In the same month Barnett's signature was one of about a dozen to a petition asking the Sheriff of New South Wales that on some day before the imminent departure of Governor Darling from the colony the sheriff would call a public meeting to consider the propriety of voting an address to His Majesty in England on three grounds, the last and most pertinent of which was

> ... For the benefit conferred upon the Colony, by the recall of Lieutenant General Darling and the appointment of a successor in the person of Major General Bourke, and praying that His Majesty will be pleased to adopt such measures as may be calculated to prevent the recurrence of various grievances, which have taken place during the existing administration.

Darling, meticulous in such matters, duly forwarded this letter to the Colonial Office in London. Against Levey's name had been penned (by either Macleay or the Governor), not the phrase "a person of the lowest class" of some years before, but the even more contemptuous "an insolvent Jew".

Governor Darling's departure from the colony was celebrated by a large portion of its population with bonfires and drunken jubilation. Wild, indeed, was the outdoor party held by Wentworth in the grounds of his home at Vaucluse.

If Darling could be said to have been the wrong man for the time, it could also be said that his successor, Bourke, was the right one. But each owed much more to the work of his predecessor than he perhaps realized. Darling reaped the full effect of Macquarie's humane treatment of convicts and ex-convicts.

Macquarie had given them back their manhood by making it possible for them to prove that they could be useful, successful citizens. Darling was unable to handle these successful ex-convicts who not only believed they had a stake in the country and its government, but were determined to say so. He was not the man for them, because he never doubted that he was right and they wrong. But despite them and his own nature, Darling achieved much for the good of the colony during his term of office, and was certainly not quite so black as the pro-emancipist newspapers occasionally painted him. That he was a stern moralist and something of a military martinet were two of the reasons why he often could not see "the wood for the trees" when dealing with the more unruly and irrepressible colonists. He was not accustomed to being publicly sneered at, to being criticized, lampooned, and censured in the newspapers, or to being disobeyed by those under him, and he had to endure all these things during his term as Governor. But although he was hounded even on his return to England by the more vituperative and vindictive of his former charges, neither they nor their supporters were able to harm him. He had done what he believed he had been sent out to do, and if he had been a little too strait-laced, a little too unbending and superior, he had at least stuck by his principles. His successor proved to be his opposite, in that he at least knew how to temper the wind to the shorn lamb without loss of dignity.

All this time Levey continued to live in the small building in George Street which was put up by Solomon Levey. It was not until December 1831 that he advertised he was about to leave the premises and would dispose of his stock by auction. Already hope was flaring within him again, that incredible optimism which needed but the tiniest spark to set it glowing. A new governor was coming. The hated Darling could be forgotten. His anti-theatrical toadies and weathercocks could be forgotten.

Levey was again a signatory, this time one of thirty-seven, to a petition to the sheriff asking that a public meeting be held to address Governor Bourke on his assuming government. It was beginning to look as though the *Australian*'s prediction of the year before was likely to come true. Even if nobody else thought so, Levey did.

Levey's next venture, and one he felt sure would be a temporary one only, was his "Reform Auction Mart", in which he held nightly auctions, the reform being his willingness to lend cash in advance without interest on any goods sent in for sale. This and his watchmaking business kept him going until April 1832, when the *Gazette,* unabashed by any of its earlier attitudes to the establishment of a theatre in Sydney, broke the news that His Excellency the Governor had signified his assent to a licence being granted to Mr. Barnett Levey for dramatic entertainments in Sydney. Said this newspaper: ". . . so that we very shortly expect to see the very pretty little theatre at the rear of the Royal Hotel opened with as efficient a company as can be obtained in the Colony".

The newly-arrived *Herald* now joined the chorus, announcing that the theatre was to undergo extensive alterations and repairs. For Levey, just waiting the opportunity, had not only advertised the immediate sale of his stock in trade at the Reform Auction Mart, and his watch and clock business, but, fired again with grandiose schemes, had announced that the theatre ceiling would be removed (i.e. raised) and another tier of boxes would be added to the auditorium. By the next month these projected improvements had grown to "the windmill to be taken down; the ceiling to be elevated at least 12ft, and a gallery and a second tier of boxes to be added". For the first time a tentative opening date was mentioned — "in about ten weeks hence". It is to be feared that the news of these alterations, however they leaked out or were distributed, were garbled by the time they reached publication, for the theatre already had a "second" tier of boxes.

Again Levey ran into financial difficulties because of his grand schemes. He evidently planned to raise the theatre ceiling, though possibly only at the back of the theatre, so as to permit the construction of a gallery which would run at a sharp angle from the

71

front of a planned third tier of boxes up to the back wall, thus increasing the theatre's seating capacity by more than a third. The lowest tier of boxes was also to be raised a little, because it was too close for the comfort of the occupants to the benches in the pit, the rowdiest area in the theatres of the period. All this had to be paid for, which meant that money had to be obtained somehow, and so Levey applied for a licence to hold some of his At Homes, not in the theatre, but in the saloon of the Royal Hotel. He was granted permission to hold a series of these on 10 and 17 September, and on 1 and 18 October 1832, to enable him to meet the necessary expenses of providing scenery, properties, dresses, and decorations for his theatre.

For the first of these At Homes Levey again put on the cloak of Mathews and gave more or less the same performance he had given in 1829, except that this time he introduced a few more characters and polished up the earlier ones.

The Royal Hotel saloon was 60 feet long, 30 feet wide, and 17 feet high. In this space Levey had installed a small stage under the "orchestra", complete with curtains and footlamps, and benches for the audience. On the first night of his At Home season the room was so crowded that thirty had to be turned away. And because the room was so crowded those at the back chose the best possible way of seeing what was going on on the stage — they stood on the benches instead of sitting on them. But apart from the occasional disagreement this caused until those standing were finally persuaded to sit down, the evening was very successful. The *Gazette* concluded its favourable review with a specially written quatrain:

> Then let us sing, long live the King!
> And Levey, long live he!
> And when he is "At Home" again,
> We *will* be there to see.

With this practical tryout of the saloon "theatre" it was found that the stage was too low for the comfort of those seated at the back, so for the second performance it was raised to 18 inches in height. The members of the orchestra were moved, for this second performance, from their "balcony" to the front of and facing the stage, as in the average theatre. There is no doubt that soon after this the saloon "orchestra" was done away with.

Seats for these At Homes cost five shillings each, and the performances attracted everybody from Chief Justice Forbes and Sir John Jamison to "gentlemen bruisers amusing themselves by disfiguring each other's faces".

Although Levey had stated quite clearly in his original advertisements that his entertainments were to be "At Homes à la Mathews", in reporting the second performance the *Gazette* said it found little of Mathews but a great deal of Levey evident.

> Although Mr. Levey designated his entertainment "At Home;" and although the plan is somewhat like that of Mathews, yet it is not an imitation of Mathews "At Home," nor of Yates "At Home," nor of anybody else "At Home" that we remember having seen. It is Levey "At Home" — he conceives a general outline of the picture he wishes to draw, and leaves the filling up, the lights and shadows, to chance or the inspiration of the moment — whereas, the entertainments of Mathews and of Yates are usually the compositions of some of the first comic dramatists of the day. Levey, therefore, in addition to the undoubted humour which he possesses, is also entitled to the very rare merit of originality.

For the performance on 1 October Levey put on what he claimed was a new programme, which was little more than yet another variation on the first Charles Mathews At Home, even to the inclusion of the legal gentlemen presented in that programme. This entertainment he held in his still unfinished theatre "for the better accommodation of his friends, and to prevent irregularities". It also gave him the opportunity to increase admission charges to six shillings for a seat in the boxes, and four shillings for the pit. He also, for the first time, called in a stage assistant, a Mr. John Meredith of the Standard Tavern, George Street. Mr. Meredith, it was said, was no less stage-struck than

Mr. Levey himself, but he fancied himself as a tragedian. The *Monitor* was not impressed by either his ambitions or his performance, and accused him not only of being imperfect in his part but also of having used a naughty word in the hearing of the ladies in the audience.

> We begin to suspect that Mr. Meredith's abilities do not lie either in tragedy or comedy; but in melo-dramas, such as performed at Sadler's Wells and the Surrey Theatre. If so, there is little hope for "the *theatre*" in New South Wales; for we had always understood that Mr. Meredith was a crack tragedian and could recite well from Shakespeare.

Levey, this newspaper decided, trod the stage very well and his "attitudes" were good, but his voice and pronunciation were suited solely to low comedy. Then, after gazing into the crystal ball without which no editorial office is complete, the *Monitor* forecast that Mr. Levey would no doubt make a clumsy attempt to establish a theatre. "Though clumsy, however, it will be sure to ruin *him*. For in the first place, if Mr Meredith is to be the crack actor on our Australian stage, of what description of performers will be the jack-puddings who will have to take the *second and third-rate* parts?"

With these findings the other newspapers both agreed and disagreed. *Hill's Life* also heard the naughty word, but otherwise enjoyed the performance. It said of Levey that his talent as an imitator was unquestionable. "If he would take pains to *cultivate* his powers," it said, he would prove a humble disciple of Mathews, "who is so inimitable in his imitation of original characters." The *Gazette* was all enthusiasm, and regretted that the *Monitor* should have gone to such pains "to break a butterfly on the wheel". It also denied that Meredith had used a naughty word.

In these reports Levey had a first taste of the conflicting views and opinions dramatic representations in Sydney were to call forth from the press. Rarely were these reports the work of the same man twice running, for on odd occasions the editors themselves attended to criticize, sometimes they sent a reporter,

sometimes they paid an outside contributor to report, and sometimes they merely reprinted (with acknowledgments) a fellow
editor's report holus-bolus from his newspaper.

That the criticism, deserved or not, rankled, Levey showed at
his final At Home performance before the opening of his first
dramatic season. At its conclusion he came forward and delivered
an "Epilogue" which he had written himself, answering the
Monitor's criticisms and finishing with a couplet which is the
only scrap of this interesting piece of work to have survived. He
intended, he said, to appear:

In comic line in Colman's plays —
And read the lines of Shakespeare's rays.

Some days later he announced that he would award an engraved
silver medal for an approved "Opening Address" to be spoken
at the first night of the Sydney Theatre Royal.

7

With Great Éclat

Barnett Levey was granted his theatre licence by Governor Bourke on the understanding that no convict would be employed at the theatre, a condition quite easy for Levey to accept. The catch now, of course, was that he did not own a theatre. Either he took matters in his own hands, as usual, or he came to some arrangement with the new owners, Cooper and Levey, for he announced on 30 April 1832 that the ceiling of the disused theatre was to be raised and another tier of boxes added. This statement was repeated on 11 May and 9 June. By August it was being said that the theatre should be ready for use, with the alterations completed, in two months' time.

It seems from these and subsequent reports that Levey's plans for "his" theatre did not meet with the approval of the owners, and that he had some difficulty in bringing them up to scratch — in persuading them he knew best what he wanted. Work on the theatre, if it ever really started, seems to have stopped altogether for a time. Perhaps whatever difficulties there were had been brought about by the *Monitor*'s remarks after Levey's At Home in the theatre. This newspaper finished its far from laudatory notice of this performance with a "warning" directed at the theatre owners, to which they must have paid attention: ". . . and we do think that the representatives of Cooper and Levey will inflict an injury on Mr. Levey and family if they should be induced to enlarge the present theatre on *his representations*". This statement makes it clear that despite the many paragraphs published on the proposed renovation and reconstruction of the theatre nothing had been done. The words "if they should be induced to enlarge the present theatre" give the game away. Levey had been trying to force the owners into action by publishing, or causing to be published by means of newspaper "puffs", his, not their, intentions.

There was not another performance in the theatre, but from his At Homes Levey apparently raised enough money to enable him to embark on a new scheme. He no longer owned the theatre or the hotel, but if he could not use the theatre (because the owners would not carry out the changes he wanted) there was nothing to stop him from sub-letting the hotel saloon from the lessee, and turning it into a theatre. This he did. At the same time he seems to have played a number of very clever cards to manoeuvre the theatre owners into a position where they would agree to do what he wanted.

First it was announced in the Press on 17 November 1832 that the "old" theatre could not be completed "in the time originally projected", but so as not to disappoint the public Mr. Levey would fit up the hotel saloon with a tier of boxes and other requisites as a temporary theatre. A subsequent announcement fixed the opening day of the saloon Theatre Royal as 26 December 1832. This theatre, it was said, would be used for six months, "at the end of which time the new theatre fitting up in the building of Messrs. Hughes and Hoskings at the Market Wharf shall be completed". Levey thus let the public and the owners of his original theatre know that he would not be stopped from conducting a theatre; that he would conduct his saloon theatre for six months and would then move into an entirely new theatre in another building. Cooper and Levey, the implication was clear, would be left with an incomplete, unprofitable empty theatre which they could not use, for even supposing there was somebody else willing and able to open it Sydney could not support two theatres. Cooper and Levey capitulated. The *Herald* of 3 December carried their advertisement calling for tenders for alterations to the theatre — plans and specifications by Mr. Verge.

Levey's victory was announced four days later with a calm press statement that he had altered his arrangements with regard to the theatre. "The old one being far advanced in repair will require a much shorter time in completing than the proposed new one at the Market Wharf, besides which it has the advantage as to situation." This was no doubt a face-saver inserted for Cooper and Levey's benefit. It seems likely, bearing in mind all that had gone before, and the fact that almost twelve months were to pass before the changes to the old theatre were completed, that work on the old theatre had not even started. But Levey had gained his way, and was prepared to be magnanimous.

The architect who designed Levey's first Theatre Royal, the one now owned by Cooper and Levey, was Francis Greenway, who had last been in England, at Bristol, in 1813. The man who converted the saloon of the Royal Hotel into a theatre for him, and then re-designed and enlarged the original theatre, was John Verge, who was last in London in 1828. Both men were therefore familiar with the Georgian style in theatre architecture. Between Levey and Greenway was devised what must have been a perfect little Georgian theatre, used for the first time, as we have seen, on 20 August 1829. As late as 1840 it was decribed nostalgically as "a pretty little theatre" in which the sound was said to have been better than in the "larger" Victoria Theatre which succeeded it.

The saloon Theatre Royal opened as planned on 26 December 1832. Levey and his company, who were unnamed in the theatre advertisements and burst on the public as a surprise, presented Douglas Jerrold's *Black Ey'd Susan; or, All in the Downs,* and the farce, *Monsieur Tonson.* Box seats were five shillings and pit seats three shillings, so that the opening night held a house of about £90, but quite possibly more.

No less than three separate references show that the saloon theatre was fitted up to seat 500 persons. In fact, for one performance the *Herald* said 600 people were jammed into this small theatre. As we have seen, the saloon of the Royal Hotel measured 60 feet by 33 feet and was 17 feet high. In this space Levey had had a stage fitted, a pit, and one tier or gallery of boxes which ran around the three walls of the room, the proscenium and stage filling the fourth wall. The *Currency Lad*, a newspaper of the period, described this theatre in its issue of 22 December 1832, four days before it opened.

> Those who expect to see a "Drury Lane" or even an "Adelphi" will find themselves egregiously deceived, but those who may go with no higher expectation than to witness the first playhouse in a young colony, will be agreeably surprised. The stage is on as high an elevation as the place would allow, with the usual foot lamps. The orchestra is in the usual place and well arranged. The floor of the saloon forms the pit, the seats being on a gradual rise, and capable of accommodating 350 persons. There are six private boxes, three on each side, which with those opposite the stage will hold 150 more...

Allowing in this saloon theatre a possible depth of 20 feet for the stage, the auditorium would then have been 40 feet in depth, its width being 33 feet. Ingress and egress for the actors would have been through the door, now at the back of the stage, which led from the saloon into the original theatre. With three boxes to each side wall, each box must have measured about 13 feet wide and perhaps 5 feet deep. With this measurement there could have been two 12 feet wide boxes facing the stage, on the back wall of the saloon; or, if there were three, each could have been 8 feet wide. The pit stretched the full width of the room, under the side boxes but not under the "front boxes" on the back wall. The space here would have been needed for the entrance and circulating lobby for the audience to find its way to the pit seats and up the small stairways to the box seats. The stage must have been, in the most graphic sense of the word, "miniature". Said the *Gazette*:

> ... The stage is, indeed, so small — unavoidably so, however

— that the performers have not space to move about in; their action consequently seems contracted, and their altitude not a little increased. The ladies, for instance, looked unfemininely tall; and Mr. Meredith, to all appearances, had added at least six inches to his height. . .

Levey's first playbill announced that *Black Ey'd Susan* and *Monsieur Tonson* would be performed on 26 December, *Black Ey'd Susan* and *Fortune's Frolic* on 29 December, a repeat of the first programme on 31 December, *A Tale of Mystery* and *The Village Lawyer* on 1 January 1833, *A Tale of Mystery* and *Fortune's Frolic* on 3 January, and *A Tale of Mystery* and *Monsieur Tonson* on 5 January. Seats in the boxes were five shillings, and in the pit three shillings. Doors opened at half-past six, and the performance started at seven o'clock. At nine o'clock half price was to be allowed.

In all his theatrical arrangements Levey showed that either by personal experience or meticulous observation he had gained a wide knowledge of theatre practice before his arrival in Australia. He called his theatre the Theatre Royal and his players "His Majesty's servants", when in fact the theatre had no royal patent and his players were merely the public's servants. This could be dismissed as pretension on his part, but in fact it went deeper than that. Levey was a man truly enamoured of the theatre, and of Levey as the man who established the theatre in Australia against "incredible odds". If he saw his theatre as a miniature Drury Lane or Covent Garden, patent and all, what harm was there in that? Even the newspapers humoured him by allowing the use of the royal crest above his advertisements. Everything about his theatre, Levey decided, had to be as "professional" as possible, even though no one associated with it in its early years was more than an amateur by any standard.

And in the matter of half price Levey was also following a well-established English precedent. As early as 1763 riots broke out at Covent Garden and Drury Lane because the management decided to abolish the half-price system. Half price grew out of an earlier theatrical practice of allowing people into the theatre free after the third act. As theatre programmes grew longer, sometimes as many as three pieces being given on the one night, and much more could be seen after the third act of a drama than used to be the case, the practice of charging half price after the third act was adopted. It survived to as late as the 1870's, as an artistic as well as economic necessity, for it ensured that the theatre and its coffers were full for the "strong" scenes or pieces in the programme.

Black Ey'd Susan was one of the first of a host of nautical dramas peculiar to the English theatre which had a stage life of up to seventy years. So popular were they that as late as 1856 one critic wrote of the productions at a London theatre: "The shipping interest is here represented — its playbills ought to be posted at Lloyds. Vessels are wrecked in latitude O.P., longitude P.S. As you enter you smell the 'distempered sea.' You sniff the brine of the 'set waters' and feel the dusty spray of the canvas waves."

Black Ey'd Susan was first produced at the Surrey Theatre on 8 June 1829, with T.P. Cooke playing the part of William. It was an immediate success, and set a record by running for 400 consecutive performances. So popular was it that even Covent Garden insisted on presenting it, and T.P. Cooke used to finish his performance at the Surrey and, in costume and make-up, walk to Covent Garden and go through the same play there. As a play it had an extraordinarily long life. It was still being presented in Sydney in the 1860's, while in London it underwent various transformations in a life which lasted almost to the end of the century. The Kendals presented an altered version at the St. James's in 1880 under the title *William and Susan*. The same plot was again used at Drury Lane in 1891 in *A Sailor's Knot*. It remained for "matinée idol" William Terriss to conceive the novel idea of presenting it under its original title at the Adelphi as late as 1897, where it proved as popular as ever with audiences.

Monsieur Tonson, one of the farce afterpieces which were customary in the eighteenth and early nineteenth century theatre, was written by W.T. Moncrieff and had its first performance at Drury Lane in 1821. So that with his opening plays Levey was surprisingly up-to-date, one being eleven years old and the other only three.

Monsieur Tonson, as usual with a farce, is largely a play of misunderstandings, with the ubiquitous stage Frenchman as the butt. It is rather a silly piece in print, but on the stage has a life of its own which is essentially theatrical. Monsieur Morbleau, Madame Bellegarde, Adelphine de Courcey, Jack Ardourly, and Tom King (who repeatedly knocks on Morbleau's door in the hope of seeing Adelphine, and sees only Morbleau, whom he tries each time to stave off by asking if a fictitious Mr. Thompson ("Mr. Tonson") lives there) — all these characters provided a great deal of amusement for something like fifty years to audiences throughout the English-speaking world.

Considering the tyranny-overthrown-and-virtue-triumphant theme inherent in the opening of Levey's theatre at long last, the newspapers gave cursory treatment to that first performance on 26 December. The *Herald* said both pieces were well performed, and that a "correct report will be given in our next". The *Australian* "heard" that it had passed off "with great *eclat,* the utmost harmony and not the slightest disturbance . . . particulars probably in our next". The *Gazette* also "understood" that everything went off with "great éclat", but was prevented by a press of business from attending. It was left to the *Monitor, Currency Lad,* and *Hill's Life* to report the opening of the Theatre Royal with something like the seriousness it merited. The *Monitor* found that both pieces went off better than could be expected from a first essay. The house was full, and the audience so pleased that it occasionally cheered the stage. The *Currency Lad* agreed with this finding, adding that in Mr. Meredith, Mr. Cooper,* Mr. Vale, and Mr. Cook the proprietor possessed actors of no mean talent.

* Stage name adopted for the first few months by Conrad Knowles.

82

Hill's Life was also in agreement, noting that the performance "exceeded the expectations of the visitors, who cheered the stage repeatedly".

On 31 December the *Herald's* promised "in our next" covered the performance in detail, and expressed itself generally pleased apart from the need for "a little smarter motion" in the scene-shifting, and more lights throughout the house. All reports agreed that the second night's performance was better than the first. There was no mention of the prologue for which Levey had promised "the poets of Australia" an inscribed silver medal.

One newspaper described the theatre as having been crammed to suffocation, two estimated the attendance at 500, and one at 300.

Finally, and somewhat tardily (perhaps it was shamed into it) the *Australian* produced its "probably in our next" report, on 10 January 1833, as a letter to the editor from "An Old Playgoer". It was a laudatory notice by a man who was sure that the manner in which the pieces were presented would not have discredited any provincial theatre in England, and was equally sure that the performance was one of which Levey and his company could feel proud.

During this first season Levey's theatre was opened three nights a week, Mondays, Wednesdays, and Saturdays. About the middle of January Levey himself "took to the boards", playing the part of Sheepface in William Macready's comedy *The Village Lawyer,* first produced at the Haymarket in 1787. He was said to have played with a degree of humour, half-simple, half-knavish, which showed a happy idea of his part. But the real praise was received by Mr. Buckingham, who played Snark, and whose acting was given a lengthy, detailed report as against the two or three lines devoted to Levey. At the next presentation of *The Village Lawyer,* a few nights later, Levey handed over his part to a Mr. Dyball, who "sustained the character admirably".

Were Levey's audiences at all discriminating? The opening performances were not only a novelty, but the whole idea of theatre was something new to a large majority of his audiences, particularly the Australian-born "currency" lads and lasses. They perhaps neither knew nor cared whether the plays or the acting were good or bad according to other, more experienced or educated tastes. To them theatre was a fascinatingly new way of spending or getting through a night otherwise much the same as the remaining 364 in the year. On the other hand, the few who had known the London or English provincial theatre were often more critical than was necessary. From their published remarks it seems a great many of them were disappointed and even outraged because Levey's Theatre Royal was not a piece of London bodily transplanted. But in their remarks it is possible to detect a great deal of sham and pretension, and of politics and hypocrisy at the Mother Grundy level.

It was not long before the Sydney Theatre was considered to be so well established that its novelty could no longer be used as an excuse or palliative for its shortcomings. It was time for stronger measures, and the critics, those "dark sons of uncertain fathers", began to wield a more caustic pen. The first and subsequently most frequent criticism made of Levey's players was that they too often "gagged" (spoke any nonsense which came into their heads because they had forgotten their lines). A second and more serious complaint was that they used innuendos, and sometimes deliberate indecency, to get a laugh from the less reputable members of their audience. A third was that very often the prompter was the hardest worked man backstage; that his voice could always be heard when the actors' should have been.

The charge of indecency was given wide circulation in George Bennett's *Wanderings in New South Wales*. Although Bennett said he found the *tout ensemble* of the saloon theatre far exceeded what he had expected, he nevertheless played the part of hanging judge rather than critic in his account of the performance. He noted that some of the actors mistook indecency for wit, "and probably by doing so they pleased the majority of their audience". He also noticed that during the performance there were squabbles, threats, and actual combat among the occupants of the pit. Had he been

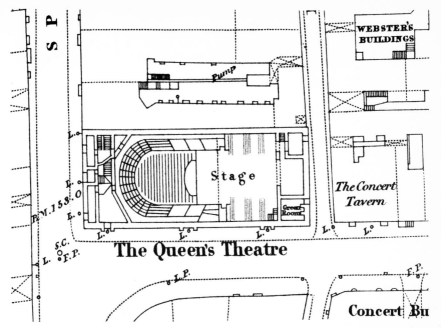

Ground plan of the Queen's Theatre, Manchester (1831), formerly the 1790 Manchester Theatre Royal. This is a typical Georgian theatre plan. Manchester Library

The architect's original drawing for the facade of the Royal Victoria Theatre, Sydney, 1838. An engraving of the facade as it was actually built, pared down by economic necessity, is to be seen in Fowles's *Sydney in 1848*. This engraving from *Maclehose's Picture of Sydney and Stranger's Guide for 1839* (Sydney, 1838)

The first Play Bill as Theatre Royal — printed in this Colony

THEATRE ROYAL,
SYDNEY.

ON WEDNESDAY, DECEMBER the 26th, 1832,
THIS THEATRE
Will open for the first time, with New Scenery, Machinery,
Dresses, and Decorations, under the management of
MR. MEREDITH.

The Pieces selected for the opening are first:
THAT MUCH ADMIRED
Nautical Melo - Drama,
IN THREE ACTS,
CALLED,
BLACK-EYED SUSAN;
OR,
ALL IN THE DOWNS.

ADMIRAL, by Mr. Vale.
CAPTAIN CROSSTREE, by Mr. Cooper.
LIEUTENANT PIKE, by Mr. Raymond.
BLUE PETER, by Mr. Richardson.
SEAWEED, by Mr. Taylor.
QUID, by Mr. Kirby.

DOGGRASS, by Mr. Buckingham.
JACOB TWIG, by Mr. L. C. Cook.
GNATBRAIN, by Mr. Vale.
PLOUGHSHARE, by Mr. Varley.
RAKER, by Mr. Hollingsworth.
HATCHET, by Mr. Hill.
YARN, by Mr. Sykes.

WILLIAM, BY MR. MEREDITH.
BLACK-EYED SUSAN, by Mrs. Love. DOLLY MAY-FLOWER, by Mrs. Weston.
Captains, Midshipman, Sailors, Villagers, &c. &c.
To conclude with that Far-famed Highly Comic Farce,
IN TWO ACTS,
FROM TAYLOR'S CELEBRATED POEM, ENTITLED,
MONSIEUR TONSON.

MORBLEU, by Mr. Meridith.
TOM KING, by Mr. Cooper.
JACK ARDOURLY, by Mr. Buckingham.
USEFUL, by Mr. Raymond.
WANTOM, by Mr. Taylor.
TRAP, by Mr. Kirby.

MR. THOMPSON, by Mr. Vale.
RUSTY, by Mr. Hill.
NAP, by Mr. Ryder.
FIP, by Mr. Hollingsworth.
WAITER, by Mr. Barnard.
SNAP, by Mr. Barns.

ADELPHINE DE COURCY, Mrs. Weston. MADAME BELLEGARDE, Mrs. Love.
MRS. THOMPSON, by Mrs Ward.

*The Performance to be supported by the Band of His Majesty's 17th Regiment, kindly
allowed by Colonel Despard, and conducted by Mr. Lewis.*

BOX SEATS 5s. PIT SEATS 3s.

an experienced theatregoer he would have been so used to seeing this in the pit of the London theatres he would not have thought it worth mentioning in connection with the Sydney theatre. He completed his brief account of his visit to Levey's theatre with a "historical" footnote which ever since has given a quite erroneous impression of the Theatre Royal and Royal Hotel.

Bennett was present at a performance of *The Heir at Law* and *Bombastes Furioso,* and it is significant that the indecency he complained of was not mentioned in newspaper reports of this performance, nor were the alleged fights. Because of the attitudes which the more literate portion of the travelling and resident population felt it necessary to adopt towards the theatre and the "lower class" colonials, their reports need a great deal more than surface reading.

By the end of January press critics were beginning to complain that "some of the dialogue" in the plays presented was "the offspring of the prolific brain of the actors, and not to be found in the author". This followed an earlier remark concerning a performance of *A Tale of Mystery,* in which one critic said the play would have been a great deal less mysterious if Meredith and one or two others had not left out so much of their parts.

Criticism of the acting also became more frequent as the critics became familiar with the actors' stock "attitudes" and mannerisms. This criticism was always in a "more in sorrow than in anger" vein, but was no respecter of persons. One actor was reminded that "dignity does not alone consist in folded arms and eye flung askance over the right shoulder". An actress was praised for the part she played in *Charles the Second,* but was warned not to grow careless on the strength of this commendation, as "she will find us just as ready to censure as to praise". Mrs. Weston's efforts as a dancer were approved on the first two occasions on which she appeared, apart from the statement that "Mrs. Weston danced a *pas seul* with some excitement to herself but evident satisfaction to the audience", but on the third the Gazette reporter found his patience was tried beyond bearing. ". . . Mrs. — we forget her name, would be, we dare say, a good partner in a country dance, and could manage to get through a quadrille; — but, a *pas seul*! 'No more o' that, Hal, an' thou lov'st me!'"

But on the whole the newspapers praised rather than blamed, and continued to laud the "indefatigible" Levey for his perseverance in providing Sydney with a theatre. Perhaps they also recognized that the members of his company had some heavy work to get through so as to keep up with the constantly changing programmes. They had to be proficient in a great variety of parts, while at the same time they had to keep on learning new ones. As the most popular play in the repertoire, *Black Ey'd Susan* was performed so many times it was comparatively easy for the actors to remember their lines in this play. But each time it was performed it was followed or preceded by a new production. On Monday night Meredith, for instance, would play in *Black Ey'd Susan* and *Bombastes Furioso;* on Wednesday night in *Fortune's Frolic* and *The Village Lawyer;* and on Saturday night in *Black Ey'd Susan* and *Monsieur Tonson*. During this week he would also be expected to learn something of his parts in the following Monday night's performance of *The Mayor of Garret* and *Charles the Second*. In addition, he and most of the other leading players had also to be perfect in whatever songs or dances these pieces called for. Levey's players were, by the standards of the time and by comparison with their fellow players in England, well paid; but they had to earn every penny of their wages. Again, this was typical of the theatre of the period. Two, or even three plays on the one night, plus divertissements of all kinds between them, were normal theatrical fare as far back as 1799, when Charles Macklin in one night played two parts in *Venice Preserved,* Harlequin in the entertainment that followed, sang three humorous songs between the acts, and danced an Irish jig between the play and the entertainment. Audiences, particularly those in the pit and gallery, could not be left to their own resources for long without them protesting, demonstrating, and even rioting because nothing was happening on the stage.

The double bill, a play and a curtain-raiser or afterpiece, survived well into the twentieth century, while in the early part of the nineteenth century to stage four plays on the one night was not considered unusual. It was not until the illness of an actress caused the sudden cancellation of a two-act drama, one of four pieces on the bill at London's Olympic Theatre, that Madame Vestris, the manager, decided to adhere from then on to the shorter bill — three pieces instead of four. She found that audiences were grateful for this opportunity to get home before twelve o'clock at night. Levey followed the fashion of his day, and sometimes gave his patrons performances which started at 7 P.M. and did not finish until after one o'clock in the morning.

8

So Much for Buckingham

Until he opened his theatre no one had ever heard of Levey's players as stage performers, apart from Meredith and Mrs. Jones. The former had appeared with Levey in his At Home, while Mrs. Jones had been one of the singers in the 1826 concerts. They were all inexperienced amateurs, a handful of whom had real talent and sufficient intelligence to foster and build on the experience he gave them. Most of them had little more than conceit or ego and sufficient imagination or vainglory to believe that, having learnt the rudiments of theatrecraft from Levey they had thus been transformed into Kembles, Keans, and Macreadys. The few — among them Meredith, Buckingham, and Knowles — clung to the foothold Levey gave them and made a life job of acting. The majority went the way of all amateurs who are content to remain amateur. A feature of Levey's theatre throughout its existence was the huge turnover in the acting ranks, by no means all of it due to Levey's own peculiarities.

A little more than a month after the opening of the Theatre Royal its unqualified success so far turned the heads of a few of his actors that they began to assume the airs of prima donnas or stars. They grew self-opiniated and assertive, and began to adopt airs and graces not only with their employer but also, in some instances, towards members of the audience. Mackie (variously spelt Mackie and Mackay) was the first to transgress. He took objection to some remarks made by two men in the audience in his hearing, and from the stage publicly insulted them by calling them "ticket-of-leave men". Levey summarily dismissed him, but, it appears, with more of politics than sincerity behind the act. Mackie was a valuable member of the stage *corps*, and Levey could ill afford to lose him for long. But this did not stop Mackie from stirring up more trouble. He was certainly a supporter if not an inciter of the moves subsequently made by Buckingham and Mrs. Weston for an increase in their wages.

With the obvious financial success of the theatre constantly before them, some of the actors attempted to gain a bigger share of the profits. Even though, as the *Gazette* soon reminded them, but for Levey most of them would have been behind a plough, they tried various ways of coercing him into giving them more money, finally threatening not to "go on" unless they were paid more. The prime leaders in this appear to have been Buckingham and Mrs. Weston, and though again he could ill afford to lose either, Levey dismissed both of them as a matter of principle. They were to have played that night, and so their places had to be taken by inexperienced and untutored players at a moment's notice. A Mr. Dyott replaced Mackie, Levey replaced Buckingham, and a Miss Bland replaced Mrs. Weston.

At that night's performance Levey and his remaining players had their first taste of "London" manners from a displeased theatre audience. There was, of course, a claque to lead the audience in its demonstration; a claque carefully primed and placed by the disaffected players, who had spread the tale that Levey had grossly mistreated them and that when they remonstrated he had dismissed them. But even so, it was customary for audiences of the time to express disapproval they might feel towards the play or the actors, and many members of the audience were genuinely annoyed when the curtain rose on the night of 18 February 1833 on the first scene of *The Castle Spectre*. Instead of the billed Mackie, Buckingham, and Mrs. Weston they saw an unknown man, an unknown "slip of a girl", and Barnett Levey with a ream of paper in his hand. Within a few minutes the audience learned that Levey was word perfect simply because he was reading his part line by line from the paper in his hand, but that the others hadn't the faintest idea of what they had to say or do.

"Off! Off!" the audience roared, and a scene of raucous confusion ensued. "Where's Buckingham? Where's Mackie? Where's Mrs. Weston?" was called from all sides of the house, and the unfortunate "unknown man", Mr. Dyott, came or was pushed forward to explain that he had only taken the part that morning, was the servant of the public, and as such would do his best to give satisfaction. "Off! Off!" the audience again roared in answer to this, and first Miss Bland and then Dyott withdrew from the yells and abuse, leaving the stage to Levey. The audience then called on him to explain, but made such an uproar that he could scarcely hear what he was saying. The impertinence of his actors in demanding more money despite contracts which quite clearly stipulated their weekly wage, the disgraceful and ungrateful reaction of the audience, and the ruination of the first play of the night would have upset most men. They sent Levey into a high-pitched frenzy. The curtain fell on this red-faced, spluttering little man dancing up and down in impotent fury at the audience's disregard of his willingness and right to give an explanation. The audience was enjoying itself and, as one newspaper reported, Levey was "permitted to perform a little ballet, but as to speech, not one word could be gathered".

Now the instigators of the disturbance decided to show themselves. They had been in the audience all the while, and had apparently arranged a signal with one of their friends among the actors. When the curtain had been rung down this player stepped on to the stage and "gave out the play", that is, he announced the programme for the next performance at the theatre. At the same time he took it on himself to deplore "the insult offered to his friend Mackie". This was the signal for Mackie to "clear the orchestra at a bound" and jump on to the stage, where, with his hat on his head in defiance of all the rules of good conduct, he attempted to explain his grievances to the audience. The abject Dyott then appeared from the opposite side of the stage and tendered a humble apology to Mr. Mackie, which he hoped he would accept. Far from accepting it, Mackie, hat still on head, struck an attitude and said clearly and disdainfully: "I can accept no apology from a puppy!"

At this point Mr. Buckingham, somewhat tardy in arriving to state *his* case, appeared at one of the doors at the side of the stage, and Mr. Meredith, the stage manager, at the other. Having "eyed each other like pointers at a covey", they threw themselves into attitude à la Mendoza (that is, they shaped up to each other, though the width of the stage separated them). Then followed a general fight on the stage in which Meredith apparently took on all those who had no right to be there. In the course of the fight grappling antagonists fell and rolled together under the curtain from the view of the audience, and then back on to the forestage again. But finally Meredith prevailed, and cleared the stage of intruders. "Some of the junior portion of the audience laughed heartily at Meredith's prowess, considering this fisticuff scene as the *commencement of the afterpiece*", one newspaper reported.

When the dust had settled Meredith made a suitable apology to the occupants of the boxes, and the second play was allowed to proceed. It was not a success, for the players who had to take the leading parts did not have Levey's "ream of paper" to jog their memories.

The next day everything was, of course, patched up. The disaffected players apologized to Levey and expressed their willingness to resume duties as before. Levey needed them quite as much as they needed him, and for a fortnight at least there was peace.

But Buckingham was still not happy, and again told Levey he was worth more a week than he had been induced to contract for. Again Levey stood by his bond and refused to increase Buckingham's pay. Indeed, according to his detractors, Levey did more than this. They said that because Buckingham's dissatisfaction was affecting the whole company, Levey decided to turn them

91

against Buckingham as that importunate actor had turned them against him. The *Monitor* aired the matter in a brief and cautious paragraph obviously meant to spring a trap so as to have the true story revealed. The newspaper said there was a rumour going around the town that Levey proposed to exclude from the stage all actors who came to the colony originally in bondage but were now free. "A free man is a free man," the *Monitor* said, "and the moment we should learn that such a report is true, we should be happy to join the public to the utmost of our power, to *raise a new theatre.*"

In the following issue of the newspaper an unusually calm and considered letter from Levey was published in which he denied that he would ever refuse a man a livelihood because that man had once committed an error. Busybodies were doing their best to interfere between him and his actors, and cause as much trouble as possible, even dictating to him to give some of them more and some less money. Let busybodies mind their business, Levey said, as he troubled his head with nobody's business but his own.

The *Monitor* said it was satisfied with this explanation, and suggested to Levey that the best way to get rid of the busybodies who were interfering in his concerns would be to send the actors to them on a Saturday night to be paid.

It should seem, that when Mr. Levey declines raising the salary of any of his actors who are *emancipists,* they try to raise a *cabal* against him, attributing his refusal, not to his desire to hire his actors according to his judgment of their merits, and to the demand he finds for their particular talents, but to the circumstances of their being *emancipists.*

The truth is that Levey would have been the last to use such a lever, for such emancipists had the obvious answer — his brother was one. There seems no doubt the true story was the one presented by the *Monitor,* that the players accused Levey of bandying the word *emancipist* about when all the time it was they who were using it in an attempt to force or shame him into giving them more money. They thought that in doing this they would put him over a barrel, but they hadn't yet learnt enough about their man.

When the *Gazette* entered the discussion it first of all criticized the *Monitor* for airing the subject, especially as the whole matter, it said, had been settled before the *Monitor* paragraph was published. The *Gazette* then stated what it said were the unvarnished facts. Buckingham had proved to be an unexpectedly talented and popular actor, but he was receiving less, under contract, than the other leading performers. Buckingham was an emancipist, the others were emigrants. They received two to three pounds a week, Buckingham received thirty shillings. He applied for an increase, feeling that with his success on the stage he had earned it, but it was refused. Some few of his "friends" then told Buckingham Levey had refused him because he was an emancipist. Buckingham tackled Levey with this, and threatened to resign, whereupon the volatile Levey immediately published a handbill stating that Buckingham was no longer a member of the Theatre Royal company. Then they thought matters over, and cooled down. Buckingham was reinstated with an increase in his salary to two pounds. The *Gazette* ended its remarks with a quotation, the most telling punch line from Colley Cibber's 1700 version of Shakespeare's *Richard III,* which held the stage for more than 150 years: "So much for Buckingham!" It very tactfully did not quote the words which precede this statement — "Off with his head . . ."

Compared with the six shillings and sixpence a day it was said some mechanics or tradesmen in Sydney were receiving at this time, two pounds was not a very high wage, but it was a great deal higher than these relatively unskilled people would otherwise have been able to earn, and certainly higher than the wage received by their counterparts in the English theatre. At about this time the top wage on the Norwich circuit was twenty-five shillings, and even as late as 1856, when Henry Irving first "trod the boards" at Sunderland, he received only twenty-five shillings a week, after working for nothing for a long trial period; and the next year in Edinburgh, as juvenile lead, only thirty shillings. In 1866 he made his London debut at the St. James's Theatre, playing leading parts for three pounds a week.

Levey may have lost whatever argument there was in the Buckingham affair, but on the other hand he had regained Buckingham and Mackie, and at that stage of his undertaking they were irreplaceable. That a lot of dirty linen had been publicly aired in the process was unfortunate, but at least Levey had learnt, if he had not known before, that any disagreement he might have with his players would, in the relatively small community of Sydney, be made as public as gossip and the publication of conflicting stories could make it; and that therefore he would have to protect himself in every way by seeing that *his* version was the first to be made public.

This first short theatrical season continued on its way, with an increase towards the end from two to three plays a night, and with minor changes in the company from time to time as new aspirants were tried out or originals withdrew or were dismissed. Houses were almost uniformly good, and criticism was restricted to occasional statements on the obvious lack of rehearsal exhibited by the players, and consequent over-use of the prompter. For this first season Levey's theatre presented to the public of Sydney, from 26 December 1832 to 6 July 1833, thirty first performances of plays and farces. Most of these received many repeat performances during the season, and it is evident that players, orchestra, backstage crews, and front-of-house staff, whatever their individual or combined failings may have been, had to work very hard under far from ideal conditions to establish the theatre and keep it working.

The plays Levey produced fall into three categories typical of the dramatic preoccupations of the period. There was the "romantic agony" type of play, complete with ghosts, demons, bloody spectres, and tortured, mad, or wronged females, exemplified by such confections as *The Castle Spectre, Inkle and Yarico,* and the like. Next there were the "man of sentiment"

94

plays, verging on the melodrama which took almost complete hold of the stage during the Victorian era, such as *A Tale of Mystery* and *The Mayor of Garret*. Finally there were the farces, as old as Garrick and as new as Kenny and Rodwell. The safe and generally revered formula of virtue triumphing over vice then as now was the backbone of most of these plays. The longer the triumph was delayed, the more obstacles there were in the path of its fulfilment, the more popular the play.

There was no further eruption of domestic politics until the season ended and ushered in the series of "benefits" with which theatrical seasons of the time customarily ended. For the more popular players these benefits provided the necessary money to get them through that bane of all actors, the "resting" period — the unemployed and therefore unpaid weeks between seasons. The benefit was a night set apart for the leading actors in a theatrical company for the theatre proprietor and stage manager, for the scenepainter and the musicians, and in fact for any member of the company to whom the public could be relied on to give monetary support. The actor or other recipient of the benefit was given the use of the theatre for the night, and once the costs of the house (including an agreed upon reimbursement to the proprietor for the loss of his normal receipts, and for lighting, property, and staff charges) had been paid, the balance was the property of the person for whom the benefit was given. He had to persuade the other actors to perform with him, without pay, but this was usually a matter of *quid pro quo*. To refuse was to be in turn refused. An alternative arrangment was the share system, safest for those who were a bit timid about the possible result of a benefit. In this the proprietor and the person receiving the benefit agreed to take equal shares of the balance left after normal expenses had been paid.

At the end of Levey's first season there were eleven benefit performances, one each to Levey, Meredith, Sippe (the orchestra leader), Allan (the scenepainter), Buckingham, Cooper (or Knowles), and Mrs. Love.* These were the "important" people

95

of the company. Mackie and Vale shared the profits of one benefit, and Dyball and Palmer those of another. A further benefit was given for a charitable cause, the Sydney Dispensary, for which all the actors gave their services free, and a final one for Mrs. Laverty.

By 17 May 1833, when the first of these benefits was given, Levey had in his company of players Meredith, Cooper, Hill, Vale, Dyball, Buckingham, Huffnell, Palmer, Mackie, Dyte (or Dyott), Fitchett, and Johnson, and Mrs. Love*, Mrs. Ward, and the Misses Mary and Martha Bland. Mrs. Weston had earlier been replaced by a Mrs. Laverty, who herself returned very soon to the obscurity from which they had both come, but not before she had, wittingly or not, created a little diversion of her own.

Towards the end of this first series of benefits Mrs. Laverty became a widow. Although she had not played with his company for some weeks, Levey generously decided to help her out by giving her a benefit — the last, in fact, of the series. It was announced as a benefit for the widow of Mr. Laverty, and Mrs. Laverty was billed to take part. This the other female members of the company said they considered to be extremely indelicate of her, and they refused their services. Their true motives will not bear too careful a scrutiny. Certainly they were not activated by a spirit of Christian charity towards a woman suddenly deprived of her husband, for there is no doubt they thought that by absenting themselves it would not be possible for the benefit to be given. It was Levey who let the cat out of the bag. On 9 July he advertised the programme for the "benefit of the widow of the late Mr. Laverty", in which Mrs. Laverty was billed to sing as well as act in *A Tale of Mystery,* and a pantomime, *The Three Wishes; or, Harlequin and the Black Pudding.* At the bottom of this advertisement Levey had a discreetly worded note: ". . . In consequence of two of the Ladies refusing to play at the above

* Stage name adopted for the first few months by Mrs. Harriet Jones, later the *de facto* Mrs. Conrad Knowles.

96

benefit, Mrs. Laverty is obliged to appear herself. The part of Selina will be sustained by a young Lady, being her first appearance on the *Sydney stage!*"

Three days later, lest they should be misunderstood, the ladies, now grown to four — Mrs. Love, the Misses Mary and Martha Bland, and "An Actress" — inserted their own advertisements in the newspapers setting out their reason for refusing to go on. They "felt it would be unjust to allow the concluding sentence of a theatrical advertisement to pass unnoticed". "Certain performers" had refused to play at Mrs. Laverty's benefit because "it was previously stated as being her intention to appear in character before the public, which, deemed indelicate, was the reason they declined giving their services." The public, presented with this "which came first, the chicken or the egg" argument, ignored it altogether and flocked to the benefit. The result was a bumper house for Mrs. Laverty, and a newspaper notice of the performance which said that all the players had acquitted themselves well, "and notwithstanding the delicacy of Mrs. Jones, or Mrs. Love, or Mrs. Hatred, and the other touching and coy parties who designated the appearance of Mrs. Laverty as indecorous, she seems to have realised a good penny."

With the first season and its benefits concluded, and no date yet announced for the opening of the new season, Levey's players found themselves faced with what looked like a long period of unemployment. No play no pay was the practice, and for this reason Meredith and a few others decided to rehearse some plays and present them in Parramatta. Had they set fire to his theatre Levey could not have been more outraged. Not only did he regard their action as desertion, but also as theft of his property. It was *his* theatre, they were *his* players, and all of them had learnt *his* plays. In no time advertisements were pasted all over Sydney castigating the "deserters" and labelling them "strolling players". In truth, Levey was not so much worried about desertion as he was about opposition. Even though Parramatta had no theatre, and the plays were to be presented in the "long room" at Nash's Woolpack Inn, there was still the possibility that they would take so well as to warrant a more permanent set-up.

He need not have worried. Under the control of Meredith as stage manager, Palmer, Buckingham, Dudley, Mrs. Jones and the Misses Bland determined to put on a three-week series of plays. A stage was erected, and the seating divided into two classes, front seats four shillings and the back, "which answers to the pit", two shillings and sixpence. The opening programme was *Inkle and Yarico* and *The Spectre Bridegroom*. Attendance at the first performance was affected by bad weather, and Meredith did little more than clear expenses, as the "theatre" was only half filled. There appear to have been two more performances, which were fairly well patronized, and then the close of the campaign was announced because of "sufficient encouragement not being held out to remunerate the manager". Meredith and his players were bitterly disappointed by the lack of interest; so disappointed, in fact, that they resorted to the alcohol so conveniently available in the building which housed the theatre. As a result the final performance was later described as "the most disgraceful exhibition that can be conceived". The performers were *all* the worse for liquor, it was said. "The audience, finding they were defrauded, rushed the stage and started to pull it to pieces about the actors' heads. Mr. Nash, who is highly respected by the townspeople, was forced to go on to the stage and beg them to desist", the report said. The audience "retired vowing vengeance on the performers".

The end of Levey's first season also provided the *Gazette* with the opportunity to voice the expectations and disappointments the season had aroused, and to add advice on how the next should be conducted. Levey, it felt, was not firm enough with his employees. He had allowed himself to become the servant of those who should have obeyed him. With this, of course, the public had nothing to do. They and the *Gazette* looked solely to Levey for what was theatrically right, for decorum on the stage and in the audience. Levey's sins were of omission rather than commission, and although the *Gazette* felt it could say much on this subject, it would for now content itself with the hint.

When the "Theatre Royal" (!) after much note of preparation, threw open its doors, it is in our knowledge that several families of respectability in the colony, professed an anxious desire to promote the interests of the proprietor. Some individuals of them attended the first representations at the theatre, and then were seen no more. Why was this? Because the low-bred ruffian, the courtesan, the *everybody* who paid his or her money, asserted a right to station him or herself where he or she pleased, until, at last, the audience was nightly composed (with a few exceptions) of equivocal characters and "young men about town."

Levey, who by this time had gained a little wisdom, made no answer to these charges but contented himself with announcing the opening not only of his new season but also of his new "old" theatre, the original Theatre Royal. His first advertisement, on 23 September 1833, announced that the theatre would be opened on 5 October with *The Miller and His Men,* and *The Irishman in London.* Mr. Cavendish was announced as stage manager, and Mr. Knowles as acting-manager, or the man in charge of the players and the play. Admission prices were to be: Dress circle five shillings; second tier of boxes four shillings (two shillings and sixpence at half price); pit three shillings (two shillings at half price), and gallery two shillings. There was no half price for the dress circle or gallery. Subsequent advertisements listed the players as Harpur, Buckingham, Grove, Knowles, Vale, Dyball, Hill, Mackie, and Dyott (now Dight), and Mrs. Dawes, Mrs. Coveney, and Mrs. Love. The scenery was by Messrs. Duddridge and Fitchett, machinery by Messrs. Fitchett and Clarke, decorations by Mr. Allan, and dresses by Mr. Aldred. The nights of performance during the season were to be Mondays, Thursdays, and Saturdays. Meredith and a few others, it will be seen, were either dropped out or dropped out of their own accord.

The final advertisement for the new season, published for the performance that night on 5 October, informed the public that the Sydney theatre would commence its season that evening

"... when His Majesty's servants, at the first rise of the curtain, will sing the National Anthem — God Save the King. After which an original address, written expressly for the occasion by Mr. Knowles, and to be spoken by him."

Whether the *Gazette's* strictures on Levey's theatre were warranted or not, the first season had proved what Levey had felt for many years to be the fact — Sydney not only wanted a theatre but was also willing to support it. Now fully launched on the treacherous and unpredictable seas of theatrical management, Levey had already experienced some of its squalls, and had not always shown himself to be the wisest of captains. He was to learn as he went. Meantime he had established a new industry in Sydney, one which, with the opening of his new theatre, would provide employment for more than one hundred people. In addition, his activities had helped to swell the annual profit of the various chandlers, haberdashers, hatters, clothiers, and other stores from which he bought his theatrical supplies, from canvas to dress lengths, from candles to men's slops. And his theatre was also an unforeseen and unexpected boon to Sydney's infant printing and newspaper industries. From no other source in the town did so many orders emanate for advertisements, handbills, and "bills of the play" or programmes.

By another of those coincidences which occasionally dogged Levey's activities, on the day his final advertisement for his opening performance appeared the *Gazette* carried a paragraph announcing the retirement from his fashion and haberdashery store in Pitt Street of Joseph Wyatt, another wealthy emancipist. Mr. Wyatt, it was said, had retired from shopkeeping to live on his means, "acquired without a breath of calumny". He had also in the course of business amassed a fortune in money and property. He was now entering into a "retirement" which was to bring him much more before the public than his earlier business undertakings had ever done.

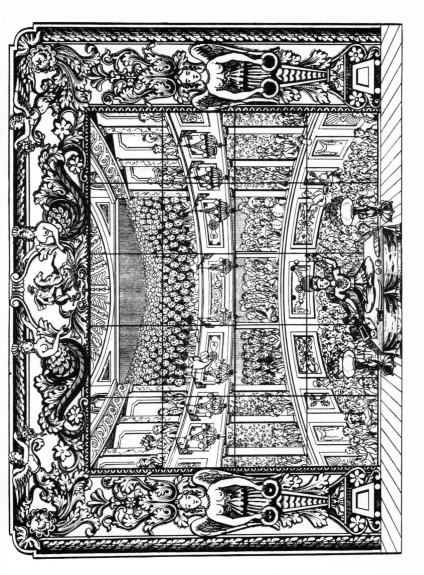

Mirror curtain in use for a while at the Queen's Theatre, Manchester. Shows auditorium of theatre. Victoria and Albert Museum

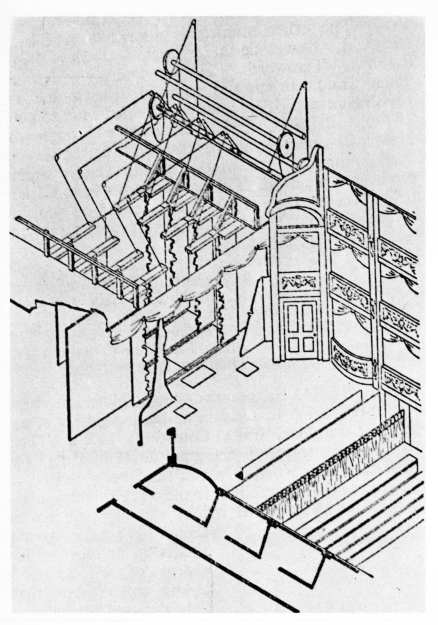

A cut-away drawing showing the wing and groove system of the eighteenth and early nineteenth century stage. *Chambers' Encyclopaedia*

9

The Drama Flourished Here

The first thing about the average Georgian theatre that strikes the modern inquirer is its smallness. Not only was the theatre small, but it was the custom of the period to jam the audience in as tightly as possible on bare-bench seats under conditions which would not be tolerated today. In some theatres a baize or carpet covering was a concession to seat comfort. A full house meant a jammed side-to-side, knee-to-back gathering. This small auditorium was the outcome of many theatrical and other conditions of the day, among which was the stage depth, the incursion of the forestage into the auditorium, the kind of lighting used — candles and oil lamps, which frequently burned out before the end of a performance — and the physical smallness of the people compared with those of today. Even in the Sydney of the 1830's, among the English and Irish who had come to Australia either as convicts or emigrants, the average height was from 5 feet 2 inches to 5 feet 4. This is borne out by advertisements in Sydney newspapers for absconding convicts, which listed full particulars of up to ten or twelve men at a time, the majority of whom were described as of little more than up to 5 feet 4 inches. Barnett Levey was 5 feet 2 inches in height.

Another reason for the large capacity of these small theatres was the indifference of the audience to what today would be considered gross discomfort and would not be endured. They thought nothing of sitting tight-packed and cramped for hours on end on narrow, hard benches, especially as there were no accepted restrictions on the manner in which they voiced their approval or disapproval of the play, the players, or the theatre management. Nor did they seem to mind standing in depth behind and overlooking the boxes.

London's largest theatre in 1790 was Covent Garden. It was 86 feet long from the stage opening to the back wall of the gallery, 56 feet wide, and 31 feet 6 inches high from the floor to the ceiling, with a higher slope over the gallery. Only 1 foot 9 inches was allowed for seat and void, though a writer of the time said a moderate sized person could not conveniently sit in a less space than 1 foot 10 inches from back to front, or comfortably in less than 2 feet.

England's provincial theatres, of course, were smaller than this. The Ipswich Theatre Royal, for instance, contained within an 84 feet by 40 feet space both stage and auditorium, and when we come to the Georgian Theatre at Richmond in Yorkshire (still in use, though greatly restored) we find the same general architectural pattern contained in the smallest space of all.

The Richmond theatre was opened in 1788, the year in which Australia was founded, and twenty-two years after the Bristol Theatre Royal (still in use) was opened. The auditorium measures only 26 feet 8 inches long by 24 feet wide. The stage is an inch longer, and the same width, so that the theatre is contained in an area of no more than 53 feet 5 inches by 24 feet. The proscenium opening is 15 feet 9 inches high and 17 feet wide. Yet in this space up to 400 people were accommodated.

In this same period Ireland was dotted from one end of the country to the other with provincial theatres, a few typical ground dimensions being: Ennis (1790) 50 feet by 30 feet; Limerick (1770) 80 feet by 40 feet; Cork (1736) 88 feet by 44 feet, and (1760) 136 feet by 60 feet; Derry (1789) 80 feet by 40 feet.

In the always oblong space of these theatres the stage occupied half or almost half. In the other half was accommodated the auditorium. Distinctive features of this auditorium were the balconies or verandas which lined its three walls, divided into boxes in the manner already described. The pit of the auditorium (where today's stalls are located) always sloped from just beneath the front boxes down to the stage, which was 4 feet and sometimes 5 or more above the ground level at that spot. Pit seats were again benches. From about 1785 it was the custom to floor over the pit of these theatres for balls and other social gatherings. Thus is explained the discrepancy in auditorium decoration above the base line of boxes and below it in the pit. When the pit was floored over there was an unbroken expanse from the back wall of the stage to the front boxes in the auditorium. This fashion or practice was followed in Levey's Theatre Royal, where he used to hold costume balls, and also in the later Victoria Theatre in Pitt Street, which before it was put into use as a theatre was first opened for a St. Patrick's Day ball, when the pit was floored over in the way described.

By May 1833 good progress had been made with the work on Levey's new "old" theatre, or theatre proper. It was announced that the lower tier was to be composed of the dress and private boxes, and there would be two upper tiers of boxes. The theatre, contained in its space of 86 feet by 33 feet, would measure 45 feet from the drop curtain to the front of the centre box (facing the stage), and the pit, extending under the side boxes, would measure 30 feet across. This means that the stage had a depth of 25 feet to 30 feet, allowing for the depth of the boxes on the back wall as well as the depth of the auditorium from curtain line to centre box. An advertisement in September mentioned the dress "circle" of boxes, and Maclehose in his *Picture of Sydney and Stranger's Guide for 1839* mentions the new "old" theatre as having a "neat circle of dress and private boxes". This means that Verge changed the auditorium shape from the traditional square-ended U plan to the circular-end or true U-shape.

While a certain amount of conjecture about the reconstruction of this theatre is unavoidable, because of the lack of complete evidence, there is not much room for gross error. The theatre pattern of the period was a "set" one, and we know the dimensions of the theatre building, of the saloon into which it opened, and of the rooms above both — which were 10 feet high. It may safely be assumed, therefore, that to install the gallery the original ceiling (which was the floor of the 10 feet high room above) was taken away and all or part of the exposed area was used to provide room for the gallery (which, for the depth it required, must have stretched back over the roof of the saloon), and to better the sound and ventilation.

It was said of this theatre that it was "a very pretty model, quite equal to the theatres in the country towns of the United Kingdom", and "it is a better theatre than three-fourths of those in England and Scotland, where the towns boast of their thirty and forty thousand inhabitants". Sydney's population in 1833 was 16,232. A third newspaper described the proscenium or stage front of the theatre as "fully equal to most of the provincial theatres in England, and may stand comparison with a few in London".

The house on the opening night, 5 October 1833, was said to present "a very splendid appearance" with its boxes lined with red baize and studded with golden-headed nails, its due measure of candles and lamps, its gilded stage doors each with a mirror above, and its green baize front curtain. When this curtain was raised a "skilfully executed drop scene" was exhibited.

Of the colour scheme in general there is no record, and it is tempting to think that it was one of those bright, freshly-iced cake schemes beloved of Sadler's Wells and other London theatres — a subtle use of white, pinks, pale greens, blues, and gold — even though such decorative schemes were quickly discoloured by the smoke and heat from constantly burning oil lamps and candles. On the other hand, the traditional colour scheme for English provincial theatres of the period which Levey seems to have used for his pattern was: green curtain, red-lined boxes, and green woodwork.

Entrances to the theatre were, as before, through the saloon of the Royal Hotel, to the lower and upper tier of boxes, and down the side laneway to the pit doors, and perhaps also to the gallery.

As an indication of how this Georgian architectural style persisted it is only necessary to turn to a description of the "iron pot" theatre built in Melbourne in 1855 by actor-entrepreneur George Coppin. This iron building was prefabricated in England, sent out in parts, and erected in Melbourne. The building was 88 feet long, 40 feet wide, and about 24 feet high from the ground level to the roof peak. "As the floor level of the pit will be sunk five or six feet below the ground level, there will be considerable altitude in the interior", one newspaper reported. The gallery supporting the boxes along three sides of the auditorium was 24 feet deep at the end facing the stage (to provide for the gallery seats), and projected 8 feet from either side wall. The prevailing colours used in the interior of this theatre were green, pink, white, and gold. The ceiling was painted a blue-white, spangled with gold stars.

Barnett Levey's Theatre Royal was said to be capable of seating 1,200 people, a surprising figure in view of the claims made for the Victoria Theatre, which has been described by many writers as capable of holding up to 2,000 people. In fact, the Victoria's "comfortable" capacity when it first opened was no more than 1,600 people. A report in the *Australian* of 17 May 1833, before Levey's Theatre Royal was opened, said "it is calculated to hold nearly £250, or 1,200 persons". The only other reference to this theatre's capacity to be found conflicts with this, but not so very much if it is remembered that the saloon theatre with its pit and one tier of boxes held 500 persons. In fact, this figure of £250 seems almost certainly to be a misprint for £150. Maclehose, in the book already mentioned, describing the Theatre Royal with its two tiers of boxes, pit, and gallery, said "the house is capable of containing in admission money about £130". This figure is nearer what must have been the true one than the previously quoted £250. Assuming that the pit and first tier of boxes would hold at least the 500 people the saloon theatre held (they almost certainly held more), this gives us no less than £90 in admission money for that part of the theatre alone, working it out at 350 pit seats at three shillings each and 150 box seats at five shillings each. To clinch the argument (still working on the thrice-repeated 500 capacity for the saloon theatre), if 150 is allowed for each of the three tiers of boxes (a total of 450), 350 for the pit, and 300 for the gallery, the figure of 1,100 is arrived at. But the pit and box areas in the new "old" theatre were slightly larger than those in the saloon theatre, which would account for the extra 100 at least. If we take 350 people at three shillings (£52 10s.), 150 at four shillings (£30), 150 at five shillings (£36 10s.), and 300 at two shillings (£30) we get a total of £150.

None of these figures, of course, either for capacity or door-takings, takes into account the half-price system. It is not inconceivable that a packed house at the Sydney Theatre Royal could have accommodated 1,600 people.

Of the first performance of *The Miller and His Men* and *The Irishman in London* the *Herald* said on 7 October that with very few exceptions everything went off well. The *Gazette,* on the other hand, found a want of organization, a negligence in the management of the scenery, and a jerking stiffness in many of the actors. The *Monitor* said that its reporter's account of the opening performance was so much more severe than that of the *Gazette* it preferred to reprint that newspaper's account rather than use the reporter's. But it did add a rider to the effect that none of the actors seemed to know his part. The *Herald* then took it on itself on 10 October to print a second and fuller report of the same performance, possibly to correct what it felt to be an imbalance or unfairness in the reports by the other newspapers, or to make up for the brevity of its initial report.

It praised the appearance of the theatre as a credit to so young a colony as New South Wales, and then admitted that *The Miller and His Men* had passed off tolerably well, but for the total failure of the explosion in the last scene. This, said the *Herald,* was remedied at the next performance of the play. The scenery was good and the music excellent, the performers exerted themselves with success, and *The Irishman in London* went off with considerable *éclat*. Its only real criticism was of the female characters, "the whole of whom, we trust, will improve by practice, as we thought them very inanimate".

It was now left for Sydney's remaining newspaper, the *Australian,* to make its pronouncements, which it did six days after the opening performance. This newspaper was not only the only one to mention that a specially written prologue had been spoken at this historic performance, it also printed it in full. The verse was the work of the cleverest member of Levey's company, the actor Conrad Knowles, and was spoken by him. As it is the first prologue spoken at a Sydney theatre of which there is a record (one is said to have been spoken at the opening of Sidaway's theatre, but no copy exists) it is, bad verse though it may be, of some significance.

The *Australian* was thorough in its treatment of this first performance. It described the curtain rising "sharp at seven-thirty", to disclose the whole company assembled on the stage, with Mr. Levey in the centre "standing like a patriarch in the midst of a numerous progeny". The orchestra struck up "God Save the King", which the assembled actors sang "in such a way as to prevent us being very loud in its praise". Mr. Levey, it appears, was so carried away by a combination or ferment of pride, excitement, enthusiasm, and patriotic fervour that he moved forward far in advance of his company, "as far as the stage (i.e. foot-) lamps, and seemed unwilling to stop even there". After this the drop-scene fell, leaving alone on the stage Mr. Knowles, who came forward to deliver his address.

> Patrons and Friends! (for by these names so dear
> We sure may call on all assembled here);
> At length we view, — view with honest pride,
> A Pile, for which full many a heart hath sighed.
> The Drama's Temple, — where for many a night
> The Muse's star shall reign with halo bright.

107

Thro' weeks of toil and months of anxious care,
Laborious nights, where rest had scarce a share,
This was our thought, — this was our only aim,
To found a temple, for the drama's fame.
Tho' disappointment threatened with her blast
And adverse fortune oft her clouds o'ercast,
At length we triumph, while our hearts rebound
We gaze exultingly on all around.
Now view our work — may each friendly heart
Approve, — cheerfulness to ours impart.
Say — have we raised a building to the view
Worthy the drama — not unworthy you?
Here are some friends, whom oft before we've met
Whose kind forebearance we can ne'er forget; —
Who pardoned faults, — faults glaring as the sun,
Encouraged all, — depressed the minds of none,
And here are some, whose welcome smile tonight
We hail the harbinger of days more bright;
Let them smile on, 'tis they our labours crown,
And may we never make that smile a frown.
What tho' we boast no Garrick's tragic powers,
What tho' a Kemble's talent be not ours?
What tho' a Siddons, whose Majestic sway
From every rival bore the palm away;
Whose every action, look, a tear could draw,
Entrance the heart, or fill the soul with awe?
What tho' she be not here? — we may yet seize
The humble meed of praise, desire to please.
— Tho' here its alien sons tune not the lyre,
Still, music charms us with her thrilling fire,
— Ours is the simple song, whose tones impart
The softer feeling, — and pleasure to the heart.
Our talent is not great, yet still tho' small,
We call it forth in efforts to please all
— For, while Australia's sons support our cause
And greet our humble effort with applause,
While her fair daughters meet us with a smile
And beauty praises — beauty void of guile,
So long our pride shall be their praise to gain,
Strive their esteem to win — nor strive in vain.
— Here we commence! here then we make our stand,

Friends of the Drama! Lend a fostering hand!
And while our stage, life's real glass, shall be
A well drawn picture of morality,
While virtue's cause is seen to flourish here,
And vice her hideous head hangs down with fear,
So long with confidence, we'll here appeal
Nor shall a doubt impede our ardent zeal.
Advance Australia! and advance, the Stage.
Let every hand, let every heart engage,
Let every voice be raised in one loud strain,
And bid the Drama prosperously reign —
Let it be told in History's bright page,
The Drama flourished here in this our age;
Australians yet unborn the stage will view,
And proudly say it owes its rise to you.
Ours is no merit, yours alone, the pride, —
Yours is the Glory, — let each heart decide.
And now to obey the Drama's ancient laws,
Ere we commence, one moment let us pause,
And breathe a welcome, every kindred mind
Will meet our greeting with a heart as kind.
Then welcome all! Long may we tread the Stage
Your smiling approbation to engage —
Long may you sit our Judges — and decide
On every action, while with heartfelt pride
We hear our sentence, and in you confide;
Long may the Drama reign, — and we confess,
Patrons and Friends, 'tis you command success.

The prologue over, the newspaper said, *The Miller and His Men* was got through "in a manner we can neither condemn nor admire". But it added that it did not intend to be as severe on these *debutante* players as the *Gazette* had been. "A first appearance is an awful affair ... and we shall therefore suspend our judgment." For the scenery, decorations, and machinery it had nothing but praise. What it did find worthy of criticism was something which the *Monitor* had also found disturbing — the dress circle. Said the *Australian*:

... The only thing which appeared to us incomprehensible was, the meaning of the *Dress Circle,* for a more heterogeneous

109

assemblage of *dresses* can scarcely be imagined. Here were gentlemen with their hats on (one of whom had actually forgotten to take his pen out of his ear) and their ladies with infants at their breasts — we hope to see this corrected.

The *Monitor*, because gentlemen were there in all sorts of dress *except* full dress, pronounced the term "dress circle" to be so much humbug.

That Levey knew the fare his audience expected is evident from the choice of plays with which he opened his theatre. *The Miller and His Men* had all the necessary ingredients to thrill and delight the audience of his day, and although it was by then twenty years old it still had as much theatrical life in it as the newest production at Covent Garden. It was written by Isaac Pocock, and has been described as the one enduring drama of the Gothic sunset. Although its author wrote two plays a year for many years, this is the only one still remembered and the only one to prove popular, not alone because of its plot and such sentiments as: "Do riches without love give happiness?" or, "I pine for virtue and freedom", but also because of the grand explosion with which the play ends. The story is of Lothair and his attempt to rescue his beloved Claudine, held prisoner by bandits in their den below the mill. Lothair joins the band with the intention of firing their powder magazine and blowing them sky-high, but he is beaten to this goal by the unfortunate, wronged, and vengeful Ravinia (an apt name on the author's part to indicate the depths of her despair), the miller's prisoner. For the mill is a cover for a desperate band of ruffians whose leader is the miller. For added interest there was the music specially written by Henry Bishop, who at the time the play was first staged held the post of composer to Covent Garden Theatre. His subsequent compositions for the theatre endeared him to Victorian hearts, and in 1842 he received a knighthood.

The Irishman in London; or, The Happy African also had its first performance at Covent Garden, in 1792. It was a lighthearted and highly amusing farce which William Macready the elder is said to have written from James Whitley's *The Intriguing Footman; or, The Humours of Harry Humbug,* given its first performance at Shrewsbury a year earlier. Throughout the period and well to the end of the nineteenth century the plots of plays and novels were looked upon and treated as anybody's property, and many a shrewd man of the theatre rewrote a previously inept play, or dramatized a novel to turn it into a commanding success, Garrick among them, re-titling it and claiming it as his own.

111

10

Staging a Play at the Royal

When the people of Sydney attended a performance at the Theatre
Royal what did they see? How, if at all, did what they saw differ
from what today's theatregoer sees when he enters a building
which today we have to qualify with the words "legitimate
theatre" to indicate that it is live and is not a musical comedy.
It has been said that the living theatre is contained not in the drama
but in the staging of a show. Since shows were first staged this
word-versus-scenery argument has been a live force in the world
of the theatre — whether theatre lies only in the dramatist's
words as interpreted by the actor, or whether these not only
should but must be bolstered by adequate scenery, costumes,
and all kinds of "business" and eye-arresting movement. Shakespeare wrote exclusively for the theatre of the word, because he
did not live to see the fruits of Italian theatrical ingenuity transferred from the court masques in England to the Restoration
theatre. But that he would have approved of "stage show" is
implicit in at least one of his plays, *Coriolanus,* wherein Volumnia
says: "Action is eloquence, and the eyes of th' ignorant more
learned than their ears." There is no confusion here between
"stage show" and "action"; they are one and the same — that
part of a stage presentation which makes it essentially theatrical,
of the theatre, and not something for the ear alone.

For plays have always been presented in theatres, aside from
such offshoots as the performances given by travelling players,

112

who had to play how and where they could. From the time of
Shakespeare onwards the growing sophistication of audiences and
theatre people called for "action" of a more and more detailed
kind until, inevitably, the stage was reached where half- and
even three-quarter-hour waits between acts or scenes were necessary so that the elaborate and costly scene changes of the new
order could be made. In this sense "action" became moving
waterfalls, running rivers and stormy lakes, moving trains and
ships, horse races, explosions, fires, and earthquakes presented
with the utmost realism of which the stage staff was capable.
In the process of this journey from the word to the thing something
was lost and something gained.

To achieve a real understanding of the early nineteenth century
theatre and its stage we must not allow ourselves to accept genera-
lities or bold statements about either its superiority or inferiority
to the stage of today. We must ask, in fact, "How did it work?
What, for instance, did the eyes of the ignorant audiences of the
Sydney Theatre Royal, more learned than their ears, actually *see*
in 1832 and later?"

The printed versions of the plays presented at this theatre will
tell us remarkably little. They are not "the living theatre" until
they are placed on the stage. They will tell us, apart from the
dialogue, such strange things as "Exit L", or "Exit R" — which
is simple enough, as these mean no more than exit, or leave the
stage to the left or the right. But what are we to make of this,
from Douglas Jerrold's *Black Ey'd Susan,* produced in the saloon
Theatre Royal in 1832: "Act I, Scene IV. A View of the Country,
1st grooves"? Or this: "Act II, Scene I. A View of the Downs.
The Fleet at Anchor, 6th grooves"? Equally mystifying are the
instructions at the end of Act III, scene 2 — "The scene closes."
We know it is the end of the scene, for it is followed immediately
by Act III, scene 3. Similarly mystifying stage directions are
to be found in other plays of this period. Thirty years after
Black Ey'd Susan was first produced in London Dion Boucicault's
The Colleen Bawn was produced, and in it we find such directions

113

as: "Exit Danny through window — change"; and, "Cottage R. 3 E., set pieces backed by Lake; table and two seats R.C."; and, once again, "The old Weir Bridge, or a wood on the verge of the Lake, 1st grooves", followed by yet another scene change, "1st grooves". Throughout all these plays the movement on and off stage of their characters is indicated by the symbols "L. 1 E., L.U.E., R. 1 E., R.U.E., or R. 2 E." Further, in newspaper reports of performances at the Sydney theatre comments such as the following will be found: ". . . the scene-shifters were never at their posts, hence there was a mixture of scenery which was quite *outré*. The sides of a man-of-war, and the back of a cottage parlour but ill-agreed together." How did a man-of-war and a cottage parlour get mixed up? Even more puzzling, how did the *side* of one come to be with the *back* of the other? All through these reports phrases such as "the scenery was intolerably managed", and "a little smarter shifting of the scenery is necessary" are repeated again and again. Even the small theatre in the Argyle Rooms in Hobart, Tasmania, in the same period, does not escape.

> . . . the side scenes are seldom changed, so that for a cottage scene, we have the three first side scenes of a marble hall, and the next a forest side; and when the performers present themselves on the stage, it is not unusual for them to seat themselves bang down on the fire,

says one report of this theatre. Why was this?

In a report on Sydney's Theatre Royal when it was being built in 1828 it was said that "the stage possesses the due quantity of preparations and trap-doors for the entrance and exit of the usual number of ghosts, with good measure for the grave in Hamlet. . ." Today, stage trap-doors are practically unknown, or at least very infrequently used. Why were they thought important enough to warrant special mention in this 1828 report? In elucidating these mysteries we will discover exactly how the early nineteenth century theatre worked, and in what way its stage differed from the stage of today.

In the Shakespearian theatre the actor was the most important

114

stage element. He had no scenic background, although such stage properties as beds, thrones, tables, arras or tapestries, and other movables were often used. In the theatre which immediately succeeded it, which gained its impetus from the elaborate court masques designed almost exclusively all over the world in the style laid down by Italian artists and architects, the actor was still important, but of almost equal importance now was the habit of playing in front of a scenic background, and the use of stage machinery to provide moving clouds, dissolving views, and the chariots, ships, birds, and other devices in or on which actors during a masque or play made some of their entrances and exits. Scenery at this time was an accompaniment to the play.

At some period towards the end of the eighteenth century, or perhaps even earlier, the stage setting began to occupy more of the stage depth, and the tendency grew for the actor to move back with the scenery and to play *in* it rather than in front of it. As he moved back, so the need for the long or deep forestage (three proscenium doors on each side, facing each other) ceased to exist. Soon the usual stage front was a small forestage with a doorway on either side of the proscenium arch, each with its balcony or window above. Then, as the nineteenth century progressed these proscenium doors and the last vestige of the forestage finally disappeared, and the actor and the scenery retreated wholly behind the proscenium arch to create the picture or picture-frame stage which is with us to this day.

We know that Levey's Theatre Royal was, in effect, the Georgian provincial or smaller London theatre transferred to Sydney, so we can conclude that its stage was worked in the same way as those in the Georgian theatres throughout the length and breadth of England, Scotland, Wales, and Ireland. This early nineteenth century stage, in its design and fitments, was a working copy of that evolved or laid down by the Italian architect and designer Andrea Pozzo in 1693, and used by Inigo Jones in his staging of court masques in London in that century. With a knowledge of the workings of this and the eighteenth and nineteenth century English theatres in mind, it is obvious that Levey's stage conformed with the following principles, considered usual and desirable in the England of 1819.

Pozzo described his stage as a recess from the great room where the spectators sit, "in the form of a truncated pyramid, the base being what is called the *curtain;* and the vertex, which is the remote end of the pyramid, is called the point of contraction". From this it will be seen that the ideal stage setting was considered to be one capable of "representing an extended space in a small compass". For this reason the scenes sloped down from the top (that is, they were higher at the front curtain than at the back of the stage), up from the bottom (that is, the stage was raked, or inclined from the front to the back), and the sides or wings were angled or "stepped" from the front to the back.

Pozzo laid it down that a building to be used as a theatre should be divided into two equal halves, one for spectators, the other for the "theatre" or stage. Because of the insistence on diminishing perspective settings the stage floor was sloped up from the front of the stage to the back, an elevation of one foot for every ten feet of depth, so that a stage 25 feet in depth was 2 feet 6 inches higher at the back than at the front curtain. However, as the actor (and the dancer and acrobat) began to move back into the stage setting this slope was found to be too great for safety, and by 1819 the accepted gradient was no more than 1 foot in 12, and often less. Obviously, with scenery which diminished in height the further back it reached actors had to play well downstage, close to the footlights, otherwise their height made nonsense of the supposed buildings or trees at the back. Largely for this reason a longer or more extended perspective point was ultimately adopted, scaled to human height as the actors began to play more in the scene than in front of it.

The stage itself was a much simpler, more cut-and-dried affair than today's; and, unlike today, the scene-designer did not have to start with a bare stage. The basic elements of the early nineteenth century stage, which were more or less permanent, were

116

the wings (up to six or more on either side of the stage), the back
scenes or flats, and the borders (which hung from above and met
with the top of the wings). The usual arrangement was a pair
of wings, one on either side of the stage, with a pair of flats
directly behind them, repeated six or more times and finishing
with the final pair of flats. Each set of wings and flats was made of
canvas stretched on a wooden framework, the flats (in two halves)
being together large enough to fill in the space left on the stage
between the two wings. Both wings and flats moved in grooves
in the stage floor, and in a set of movable grooves at the top which
could be raised or lowered like an arm, or the half of a suspension
bridge, to fit on top of the flat or wing. Each set of grooves was
numbered consecutively from the front of the stage to the back,
so that when the stage manager, reading the directions given in
his play, found the previously quoted "A view of the country,
1st grooves", he would set his stage as follows. First there would
be the wings on either side of the stage that "matched" the act-
drop or drop-scene directly behind the front curtain. Next would
come the first set of wings in the first grooves, painted to represent
trees or the sides of a landscape view, and directly behind them
he would place the flats painted to represent a country scene.
When the time came for the scene to be presented to view the
stage prompter would blow his whistle, which he wore on a string
or chain around his neck. Immediately the scene-shifters on either
side of the stage (one to each wing, one to each flat, ideally)
would push the wings the short space needed to bring them
slightly forward of the act-drop wings, and the two halves of the
flats until they met (often with a loud clap or crash) in the middle
of the stage, parallel to the front. The presence of the vertical
"join" or middle "seam" in the centre of the back scene which
resulted was an accepted convention of the time. Nevertheless,
as early as 1853 London theatre enthusiasts were beginning to
complain about this "cutting line", as this criticism of Charles
Kean's setting for *Sardanapalus* at the Princess's Theatre shows:

. . . Nevertheless we must be permitted to remark generally

that the mechanism of placing scenery on the stage, and the mode of throwing the light on it are still highly inefficient for artistic illusion, and have not kept pace with other improvements; indeed there has been hardly an advance at all for the last half century. The scenes are still in two slides, and where they meet in the centre the most delicately painted landscape is presented to the public eye, divided by a cutting line, which is also frequently disfigured with dirt from the handling of the scene-shifters. . .

Trouble arose during the staging of a play when the scene-shifters on one side of the stage pushed on the wings or flats in the first grooves, for instance, while those on the other mistakenly pushed on those in the second grooves; or when the wrong flats or wings were pulled off or pushed on at the wrong time. Thus were the sides of a man-of-war (wings) ill-matched with the back of a cottage parlour (flats). These accidents happened repeatedly, right up to the 1870's, when the groove system of stage setting was finally superseded by the free-standing canvas setting which made possible the box-set, or set in which the only entrance was through the door or doors provided, as in a real room. With the groove system, of course, actors could enter or leave the stage right or left through the gaps between the wings. This again was an accepted convention of the time, the audience no more "noticing" these wide spaces in what were supposed to be the solid walls of a room than it "noticed" the join down the centre of a wide expanse of country. These gaps were known as "entrances", and bore the same numbers as the grooves, so that if an actor read in his copy of a play that he must enter or leave R. 3 E., or L. 1 E., he knew that he did so behind the third groove (or wing) on the right, or behind the first on the left.

But the early nineteenth century stage had other features besides the wings, flats, and borders. There were the act-drops or drop-scenes — painted canvas cloths hung from above and worked on the roller, or veranda blind principle. These, painted with some architectural or landscape scene, were usually hung directly behind the front curtain, though they were also used occasionally instead of flats, and thus became "backdrops".

There were also free-standing "set pieces". These could represent rocks, small buildings, bridges, fences, small hills or rises, or trees. They were really "cut-outs" placed in front of a painted landscape or other backing, and helped to give more depth and verisimilitude to a scene. Such a "set piece" is indicated in the previously quoted direction from *The Colleen Bawn* — "Cottage R. 3 E., set pieces backed by lake". This cottage would have had a "practical" or workable door, through which the play's characters could enter or leave as directed. The other set pieces would be perhaps a garden row, a fence, and a front gate.

The stage floor also had a number of "cuts" in it, each designed for a specific purpose. The footlights were set in an aperture in the floor of the stage immediately behind the orchestra and in front of the proscenium and curtain. They were so constructed that they could be lowered below stage level, either to trim the lamps or to darken the stage. The footlights could be raised or lowered by the prompter, who stood in the wings, by means of a lever which set in motion a system of ropes, wheels, and counterweights. They could also be set in motion by the "trimmer", who trimmed the lamps under the stage.

After the footlights came four small square traps and a large one, usually 6 or 7 feet long and 3 or 4 feet wide. All of these traps were, in effect, movable platforms worked beneath the stage by stage-hands. The small ones were used by actors who personated demons, devils, or ghosts and were consequently expected to rise from or descend to the nether regions to the accompaniment of a great deal of smoke and blue or red fire. The larger trap was used chiefly in the grave scene in *Hamlet,* though it also had various other uses.

The trap behind this group of five was usually square, and was used for the sinking cauldron in *Macbeth,* and for other plays which required the sinking or raising of people or properties. It was often used, with an understage stairway, as the entrance to the hold of a ship, or to a cellar. Long apertures in the stage floor directly behind this were used for lowering flats or wings beneath the stage for storage, or for bringing them on-stage for scene changes. These apertures were covered by a series of flaps or hinged boards, all or a few of which could be lifted and turned back as required.

As the Georgian theatre existed many years before the use of gas for illumination, it was dependent for all its lighting needs on candles and lamps. Stage lighting usually was solely by lamps, while in the auditorium, which was illuminated throughout each performance, both candles and lamps were used. Such problems as the darkening of a portion or the whole of the stage, or of illuminating given areas, were overcome by the following methods, some of which were practised by Joseph Fürttenbach in the theatre he established at Ulm in Germany in 1631, and passed on to posterity in his *Manhaffter Kunst-Spiegel,* published in 1663. He used candles and lamps with reflectors behind them. These were hung behind the proscenium and behind the scenery, and at times placed on the stage floor behind the scenes or wings. He used ten candle footlights with reflectors, each 2 feet apart. And he evolved a very simple solution to the problem of dimming the stage or scene by using iron "dimmers" suspended on cords above the lights. When the cords were released the dimmers or shades descended over the lights without extinguishing them, and were pulled up when it was necessary for the lights to come on again. This, of course, applied only to stage lighting.

We have seen that by 1819 the problem of dimming the footlights had been solved in a different way. By this time, too, a simpler method of dimming or partially dimming the stage lights was used. Apart from the footlights, stage lighting depended chiefly on side lights placed between the wings, and on single or grouped lamps hung from above, and placed on the stage floor behind set pieces and solid properties such as chests, cupboards, or other pieces of furniture. The side lights were a series of reflector-backed shelves on upright stands, with a lamp or candle to each shelf. The shelves worked on a pivot or hinge, so that when necessary the whole could be turned to face away from instead of on to the stage. Then, if necessary, the lamps or candles could be extinguished, and later re-lighted and turned slowly or quickly to face the stage again.

It is now possible to take a copy of *Black Ey'd Susan* and visualize or reconstruct for ourselves a great deal of what the audience must have seen on that night in Sydney in 1832.

The play has one main plot and many counterplots. The main one concerns William, a sailor, and his wife, the pretty black-eyed Susan. William returns from the sea after a long absence, having applied for his discharge. Scarcely has he met Susan again than his commander, Captain Crosstree, sees her and falls madly in love with her. One day he finds himself opportunely alone with Susan, and attempts to molest her. Hearing her cries, William rushes on and knocks his captain down with his cutlass. For this offence, striking an officer, he is tried by court-martial and sentenced to die, even though everyone from the Admiral down admires and sympathizes with him. At the last moment, however, the repentant Captain Crosstree comes forward with William's long-awaited discharge papers, which only a few minutes before had been delivered into the Captain's hands. William was not guilty of striking an officer, it is announced, for at the time he attacked Captain Crosstree he was no longer a member of the King's Navy. He had applied for his discharge before he struck down his captain.

We are seated in the centre of the front boxes (those facing the stage), and the orchestra, its sheet music lit by green-shaded oil lamps, is playing an overture made up of a selection of Dibdin's naval airs. The oil-lamp foot-lights throw a golden glow over the lower half of the green baize front curtain. Applause greets the end of the overture, and then the baize curtain is pulled up on its roller to reveal Levey and his full company standing before the act-drop. They sing "God Save the King", and then retire, whereat the act-drop rises and reveals the first scene of *Black Ey'd*

Susan, a view of the country, set in the first grooves. This is a shallow scene, in which a "good" and a "bad" character, Gnatbrain and Doggrass, between them establish for the benefit of the audience that the beautiful Susan is married to William, a sailor in the King's Navy, and that Doggrass, her uncle, as mean a skinflint as ever lived, also does a little smuggling on the side. Scene 2, the town of Deal, follows, and the change is made before our eyes. This is in the second grooves, and we see the "country scene" wings and flats withdrawn and the "town" flats pushed on behind the newly-revealed "town" wings.

Scene 2 also has only two characters, Raker and Hatchet, smugglers hand in hand with the villainous Doggrass. Hatchet, with the connivance of Doggrass, proposes to convince Susan that William is dead, lost at sea, so that he can marry her. For Susan, it appears, is penniless because William has been for so long unheard of, and she is living with old Dame Hatley in her cottage. Doggrass owns the cottage, and he and Hatchet plan to evict them both if Susan refuses to marry Hatchet. By this time the audience is muttering with a growing hatred for the two "evil" characters.

Scene 3, Dame Hatley's cottage, is a deeper scene, possibly as far back as the fourth or fifth grooves. The right flat has a "practical" door in it, the left a transparent lattice window. There is also another practical door at R. 2 E., whose use is presently to be revealed. Susan is heard outside the cottage singing a verse of the song "Black Ey'd Susan" in plaintive tones. She enters and bewails her fate. William has been absent now twelve months, and she longs to see him. The audience applauds in sympathetic understanding as she makes the first of the many "points" or "clap-traps" with which her part is studded: "Oh! the pangs, the dreadful pangs that tear the sailor's wife, as wakeful on her tear-wet pillow, she lists and trembles at the roaring sea."

She stands silent a moment, her head bent in mute sorrow, waiting for the applause to end. Then Gnatbrain enters through the door in the flat. They discuss the meanness of Doggrass.

122

During their conversation Doggrass is seen to pass the window, so Gnatbrain hides in a cupboard R. 2 E. just before he enters. In the approved melodramatic fashion Doggrass presses Susan for the rent, which neither she nor Dame Hatley can pay. Dolly Mayflower, Gnatbrain's sweetheart, also enters, but neither she nor Susan can bend Doggrass from his wicked purpose. He calls in his clerk, Jacob, to make an immediate inventory of everything in the cottage, and Jacob, of course, makes straight for the cupboard and reveals the presence of Gnatbrain. As the stage direction puts it: "(Pulls open the door of the cupboard, when Gnatbrain knocks Jacob prostrate, and stands, C., in attitude; Susan in R. corner; Dolly, R.C., in surprise; Doggrass standing L. corner exulting)."

How the audience cheers when Gnatbrain knocks Jacob down and "takes an attitude" of scornful defiance before the evil Doggrass; how it showers the ensuing tableau with applause.

Of course Dolly suspects that Susan and Gnatbrain have been up to something, and the wily Doggrass is too much the villain to miss such a splendid opportunity for mischief. With an expressive leer he tells Susan that it is sometimes "convenient" for a husband to be at sea. At this Susan draws herself up in righteous hauteur (there has never been anybody "purer" than the nineteenth century heroine), and makes her exit after expressing a "sentiment" which brings down a storm of applause on her retreating head.

Sir, scorn has no word — contempt no voice to speak my loathing of your insinuations. Take, Sir, all that is here; satisfy your avarice — but dare not indulge your malice at the cost of one, who has now nothing left her in her misery but the sweet consciousness of her virtue.

And so the actors continue to unfold the play's story, plot and counterplot, scene by scene, standing when directed R. 1 E. (at the first entrance on the right), R.U.E. (at an upper entrance on the right), or L. 2 E. (at the second entrance on the left). The cottage scene is succeeded by a return to the first grooves country

123

scene, and the first act ends with a scene in the smugglers' cave in which the smugglers are captured and — "the Act Closes". This direction meant the dropping of the act-drop for long enough for the cave scene to be drawn off, and the fullstage first scene of Act II to be pushed on — A View of the Downs, the Fleet at Anchor, sixth grooves.

In this scene we see William for the first time; a bluff, hearty young sailor with a salty vocabulary that set the style for stage and story sailors for almost a hundred years after he first walked on stage in 1829. Every word he speaks brings in some aspect of life at sea. Even so simple a thing as a tear in a girl's eye stands "in either eye like a marine at each gangway".

Scene succeeds scene until we arrive at the end of Act III, scene 2, with William being sentenced to hang. In the shocked silence that follows, the Admiral who has pronounced the in-escapable sentence comes forward and shakes hands with William. "The scene closes", and a gun is fired as William is escorted from the scene. That is, the scene-shifters slowly push on the two flats of the next scene, a street in Deal, to close it out.

The final scene takes place on the forecastle of the ship, with William embracing the Union Jack, shaking the Admiral's hand, and then mounting the fatal platform where the sentence is to be carried out — from which he is reprieved at the last minute by the arrival of a breathless Captain Crosstree bearing the discharge paper.

When Levey opened his "real" Theatre Royal he employed the same scenic system, so that a writer in December found reason to complain that

> the regularity of the changes in the scenery, and that pleasant and steady transition from one part of the representation to another, is accompanied with so much noise, bustle and confusion, that an eye accustomed to theatricals can imme-diately detect the most reprehensible negligence on the part of the manager. . .

Early in 1834 Levey had the wings "squared", that is, instead of being stepped forward at either side of the stage from the front to the back to make the approved pyramid, they were all placed in direct line with the wings in the first grooves, making a square-shaped stage floor and giving more room for the actors. Twelve months later the entire scenic system was changed so that it worked "upon the same principles as have recently been adopted on the London stage". This was done for Levey by a Mr. Belmore, said to be a former stage machinist or mechanist with Drury Lane Theatre in London.

What Belmore installed was apparently a version of the machine-moved wing system, and what was known as the "rise and sink" system of flats. With the former, all the wings were attached to a series of frameworks on wheeled platforms or carriages in the stage cellars. The wings were placed on these frames or "ladders," which reached up through the stage, through the specially provided slits in the stage floor. Each set of wing carriages had attached to it a rope and pulley system in the cellar, by means of which either one or the whole six pairs could be moved backwards or forwards (that is, on-stage or off) by the turn of a wheel or drum. With this system, wings out of view of the audience could be changed for the next scene simply by taking the old one off the framework and replacing it with the new. When the prompter's whistle blew for the scene change, the man in the cellar turned the necessary wheel or drum and the old pair or pairs of wings withdrew, or moved back, and the new moved forward.

With the "rise and sink" system of flats, the join was horizontal instead of vertical. One half of the flat was suspended above the stage, the other half was in the stage cellar. At the prompter's whistle the stagehand in the cellar worked the necessary wheel or lever and the under-stage half of the scene moved up to meet the descending above-stage half. Such a scene is indicated in this complaint regarding a performance of *One O'Clock; or, The Knight and the Wood Demon*.

There was a sad pause before the rise of the last scene of

upwards of three minutes; and when it did ascend the magic clock instead of being a quarter to, was a quarter past one o'clock, making it necessary to put the hands back instead of forward, spoiling the *effect* upon which alone pieces like the *Wood Demon* depend. . .

But that the "rise and sink" system had not entirely superseded the original system is obvious from the fact that an even later complaint mentioned that "half the castle hall was spliced to the half of a rustic cottage, hung with gridiron, frying-pan, etc. . ." Such mishaps in the scenic department were a constant hazard in the theatre of the early nineteenth century, where the best laid plans of stage manager and prompter were at the mercy of the unpredictable human element, despite all the ropes and pulleys mechanical ingenuity could devise.

11

We Wish Him Well

The alternating periods of theatrical prosperity and lean times, orderliness and chaos which followed each other to the end of 1833 set the pattern which was to be adhered to by Levey's theatre company for as long as it existed. The peaks during this year were the visit to the theatre by the Governor, Sir Richard Bourke, and the production of the first Shakespearian play on 26 December to mark the first anniversary of the Theatre Royal. In between were fights and law cases between Levey and his players; disturbances in the audience; too much conviviality backstage (with the proprietor himself sometimes setting the worst example); criticism of his actors and their methods by Levey, and criticism of *his* methods by his actors; slipshod stage performances, and poor houses.

Levey had at last achieved his theatre and company, for which he had fought for something like seven years, but its achievement proceeded to betray the basic weaknesses in his character, against which the ability to sing a comic song or imitate a comic character were of no avail.

By the end of October the public's first enthusiasm for the theatre had waned, for Levey announced a general reduction in salaries to his company on 26 October, and four days later the *Monitor* suggested that he should open his theatre only once a week and allow the actors a certain proportion of the receipts instead of a fixed salary. But matters were not quite as desperate as they seemed, and by 1 November Levey again had a full, even an overflowing house "which assembled to testify the satisfaction felt by the visit of His Excellency to the theatre".

The Governor was seated in a box to which had been added a special canopy of state, "as a mark of respectful and loyal distinction". On taking his seat he was greeted with three rounds of applause, "which, as it ought to do, commenced with honest uproar among the gods, and was continued with well-bred clappings and tappings of canes among the boxes". The latter, it was noted, were graced with elegant and well-dressed females of rank and respectability, who waved their handkerchiefs while the heartier and noisier menfolk extended the louder greeting.

The Governor himself had chosen the night's programme — George Colman the Younger's *The Heir at Law* and James Townley's farce, *High Life below Stairs,* in which the famous Victorian dramatist A.W. Pinero was to make one of his first stage appearances in 1879 at the Lyceum. Meredith had been re-engaged, and he and the other performers were in high fettle, forcing several hearty laughs from His Excellency. The conduct of the audience was exemplary, "no individual evincing the least disposition to give annoyance to the very respectable families which appeared in various parts of the house".

Between the plays Mr. Stubbs played an air with variations on the flute, accompanied by Mr. Cavendish on the seraphine. In this odd combination the forerunner of that lugubrious accompaniment to Victorian evangelism, the harmonium, made its first public appearance in Sydney. The critics were in agreement on its suitability for a church or a chamber rather than a theatre.

The success of this night proved that the theatre and its company were capable of achieving dramatic heights which they did not often seem disposed to attempt. Wherein lay the fault? The *Gazette* by this time was so amiably disposed towards Levey that it was almost continuous in his praise. Wherever the fault lay, the newspaper decided, it did not lie with *him.* "He has given the public a pretty theatre — superior to many we have been in at home — his scenery is excellent and his performers the best

he could procure." Its remarks were answered a few days later
by the *Monitor,* which attributed the general falling off in performances to a complete lack of discipline backstage. There were
too few rehearsals, all of them poorly attended. "Everybody is
master and everybody mistress; and when the nominal manager
ventures to give a hint or to issue an order, it is treated with
scorn, and sometimes received with a torrent of abuse quite
outdoing the gaol gang in vileness of epithet." The company
should be made to submit to discipline, first being fined on
refusing to obey an instruction, and then dismissed if that failed,
the newspaper said. And the public had to play its part. If an
actor was dismissed, it should not interfere and quarrel with the
manager, and shout for the discarded actor simply because he
was a favourite. As to the women of the company, they should,
like Demosthenes, visit the seashore and address the storm. "A
visit every morning before breakfast to Bondi Beach would work
marvels in their favour, both as to voice and general bodily
vigour, and also save rouge."

Not surprisingly, one of the ladies so censured two days later
refused to go on stage. She walked out of the theatre without
warning, in the middle of a performance. She was to have appeared
in the farce *The First Floor,* following the performance of *John
Bull.* There was a long wait between the plays, and then the
curtain drew up and Mr. Grove stepped forward to announce
that Mrs. Mackie "from some cause or another" refused to come
on the stage, and Mrs. Love had consented to take her place.
The long wait, and the off-hand explanation offered were enough
to convince the audience that it had been insulted. There was an
immediate demonstration, and calls for Levey to "show" himself.
Levey accordingly showed himself, appealed to the audience for
its indulgence, and explained that it was sometimes impossible
to restrain his performers from "taking the sulks and misbehaving".
The audience was mollified, and the farce was allowed to proceed,
with the prompter again practically presenting the play on his
own.

This absolute sway held by the audience ruled in the theatre of the period throughout the world. The famous Goethe was often its victim in the theatre he managed in Weimar. Macready and others suffered its slights in England and America, Americans were its victims in London, and in Paris the first visiting English company in 1822 had potatoes and eggs thrown at it for daring to present Shakespeare's *Othello* in Paris at a time when Corneille and Racine were proscribed on the English stage. This performance or attempted performance finished with the spectators throwing benches and chairs on the stage, and the theatre being closed by the gendarmes.

But besides demonstrating, audiences also pointedly ignored activities on the stage if the play was beyond their immediate interest or understanding. They conducted conversations and social calls from box to box during the performance. Even as late as 1837 the behaviour of the young Queen Victoria at Covent Garden was noted as she, "when Macready's Lear was fixing all other hearts and eyes, chattered to the Lord Chamberlain, laughed, and turned her shoulder to the stage". But in this she was simply following a precedent established a great many years before, when the theatre was recognized as a "time-killer, or exchange of looks and smiles... very few indeed, except the critics and the plebs, come here to look at the play; they come to see and be seen". The "unheard of coarseness and brutality" of English theatre audiences in 1826–27 was noted by a German visitor to London, Prince Puckler-Muskau. On one occasion he was at a performance of *Macbeth* by Macready, and noted at the end of his commendatory description of the play that, on the part of the audience

indeed the interest was so slight, the noise and mischief so incessant, that it is difficult to understand how such distinguished artists can form themselves, with so brutal, indifferent, and ignorant an audience as they have almost always before them.

It is no wonder, then, that these theatre manners should have

130

been brought to Australia by the first settlers and convicts, or that these should have been responsible for the closing of Robert Sidaway's theatre in Sydney in 1800, and the theatre established on Norfolk Island. And at Sydney's new Theatre Royal it was not long before actors and audience showed how unruly they could be. The first audience demonstration occurred in January 1833, when the theatre had been opened about a month. The early comers, those who had paid for their seats before the time for half price, were relatively well behaved it seems, but with the admission of the "half-price mob" a different atmosphere began to prevail. The rougher element started to throw orange peel at members of the orchestra, and to indulge in "expressions and gesticulations of the lowest and most insulting kind". From this they progressed to throwing whole oranges, and peaches. On one night the fusillade against the orchestra was so bad that every member jumped on to the stage and retired behind the wings for safety. On another occasion Mrs. Weston, an actress-dancer in the company, was hit by a peach while she was performing one of those dances which one soulless critic said she danced "with some excitement to herself, but evident satisfaction to the audience".

The truth was that Levey had found that having a theatre was one thing, controlling it another. Whatever his many faults may have been, whatever enemies his bad temper, his lack of assurance, his now fair now foul reactions to his "favourites" may have made, he was at heart a man with a wish to do well by his fellow men. He could be cajoled or importuned, but not held to ransom or tyrannized into giving as much as he could afford to the worthy labourer or the worthy cause. Nor did he ask his company to do anything he was not prepared to do himself. In the first year of his theatrical activities his must have been close to a twenty-hour working day. He interviewed would-be actors, singers, stage and theatre hands each morning from about nine o'clock; conducted or was present at rehearsals; chose the programme for each performance; distributed and checked parts and playbooks; super-

131

vised the scenery, costumes, and machinery; attended to the bookings and the daily takings; listened to the complaints and sometimes joined in the internecine jealousies and rivalries of the members of his company; and sometimes acted in and always supervised the performances for three nights a week. And he had a company that was obviously out for itself. Its members jealously hoarded every sign of public favour, seeing in it the opportunity to press for more money, to badger Levey, to take him to court, or so annoy him that he took them to court. They in fact banded against him at every opportunity. Only the *Gazette* was solidly for him, and never ceased to reprobate the culpably careless conduct of the performers. "Indeed, knowing what we do," it said early in December, "we can hardly preserve our temper when we hear the animadversions to which the proprietor is continually subjected for faults not his."

Everything about his theatre was watched with sharp eyes and reported with sharper tongues by people of all kinds, many of whom aired their findings, their gossip, and their opinions in the newspapers. Had Levey received a pound for every piece of advice thus offered before the end of 1833, "for his own good, and because we wish him well", he might well have done without his theatre as a source of income.

"An Observer" wrote in the *Monitor* that the actors were committing a fraud on the public in not knowing their parts. He suspected, "from certain appearances", that there was incredible confusion behind the scenes. The actors and actresses were "too apt to indulge" after dinner, which of course added to the confusion on the stage. There were no rehearsals, no preparation of dresses, and the passages to the stage were blocked up with women and children. As a consequence, performances were later and tater in starting. "Observer" said that on one night he had had fo pace up and down the street for an hour waiting for the performance to start. The manager, he suspected, was merely nominal, lor there was no sign of management of any kind.

The newspapers complained of a lack of light in the theatre,

The interior of the Royal Victoria Theatre during the progress of a Fancy Dress Ball given by the Lord Mayor of Sydney on 21 August 1844. A comparison with the plate of the interior of the Royal Victoria Theatre in 1848 will show how the pit area was boarded over in the Georgian theatre so that balls and other social gatherings could be held. Mitchell Library

The interior of the Royal Victoria Theatre as it appeared in 1848. Joseph Fowles, *Sydney in 1848*

and of careless attendance to what lights there were. ("We think the house might be better lighted, for always towards the end of the evening, half the lamps are extinguished, and the candles burnt out.") They complained of the smoke from the oil lamps in the orchestra and footlights, and even more of the smoke from *certain clay pipes* in the pit; of the lateness in starting; the long waits between acts and plays, and of the highfalutin airs adopted by those beggars on horseback, the actors. Never before in Sydney had one man, with the possible exception of Governor Darling, had such a volume of conflicting opinions, ideas, and grievances publicly directed towards him purely for his own good.

The *Monitor* suggested that the theatre's main faults could be laid at Levey's door, chief among them being his habit of not allowing the actors time enough to learn their parts. The actor, it said, should not simply be given a manuscript copy of his part only, but a copy of the whole play. If this was done he would be able to do something he was not then able to do — understand the plot and the object and design of the author. This, for its time, was a revolutionary suggestion. It was customary in the English theatre to issue each actor with no more than his "length" of the play to be performed. This was usually written out for him by the prompter or his clerk. A "length" was a foolscap sheet folded down the middle, on which the actor's lines and cues were written, usually about forty-two lines to the "length". Thus, unless there was a consistent and full rehearsal of the play, or unless the actor troubled to procure a "book" of the play (either of which rarely happened), "bit" players knew little more about the work they were performing than their cue, the lines they had to speak, and whatever movement or "business" these involved. The leading actors were assumed to be familiar with their parts on the opening night, even though they as well as the rest of the cast might have been given only two nights' warning of the play, for it was not the custom to "act" at a rehearsal. The star had usually played the part before, while the beginner, who was often an amateur who had paid for the privilege of playing the

133

part (or was doing it for nothing to "prove" himself), was not prepared to reveal his "secrets" until the night. Apart from this, however, it was not at this time considered good form to show off at rehearsals by acting. Rehearsals were therefore perfunctory affairs at which sometimes only one or two actors would appear, and were usually conducted by the prompter, who had all the moves and business marked in his copy of the play. V. Clinton-Baddeley notes in his *All Right on the Night*:

> When Kean first rehearsed Shylock at Drury Lane in 1814, "so little interest seemed to be attached to the event of Mr. Kean's success," writes Thomas Dibdin, "that, through one excuse or other sent by performers for non-attendance, there were, in some scenes, only the new actor, and myself as prompter, on the stage. I apologised to Mr. Kean for this seeming neglect, which he appeared quite indifferent about. . .

When they turned up at rehearsal the leading players did little more than indicate where they would stand and where they wanted others to enter and stand. Such a haphazard, undisciplined way of producing a play could have only chaotic results — results to which players and audiences were accustomed. It also gave the opportunity to unscrupulous players to "kill" the efforts of a newcomer by never being in place or on cue, or by deliberately feeding the wrong cue. More than half the complaints so frequently made about actors not knowing their lines were as much a result of this lack of rehearsal and dangerous ignorance of the play as of the dilatoriness or spite of the players. When the prompter banded with the old hands against a newcomer, as sometimes happened in Levey's theatre, wrong cues were fed by the actors, which were correctly answered by the prompter in as loud a voice as possible, creating complete confusion on the stage.

Like a breath of fresh air in dispelling this fog of complaint came the *Australian*'s finding that theatricals were beginning to look up, and that the last two or three pieces brought out proved that many of the actors possessed all the requisites to make them good ones, needing only time and application to mature them. "Many affect to draw their comparisons between the acting on the Sydney and London boards. Now, although this is both unfair and ridiculous, still we do not think, that after all, it suffers so much by the comparison."

The *Gazette,* too, giving credit where credit was due, highly praised a performance of Sheridan's *The Rivals.* The characters, it said, with one or two exceptions were well cast, and it was well acted. It was the best hit "the indefatigible proprietor has yet made". Nevertheless, Levey talked of closing the theatre, the newspaper said. Surely the public will not allow this? It would be a shame, a disgrace to the people of Sydney if he was obliged to close his doors for want of encouragement.

Meantime Levey continued on his way, leaving the stage management and the management of the actors to Meredith, and searching unceasingly for that additional novelty — a dance, a song, a solo performance on a musical instrument, or acrobats — which would provide a new interest for his quickly jaded or sensation-hunting audience. Early in December he provided his patrons with the spectacle of a man walking up and down a tight-rope which had been stretched from the gallery down to the pit, a form of amusement taken over by the theatres many years before from the travelling fairs. Soon after this novelty was introduced a boy was added to the act. He proved so successful that he outshone his mentor or partner, not only walking but also lying, kneeling, and even dancing on the rope. Strangely enough the same kind of performance had been presented at Sadler's Wells in 1816, with a boy performing "far more effectively than a recent similar performance at Covent Garden". Then, it had apparently been a woman who had performed on the rope, but now "instead of gazing in terror lest a clumsy mortal fall, we are pleased with the apparent realisation of a fairy's flight".

Levey also tried to woo the public with longer programmes. A bespeak, or specially requested performance, was given for the captains of the ships in port, who had promised to bring their

135

friends. For them Levey presented another performance of *The Rivals,* followed by a sailor's hornpipe by Mr. Mackie, a comic song by Mr. Levey, a song, "The Sailor's Tear", by Mr. Grove, a "Scotch" dance by Mr. White, and the comic song "Corporal Casey" by Mr. Meredith, the whole to conclude with the farce *What Next?*

A fortnight later the first of the triple bills made their appearance, *The Spectre Bridegroom, The Village Lawyer,* and *Monsieur Tonson,* all on the one night, with entertainments between.

In early December Levey, in an advertisement, offered a partnership to any person or persons willing to supply a small capital and take an active part in the management of the theatre. By this time he had lowered his admission charges, announced half price to all parts of the house, provided whatever novelties he could, and offered by advertisement to give a trial to any amateurs who thought they could do better than the members of his company — but he still could not control his actors. Therefore, only those who were prepared to give their personal attention to the management of the theatre need apply for the partnership, he advised.

He had had trouble with Mr. and Mrs. Mackie, and soon he was to have trouble with Mr. Palmer. He had also dismissed Mrs. Jones, for her alleged rudeness to the public. These upheavals had been reported and mis-reported as usual in the press, and had not done the theatre any good, even though they were not Levey's fault. He had also had to take a Mr. Harpur to court, or rather Mr. Harpur had taken him to court.

Charles Harpur, later to become known as an Australian poet, featured in the first two or three plays at the start of the season, and was then heard of no more, though for some little time after that he must still have been on Levey's payroll. A youth of about eighteen years of age with vaunting dramatic ambitions, his few appearances had brought him nothing but censure from the press. Levey did the only practical thing — kept him off the stage. Harpur took him to court to recover three pounds he said Levey owed him for services performed.

136

Harpur told the court he had played Count Friberg in *The Miller and His Men* and Captain Arlington in *The Mutiny at the Nore,* which was quite true. He added that he was prepared and equipped to play a number of other parts, from Romeo to Gadabout in *The Lying Valet,* all for three pounds a week, and find his own costumes and make-up. At this stage Levey told the court he believed Harpur knew as much about theatricals as the candle-snuffer's apprentice, and he had therefore discharged him. Harpur disputed this assessment of his talents. An element of farce was introduced into the hearing when Levey wagered Harpur that if he would stand on a table in the court and recite a portion of any play so that it should win the applause of those present, he (Levey) would pay the three pounds demanded. Harpur, the press report states, threw himself into "attitude" amid roars of laughter, and shouted "Do you take me for an ass?" After a further exchange of pleasantries, Harpur produced a paper showing the terms of his engagement at the theatre, which Levey countered with another signed by Harpur showing that he had consented to withdraw from the theatre for one month, at the end of which Levey was to re-engage him if funds permitted. The case was dismissed.

There were no doubt many reasons why Levey's actors should have attempted Shakespeare, but not the least of them must have been because of a benefit performance given on 12 June 1833 for two of the lesser players of the company, Dyball and Palmer. This performance had a house packed to the doors to witness a comedy, a melodrama, and Palmer in the Tent Scene from *Richard III.* One of the few newspapers to comment on this benefit performance disposed of the Tent Scene with the comment that it "was not beyond mediocrity, the stage is not large enough for such an exhibition". There, perhaps, the matter would have rested, had it not been for at least two things which remained to disturb the players' equilibrium. One was that Palmer had apparently annoyed one or two of the Theatre Royal's would-be trage- dians by stealing the Shakespearian limelight from his "betters"

137

(these being, in their own opinion at least, John Meredith and Conrad Knowles). The other was the decision by Barnett Levey announced on 20 December, to celebrate the first anniversary of his Theatre Royal on 26 December with a programme consisting of *Richard III* followed by a pantomime. To top it all there would be a display of fireworks and a large fire balloon which "will ascend in front of the hotel, at the cost of the proprietor". If it was novelty his audience wanted, then here was novelty and to spare.

Reading between the lines of subsequent announcements and reports the impression is gained that while this decision delighted Meredith and Knowles (who more than likely had helped to engineer it, and had certainly appropriated the best parts for themselves), it infuriated Palmer because he — of them all, the only one who had "done" the Tent Scene — had been relegated to one of the least significant parts. He was not one to take the implied insult without a murmur, and so he not only "left" the theatre on the morning of 26 December, but also told his tale of woe during the day to all his taproom cronies and whoever else would listen. Their numbers were surprisingly large.

The version of *Richard III* staged for this anniversary performance was Colley Cibber's, first performed in 1770 and still popular in many parts of the world as late as the 1920's. Cibber changed the play so that almost all the emphasis was on Richard. He cut lines, juggled scenes, dropped characters, added lines from at least four other Shakespeare plays and hundreds written by himself, and made of the play a melodramatic hotch-potch beloved of actors and audiences throughout the English-speaking world. Even so, his is a theatrically bold version, still thought superior to the rearranged *King Lear* and *The Tempest* prepared by Nahum Tate and Dryden respectively.

From the newspaper reports of this performance it is known that Meredith played Richard, his wife played Queen Elizabeth, and Grove played Catesby. Knowles was also in the cast, but although he was said to have been the only adequate player of them all the part he played is not mentioned.

138

The four newspapers damned the Royal's performance of *Richard III*, but it seems they damned something they were largely unable to hear, and at times could not even see. For this gala night the house was packed to the doors, and long before the rise of the green baize curtain people eager to gain admittance had been turned away. When the curtain did rise, however, there was not the expected or customary hush for the opening of the play. No sooner did Meredith appear on the stage as Richard than the theatre was filled with cries for Mr. Palmer. For some time there was so much noise it was impossible for Meredith to be heard, but when a lull finally did come he stepped forward and announced that Mr. Palmer had that day left the theatre of his own accord and would not be appearing. "From that time forward there was an incessant roar in the house so that the speeches of the actors . . . could but be imperfectly heard." It can be assumed that the Palmer-primed majority of the rowdies hoped to see that actor as Richard, and not Meredith. But as Meredith was to prove again and again, it took much more than an uproarious audience to make him withdraw. The play progressed amid a continuous demonstration by the audience. "The pit and galleries hissed incessantly and the boxes laughed incessantly, joining ever and anon in the hissing", so that the play and the players deteriorated to such an extent that not only lines were forgotten but also cues. The ghosts, for instance, arrived too soon for their scene, and when the curtain rose they rushed off the stage "leaving their cerements behind them". Women had to be rescued from the pit, the most unruly area of the house, and took momentary refuge on the stage, from where they were conveyed out of the theatre. The musicians were forced out of the orchestra pit, and members of the audience started to climb on to the stage despite the spikes fronting it and designed to prevent such a happening. Then followed an even wilder scene during which Meredith threw two or three men down into the pit as fast as they climbed up from it. The inglorious night finished, at the end of the pantomime, with Mr. Grove trying to announce from the stage the bill for the next night, while a number of boys who had clambered on to the stage untouched mimicked him, "to the infinite amusement of the *gods*".

After the performance the much publicized fire balloon consumed itself long before it reached the earth, and thus put quietus to an altogether dismal night, whose total failure was largely due to the machinations of one dissatisfied actor.

12

Short-Lived Hope

Barnett Levey repeated his call for a partner early in January 1834, and at the same time took his revenge on the newspapers for their adverse reports on *Richard III*. There would be no more free passes for the press. If they wanted to see the play they must pay. This was the signal for a further newspaper "exposure" of the theatre's real and supposed shortcomings. It was dirty;too dark; the sceneshifting was incredibly bad, parlour wings being left with a forest backdrop, and a chair or sofa left in a forest scene; the players were licentious, rebellious, and altogether past hope. Levey had heard and read it all before, and so had the frequenters of the theatre. It served no other purpose than to confirm Levey in his belief that he had correctly gauged the annoyance his ban would cause the newspapers.

But there was yet another outcome of that riotous Shakespeare performance. The strong, pugnacious Meredith appeared in court on 5 January charged with assault. During the melée in the pit, when several members of the audience drove the musicians out and clambered up on to the stage, Meredith as quickly threw them down again. Unfortunately, one man in his downward fall caught and tore a leg on one of the stage spikes, and Meredith was charged accordingly. He was remanded to appear at the next sitting of the Quarter Sessions, but as the injured man was named Nathan, and there was wrong on both sides, Levey was apparently able to settle the matter amicably out of court.

The early part of this year was also noteworthy for another addition being made to the list of merchants, hotel keepers and auctioneers who "gave it all away" for the stage. Levey had an answer to his call for a partner, which he accepted. On 7 February it was announced that Mr. Joseph Simmons, lately from London, had taken a share of the Theatre Royal and was to have the entire management of the stage. "He will be a valuable acquisition," said one newspaper, "as Mr. Simmons is perfectly conversant with theatricals."

Simmons, in fact, was said to be the first actor with any previous experience to join Levey's company. He is said to have begun his career at the age of seventeen "with the veteran provincial actor-manager Roxby Beverley". By this was no doubt meant William Roxby, who, when he took to the stage, added the name Beverley to his and was from then on known as William Roxby Beverley. He managed the Manchester Theatre Royal for some years, and later with one of his sons ran a provincial theatre circuit. His most famous son, of the same name, was a noted artist and scenepainter of the nineteenth century.

Simmons, it was said, was a "quick study" (i.e. he could memorize parts very quickly) and a hard worker, and soon made his debut in London and a name for himself as a versatile actor. He certainly proved his versatility on the Sydney stage, but the general truth of the claims made for him has yet to be established. Perhaps Simmons was merely the first of a long line of ambitious amateurs who told the gullible Levey they had performed in the London theatres.

Simmons made his debut at the Theatre Royal on 17 February and earned the usual mixed remarks from the critics. One found his performance had too much rant and too little feeling; another, that with a little more study and less action he would become the first in his line on the stage. The play was variously referred to as *The Gambler's Fate; or, The Hut of the Red Mountains*, and *Twenty Years of a Gambler's Life*. It was, in fact, H.H. Milner's *The Hut of the Red Mountain; or, Thirty Years of a Gambler's Life*,

142

a rehash of a plot used many times in England and France. Edward Moore's *The Gamester* (1753) holds the initial plot, while most of the trimmings were taken from Ducange and Dinaux's *Trente Ans; ou, La Vie d'un Jouer* (Paris, 1827).

The hope was expressed in many quarters that Simmons would be able to supply, as acting-manager, that firm control over the players which so far had been lacking. It was short-lived. Before the end of February there were further complaints about the actors and actresses. The theatre, it was said, was a school "where the teachers are at the mercy of most wayward and unruly pupils, who in proportion as they require strict discipline, mutiny against it". It was noted as a fresh sign of their irresponsibility that during a performance of *Catherine and Petruchio,* Garrick's truncated version of *The Taming of the Shrew,* they had laughed on the stage, whispered together, and some had even made significant signs to persons in the house.

The season ended in March or early April, and soon afterwards Levey announced the disciplinary action he had decided to take against his unruly players. It is easy to imagine Levey and Simmons having many discussions about what must be done to bring the actors into line, considering suggestion after suggestion and discarding them all until the right one had been found. Levey refused to allow the actors to have their usual end of season benefit. With one bold stroke he had hit them where it would hurt the most, in the pocket, and deprived them at the same time of an opportunity to retaliate, for as the theatre was closed there was no audience for them to call on for support against Levey. The actors were thus faced with a long period without pay, at the end of which, Levey no doubt hoped, they would come back to him much chastened and ready to accept his terms. Those hit hardest, of course, were the leading players, some of whom had been deprived of anything up to ninety pounds by Levey's move.

Publicly Levey explained that he had two reasons for refusing the actors their benefits. One was that the salary he paid them was at least 50 per cent higher than it would be if he allowed

143

benefits; the other was that he wished to prevent the congregation of the rabble, and the riots and other disgraceful scenes which he said had marred last season's benefits.

Both these "reasons" were untruths, as everybody knew. Knowles answered them in a letter to the *Australian*. He said that no other theatre in the world had ever refused its actors their benefits. As to the 50 per cent, he, Knowles, was still receiving the same salary given him fifteen months before — three guineas a week. Several other performers were also still receiving their original salaries, and yet all had had benefits last season. At these some of the actors had cleared sixty, seventy, eighty, and ninety pounds, though he, because his benefit was ninth in order, had cleared only ten. As for riots, and rabble, those benefits had been among the best conducted performances since the theatre had opened. For his three guineas a week he had also been acting-manager for some time, and had written the opening address for the theatre, for which he still had not been paid. Nor had he ever refused to go on. Theatre proprietors, Knowles added, did not refuse benefits, for they were clearly a source of extra profit to them as well as to the actors once a season had ended.

Without saying it in so many words, Knowles proved that Levey was deliberately lying about his reasons for not allowing the benefits, but he made the mistake of seeming to condone those lies in refusing to say straight out that Levey was "getting back" at the actors for their misbehaviour, and that in the process the innocent had to suffer as well as the guilty.

The actors did the only thing left to them; a forlorn hope, but one that had to be tried. They appealed to the Governor for a licence to conduct theatricals at the Pulteney Hotel, which was granted. Levey made no public comment about this, but no doubt had plenty to say in private. Meantime, he was treated to the usual back-somersault by the newspapers, which had criticized him in every permissible way for not controlling his players. They now said it was mean of him to try to starve the players into compliance. Knowles, Meredith, and Buckingham had

144

attempted to present "concerts" at the Pulteney Hotel, one said, but the results had not been flattering. The *Australian* emphasized that the only possible answer to the existing stalemate lay in the phrase "union is strength". The public would not attend poor performances, or support one contending party against the other. The actors were not of any use without their theatre, or the theatre without its actors. "Amuse the public, and the public will support the play — fail to do so, and though the public may be disappointed, the players and proprietor will starve." This newspaper also pointed out that Mr. and Mrs. Mackie had left Sydney to join the newly-opened Theatre Royal in Hobart, and it would not be long before the remaining "stars" in the theatrical atmosphere would do the same. It foresaw, in fact, such an exodus that "Hobart Town will be overstocked with actors, and the pay will be proportionately diminished".

Sydney's Theatre Royal opened its new season on 19 April. The house had been repainted and decorated; the stage wings, which had been at an oblique angle to the stage front, were now squared with it; the music and lighting had been improved, while the stage machinery was now under the expert management of Mr. Phillips, "nine years foreman of Drury Lane".

Dealing with the opening performance, one critic said that the actors were "well up in their parts". Another said that there was a beggarly account of empty boxes, and the pieces went off "flat, stale, and unprofitable". The company was inferior, lacking its principal performers.

This and a few following performances were enough to reveal to Levey and the defaulting players that what the *Australian* had said was true. The public would not take sides *outside* the theatre, it would simply stay away for as long as it felt it was not likely to get its money's worth. So there was the inevitable reconciliation, and on 10 May the theatre was again packed to the doors to witness the return of Knowles, Buckingham, Meredith, Mrs. Taylor, and Mrs. Jones — the backbone of the *corps dramatique*. The plays were *The Gambler's Fate* again, and the farce, *Teddy*

145

the Tiler, and as each of the "old faces" made his or her appearance on the stage "the house burst into loud and continued shouts of approbation". All — Levey, the players, the audience — had learnt something from the split, and for some months there was to be comparative peace backstage. The only people unrepentant and unstirred by it all were the newspaper reporters, who again took up their admonitory task where they had left off at the end of the previous season.

One wanted to know how it was that the hair of Albert Germaine, male lead in *The Gambler's Fate,* which had been light brown in the first act, became after twenty years of disgrace and misery in exile *raven black.* He also wanted to know why Albert should have had a very nice suit to correspond with his hair in the last act, while his wife and child were in rags. He thus put his finger on another weakness of the theatre of the time — actors having to "find their own", resulting in all kinds of incongruous costumes, and make-up at variance with the character the actor was representing.

Towards the end of May Levey wooed his audience with a triple bill which included a novelty for some time fashionable in London, the presentation of a play by a juvenile company. The bill consisted of Thomas Morton's *The School of Reform; or, How to Rule a Husband, Teddy the Tiler,* and the very popular burlesque by W.B. Rhodes, *Bombastes Furioso.* This was first produced in Australia by the convicts at Emu Plains in 1825, and as late as the 1860's it was still being presented by amateur groups in country centres throughout New South Wales. It has a quite meaningless story which gives admirable opportunities for grotesque costume and stage "rant" at its most ludicrous. Full of buffoonery and nonsense, it yet fulfilled the purpose of comedy or farce — it made its audiences laugh. In the 1840's an attractive little edition of this play was published in London with illustrations by George Cruikshank. The play had a quality (it escapes us today) which endeared it to our nineteenth century forebears for more than sixty years. It was this that Levey's juvenile company presented, and for once the critics were united in its praise.

In its review the *Herald* made two comments which, remembering the year in which they were made (1834) were remarkably percipient. One was that one of the young actors, a Miss Winstanley, daughter of the theatre's scenepainter, would one day be a star in Australian theatricals. The others was that the "grand army" in this play would make an excellent subject for Cruikshank's pencil. Cruikshank did illustrate this play, and Miss Winstanley not only became a star in Australian theatricals, but later achieved success in New York and London.

The juveniles of the company were, of course, mostly the children of people connected with the theatre, among whom were a Jones, a Phillips, and young Quinn, the boy tight-rope walker. Of their performance the *Herald* said:

> . . . Master Jones's Bombastes was a surprising performance for such a child. His mosquito person, attired in all the trappings of war, covered with scars, and wielding as it were with giganitic dexterity a huge sword, twice as long as himself, with which he "challenged all the human race," had a most comical effect upon the audience. His singing and acting were altogether far superior to anything that could possibly have been expected. The playing of Miss Winstanley as Distaffina was on an equality with the tiny General; she is decidedly a child of genius. . . Master Phillips, as Fuzbos, made the most of his part and played admirably. King Artaxominas, by Master Quinn, was rather too tall, which made him appear out of proportion with his puny associates in love and murder.

Soon after this Levey began to get many complaints about the length of the performances, which sometimes did not finish until one o'clock in the morning. "After all," asked one newspaper, "who and what is to be seen in our theatre that can possibly compensate for a sitting of six hours?" Members of the audience could have answered that question. The triple bill did not meet with the approval of everybody, but as the majority expected it it was regularly presented.

With the arrival of the benefits in October came more trouble between the players, and demonstrations by the audience. For his benefit Mr. Palmer chose to play the name part in *Richard III*, "sustaining the character throughout very respectable" [*sic*]. Unfortunately, before the curtain rose there was a fight between Phillips, the machinist, and Knowles, over Mrs. Jones, whom Knowles said Phillips had insulted. The audience was kept waiting fifteen minutes for the play to start. Palmer came before the curtain and apologized for the delay, which this time the audience accepted good humouredly. But a fortnight later, at the benefit for Phillips, Knowles continued the squabble by refusing to perform, and the audience showed its displeasure. There was another wild scene in the theatre, in which bottles were thrown at the stage, one narrowly missing Mrs. Meredith's nose. At the following performance, at which Knowles did deign to appear, the demonstration was so violent that nothing could be heard of what was going on on the stage. The hooting of Mr. Phillips' friends, and the loud applause and shouting of those taking the other side, turned the performance into dumb show. At last it came to blows between members of the opposing factions.

> . . . Two or three *gentlemen* of pugilistic fame commenced a trial of the art on the loudest vociferators of displeasure, who resisted the attack with sticks. A beautiful battle royal scene followed, in which Mr. Levey sought to *conciliate* the contending parties, by directing against them anything but fair words. . . Who would be hardy enough to express his approbation at any particular excellence or merit of a performer, when the experiment might cost him a black eye, or broken nose? or from pursuing a contrary course, render his head subject to the discipline of a cudgel?

Levey, never the most equable or rational of people, by this time must have felt like washing his hands of his players. He announced at the end of October that he was going to Hobart in the hope of signing on a few additions to the *corps dramatique* from the Hobart Theatre, no doubt in the hope that he would at least be able to replace the chief trouble-makers. While he was

A command performance of *Julius Caesar* before Queen Victoria in the Rubens room at Windsor Castle, 1850. *Illustrated London News*, 9 February 1850

Eliza Winstanley as Elinor in Charles Kean's 1858 production of *King John* at the Princess's Theatre, London. *Illustrated London News*, 6 November 1858

away Miss Eliza Winstanley and her sister Ann made their debut as actresses at the benefit for their father.

Levey returned from Hobart in December, but there was no word of any acquisition from the theatre there, apart from the return of Mrs. Mackie. By this time the season had ended and plans were being made for the next. Plans were also being made for a change which Levey, contrary to his usual practice, kept secret right up to the moment when it was announced.

The new season opened as usual on 26 December with *Jonathan Bradford; or, The Murder by the Roadside,* and a pantomime. Levey had again fallen out with the press, probably this time because of the *Monitor's* claim that since the theatre had first opened the colony had received by the four female emigrant ships an importation of about 200 "loose women", all of whom had become the chief female frequenters of the theatre. Levey accordingly withdrew all free passes to the press, and reports of the performance of *Jonathan Bradford* were therefore contributed by "correspondents", who refused to be impressed despite the unusual staging problems this play presented. The *Herald* revealed as a "theatrical trick" the fact that before the first performance on Friday, 26 December, Levey had had handbills printed for distribution on the Saturday, in which it was claimed that "owing to the crowded state of the house, and the approbation bestowed on the fifth scene of *Jonathan Bradford,* on witnessing the performances in four different parts of the stage at the same time, it will be repeated".

Levey was justifiably proud of this production, for it had created a sensation in London when first presented at the Surrey and Sadler's Wells only the year before. This play anticipated by a century Eugene O'Neill's *Desire under the Elms* in showing the interior of four rooms on the stage at one time, the first example of such a setting on the English stage. It showed, on two levels, four rooms in the George Inn: the bar and a parlour on the lower level and two bedrooms on the upper level.

But Edward Fitzball's play also deserves to be remembered

149

for another reason: this was the impetus it gave to the resurrection of old crimes and their transformation into murder plays, thus establishing a tradition which has lasted to this day, and whose prolific offshoots have been the detective and spy stories which so fascinate today's theatre and film audiences. The play is founded on the real life story of Bradford, landlord of an inn, who was executed on presumptive evidence for the murder of one of his guests. It was not until many years after his death that the valet to the guest, on his death bed, confessed that *he* had murdered his master to obtain the large sum of money he knew his master carried with him. Fitzball, of course, made many changes so as to obtain dramatic unity.

Towards the end of January 1835 there was another lengthy attack on the Sydney theatre, this time as a letter signed *Eumenes* in the *Herald*. The writer claimed that "the higher classes of our society have utterly renounced the theatre". He then proceeded to so over-colour his picture of the theatre and the social evils he said it engendered and bolstered that he displayed little more than his ignorance and steel-cored prejudices. He also included the "degeneracy of the British stage" in his strictures, asserting that because of this Covent Garden and Drury Lane were nearly deserted by persons of rank and fashion. Sydney's theatre, he said, was notorious for its scenes of indecorum and disorder, vulgarity and vice. There was also, he hinted, a lot to be desired in the moral deportment of individual members of the company, though this topic was "too delicate for public animadversion". He pronounced the introduction of the drama into New South Wales as a total failure, and warned the proprietor that if there was any justice in the world he would either mend his ways or almost certainly expect the suspension of his licence to hold theatrical entertainments.

The letter was answered a few days later in the *Australian* by Knowles, who denied that the higher classes of society had utterly renounced the theatre, for the simple reason that "proof to the contrary is before my eyes night after night". The stage, he said,

150

had been responsible for the reformation of many individuals known personally to him; men who instead of spending nearly the whole of their wages at an alehouse, as formerly, were now to be seen, quiet and sober, seated in the theatre instead. As for misconduct among the players — "Are not players men?" Why should they not quarrel? Did *Eumenes* expect them to be demigods? Neglect of study by the players was admitted, but in extenuation of his own case at least, Knowles said that recently he had had to learn 1,500 lines in three days to master a part. "I acknowledge I was imperfect; although one night, after a hard evening's work at the theatre I did not lay the book from out of my hands until six o'clock the next morning."

Knowles concluded by saying that he had come forward, not as the champion of Levey or Simmons, "but as the advocate of nearly 100 persons who earn their living at the theatre, and whom this writer by his cold-heartedness and cruelty, would deprive of a morsel of bread." *Eumenes* was silenced.

Following this there were repeat performances of Miss Winstanley in *Clari,* and Knowles's attempt at *Othello,* which was said not to be very successful. Performances of *Pizarro* and *Venice Preserved* followed, then came Simmons's farewell performance, for he and Levey had apparently (or perhaps inevitably) fallen out, and his offer to renew their contract was not accepted. On the other hand, their parting may have been due to the fact that by this time, February 1835, Levey's "secret" had leaked out. He had leased his theatre and company to a group of six Sydney businessmen, who henceforth would be responsible for its conduct.

At Simmons' farewell performance, when the curtain had fallen on the first piece, Levey came on the stage to make an announcement. His appearance was greeted by a storm of hisses from the audience, followed by such a barrage of shouts and yells that for a long time he could not make himself heard. After a while it was sufficiently quiet for him to announce the plays for the next performance, and to attempt a eulogy of his late partner, when the loud, insistent yells of "Off! Off!" at last forced him to retire.

151

The combine leased the theatre from Levey for two years at an annual rental of £1,300, sufficient indication that despite its real and alleged irregularities it was certainly not losing money. Levey could not manage it. Right up to the last moment he was engaged in a public argument with Mrs. Taylor, now the theatre's leading lady, publicized by press advertisements from both parties. Now she would consent to return to the theatre at one pound a night, now she would not. He was not firm enough in his dealings, and did not always stand by his word. By his ever-present but always fluctuating habit of favouritism among members of the company he invited the formation of backstage cliques that were constantly changing membership as now this and now that one fell out of favour. Nor was he physically well. He was drinking more than was good for him, the victim of his love of conviviality, and was in a constant state of nervous tension as the result of the many situations which he called into being but could not resolve.

On 10 April 1835 he announced by advertisement that he would bid the public goodbye for a term at his benefit, to be held that evening. He promised that at this he would present an address to his friends.

Levey's benefit performance was ignored by the press. Although the newspapers were not at all consistent in reporting benefits (more often than not they merely mentioned that a benefit had been held), this was surely one which should have been reported. They accepted his paid advertisements for the night, and left it at that. As a consequence, the points made by Levey in his farewell address, whether of explanation, justification, or complaint will never be known. Instead, the fickle press, with an indecent "off with the old love, on with the new" haste, welcomed the news of the new management and gave it frequent puffs — for a while.

13

Australia's First Hamlet

"That dismal old guy 'Amlet" first questioned his father's ghost in Australia on 18 August 1834. To don Hamlet's melancholy, though quite unaware of his destiny at the time, a young articled clerk left his home and his family in London some time in 1828 or 1829 as member of a band of ill-fated Swan River colonists. The air at the time was alive with promises and prospects, but soon after arrival in Western Australia both vanished, and the young emigrant found himself with barely enough money to get out.

He bought a passage to Tasmania, where he secured a position as tutor at an educational establishment, teaching drawing, French, and the classics. Proximity to one of his attractive young charges led to an attachment between them, the "scandal" being responsible for his dismissal. And so the young emigrant, Conrad Knowles, said to be the son of a Wesleyan minister, next made his way to Sydney, where he lived for a time with some distant relatives who made him welcome. They were very kind to him, but he was still under the necessity of earning a living. He seemingly had no wish, or was not able to resume his previous work as a clerk or a teacher. It happened that at this time Barnett Levey was recruiting actors and would-be actors for his projected Theatre Royal. Though, as a Wesleyan, Knowles knew he would forfeit the friendship and respect of the family with which he was staying if he joined "theatricals", the temptation was too strong, and he became a member of Levey's embryo company. But he kept his defection a secret from his friends for as long as he could, attending prayer meetings by night and rehearsals by day until the night before the opening of the Theatre Royal. And he decided to use a stage name, though what he hoped to gain by this in the then small town of Sydney it is hard to see. If it was anonymity, he was soon disappointed, for the newspapers referred to him continually by his stage and his real name all through their reports of the theatre's first season. This, if it did nothing else, must at least have caused confusion in the minds of the few people who perhaps did not know that Mr. Cooper and Mr. Knowles were one and the same.

On 25 October 1832 Knowles delivered a farewell address at his last prayer meeting, and on 26 October he stood with the assembled company on stage when the curtain rose for the first time at the Sydney Theatre Royal in the saloon of the Royal Hotel.

The twenty-two-year-old Conrad Knowles played Captain Crosstree in *Black Ey'd Susan* and Tom King in *Monsieur Tonson* on that opening night, and within the next two or three days no doubt eagerly bought a copy of each of the newspapers as they came out. There were then four of these to serve Sydney's town population of about 15,000. Three of them respected the anonymity Knowles and Mrs. Jones had chosen to adopt, but the fourth (and last to appear), despite the fact that they were listed in the playbills as Mrs. Love and Mr. Cooper, uncompromisingly referred to them by their true names. He learnt from them all that his maiden appearance had been a success. He had played Tom King "in a very spirited way". He was an "actor of no mean talent", and "bids fair to be a star". He had also given a "gentlemanly and dignified performance". Subsequent reports by the critics confirmed their original findings. Knowles was "possessed of considerable merit, and a decided acquisition to the corps". All reports emphasized his "gentlemanly acting". Not until the middle of February 1833 did the first real criticism appear, when

154

he was accused of displaying "far too much of that strained and unnatural vehemence of speech and action almost necessarily resorted to by actors in the overgrown theatres at home". Success had made him over-confident, and inclined to let himself go and "tear a passion to tatters". He perhaps remembered performances he had seen as a youth in London, where the theatres were huge barns and the actor could reach the back seats of the auditorium only by large gestures and a loud, blustering projection. The style was too grandiose for the small Sydney Theatre Royal.

For the theatre's second season, which opened in the true Theatre Royal building, Knowles was made acting-manager, roughly equivalent to today's producer or director, in place of Meredith. At this opening performance he played Lothair in *The Miller and His Men,* and Old Frost in *The Irishman in London.* In the first he was said to be "stiff and awkward, and obviously uneasy", but in the second he displayed those abilities which, together with later performances in such parts as Sir Anthony Absolute, Sir Peter Teazle and many character parts in minor comedies and afterpieces, were to make the critics proclaim comedy as his forte. Knowles now settled down in earnest as an actor, and was soon involved in the petty jealousies, the failures and minor triumphs, the backstage politics and furious squabbles which characterized at least the first ten years of the theatre in Sydney. Knowles liked praise, it is obvious. It is also obvious that no critic's estimation of his work as an actor was as high as his own, and that their praise of others was gall and wormwood to him. Over the years he worked hard and long, and by choice as well as necessity overtaxed his strength and his abilities. It was no wonder, therefore, that whether it was ego, conceit, or plain love for his work which kept him constantly on the stage, he should earn another name for himself as the actor most consistently unfamiliar with the words of the many parts he played. To add to the strain there was the constant competition between the stage "leaders" and between them and the more or less even flow of newcomers. Among these was Mackie or Mackay, who, like Mrs. Jones, had first appeared before the public at the amateur concerts in 1826. He was an accomplished actor and dancer, when sober, and was highly thought of by the critics. Other "rivals" were Meredith, Simmons, Spencer, Gordon, Barton, and one or two others whom Knowles took more seriously than was necessary. If reports are to be believed, he succeeded in ousting them all. He had learnt the art of back-stabbing in a hard school.

In July 1834 the Theatre Royal Company presented Shakespeare's *Othello,* with Knowles in the name part and Simmons as Iago. With this play, for the first but by no means the last time, Knowles experienced the bewilderment of reading quite contradictory press notices of what were one and the same performance. One notice had it that he displayed "a sad misconception of the hero of the piece", and that "something more than mere stage rant is required in the Moor". Another described his Othello as "badly personified by a forced attempt at theatrical stateliness", while a third claimed quite baldly that he "played in a manner that would not have disgraced a provincial theatre in England . . . he was greeted throughout with continual applause". Iago was described simply as "tolerable". A fortnight later, early in August, the play was presented with the roles reversed. For their pains the two actors were told their performance was a travesty.

It was in this month that Knowles appeared for the first time as Hamlet — that peak to which all actors aspire who take their work at all seriously. The performance drew only one or two notices, the comments proving among other things that the writers knew remarkably little about either Shakespeare or *Hamlet.* There was practically nothing approaching informed comment on the play or the players, only the conventional or accepted "attitudes" to what was described as the work of the "immortal bard". As a result we know today practically nothing about this production as a production — how Knowles was dressed, what the scenes were like, whether the play was cut and, if so, by what lines and/or characters. The reports give the strong impression

156

that the writers expected *Hamlet* to be a good "weepy" tragedy of the *Castle Spectre* or *Venice Preserved* kind.

These higher flights by the Theatre Royal company were usually tried out on such special occasions as benefit performances. Knowles, for instance, would agree to play Hamlet or Othello at Simmons', Mackay's or Meredith's benefit and they would return the compliment in something equally grand for his benefit night. Such performances were, in the main, ignored by the press, on the grounds that they were one-night special occasions and should therefore be neither criticized nor damned. However, on the scant evidence available about this first *Hamlet* performance it is possible to form a rather blurred but still recognizable picture.

Two of the five newspapers "noticed" the performance, the others ignoring it. One found that it was a creditable attempt, that all the performers "exerted themselves", and that Knowles's Hamlet, Mrs. Taylor's Queen, and Mrs. Jones's Ophelia were the best sustained characters of the evening. The other newspaper found that Knowles looked the part of Hamlet very well, but lacked "that quiet solemnity of manner which ought to distinguish it". It said the most barbarous butchery was frequently perpetrated on the text. It liked Simmons as Horatio, but thought Ophelia quite out of "Mrs. Jones's line". Her mad scenes were said to have been highly ludicrous, and her singing of snatches of songs to some nondescript tunes "most farcical". This paper then criticized Meredith for appearing first as the Ghost, and then as the First Gravedigger. "It altogether destroys the illusion of the scene, for we defy anyone then present to forget that the facetious gravedigger had just before been masquerading in a suit of armour, as a ghost." In making this comment the writer revealed his ignorance of the usual Shakespearian production. For obvious reasons, doubling has always taken place. The only thing unusual about this performance was that Meredith should have doubled the Ghost and the First Gravedigger (which he did, no doubt, because of the "comedy" in the latter part). The traditional double in *Hamlet* has always been Polonius and the First Grave-digger. The fault, if fault there was, lay in this instance with Meredith for not clearly differentiating between the two characters.

For his playing of Hamlet Knowles was to receive real praise only in retrospect, as when one newspaper said just before his benefit in September 1835, "in *Hamlet* he was considered by good judges to be nearly equal to the best English provincial performers".

By this time (1834) the critics, who saw Knowles each time the theatre was open, were beginning to comment on the faults and mannerisms in his representations. He was accused of imitating Macready, whom he may have seen when he was a youth in London. Though the writers did not say in so many words that he had "the Macready burst, the Macready pause, the Macready gait", imitated by so many actors of the time, they did note that he had too many "tragic starts and unseemly shakes of the head". "It is plain he has seen Macready", said one critic, "and is an admirer of him — but he should beware lest his imitation of him degenerate into mere mannerism and mimicry." Knowles's playing of the part of Octavian in *The Mountaineers* brought forth these remarks, to which was added:

> . . . It is quite painful to hear one grinding his words between his teeth as if he had lockjaw, and indulging in violent convulsive action as if he were commencing a fit of epilepsy. Besides, it is quite unmeaning as well as ungraceful to see a young gentleman running his fingers perpetually through his head of thick curled hair as though it were a mop he was handling. We really would not take the trouble of giving so much good natured advice but that we take Mr. Knowles to be a man of much promise. . .

Knowles continued to play in the usual run of melodramas and comedies for a few months, and then he essayed *Hamlet* again, in February 1836. This performance was noted by three newspapers but four critics, for one of the newspapers took the extraordinary step of publishing two independent criticisms furnished unexpectedly by two "correspondents".

158

In the brief notice given by one newspaper we get a glimpse for the first time of the staging of *Hamlet* at the Theatre Royal, which on this particular night was hopelessly inadequate. Knowles's Hamlet this time, the newspaper said, was "not marked by that depth of feeling which characterised him when he sustained the part twelve months since. . ." (again that approval in retrospect). The writer then confined himself to remarks on "the shameful manner in which the scenes were shifted" and other failings during the performance. The Ghost, it seems, did not appear at all in the first act. This possibly means that the trap on which the Ghost traditionally rose through the stage floor to confront the bewildered guards, just as traditionally refused to work on this night, and that the actors on stage, rather than wait, "covered" this deficiency with "gagging", and thus made it impossible for the Ghost to come up from below stage and enter from the wings. This contretemps must have caused a great deal of consternation backstage and thrown the normal running of that department out of gear. For the rest of the play not one scene was as it should have been. The fifth scene, which should have been "A more remote part of the platform", (i.e. the battlements) was, when the curtain rose, a room — "which spoiled the effect of the speeches". The first two scenes of the third act, the writer claimed, "were for some unaccountable reason made one, and when the next scene drew up, instead of the stage being ready it appeared as if the scene-shifters had to inquire what scene ought to have been there. . ." It must, indeed, have been an off-night for the stagehands, for in addition to all this "in the course of the whole piece a chair was a piece of furniture that it was quite a favour to be allowed to see on the stage".

Contrasting this with a second and third criticism of the same performance, it is seen that they disagree with each other on almost every point. The second newspaper presented its "look here upon this picture, and on this" with something of a tongue-in-cheek attitude. One writer saw no merit whatever in the performance, while the other saw little but merit. As the newspaper said

159

in explaining the presence of two reports, "playgoers will differ as well as doctors". The first writer's sole notice of the performance was contained in his second sentence (the first simply stated the fact that *Hamlet* had been played on Thursday evening last):

> There being various opinions whether that *play* of *Hamlet* which was then played by the Sydney corps dramatique was Shakespeare's or not, we forebear entering into any particulars, until made positive as to who was the author of those sublime sentences, heard on the above evening.

Here, one could say, is a man with a grudge, or a man whose ideas of theatre had been outraged by an inept and untutored performance.

The second critic saw a different play, or perhaps each had a different axe to grind. He wrote that *Hamlet* had been performed to a respectable, intelligent, and overflowing house. The chief character was ably presented by Mr. Knowles. "It is clearly that gentlemen's *chef d'ouvre*, a hit, a palpable hit, and has been closely studied so that we had the words of the immortal bard without garbling." The Ghost was well played by Spencer (from the Tasmanian theatre, and himself a candidate for Shakespearian honours), but the same could not be said for the King and Polonius. The Gravedigger, by Mr. Lee, called down repeated plaudits, said this writer, and Osric and Laertes (Johnson and Simmons) were capably handled. Mrs. Taylor looked too young for the Queen, and as for Ophelia...! There are perhaps two words which a writer should never use in describing an actor's performance, for whether it is his intention or not they will damn it. One is to say, as this writer said of Mrs. Jones as Ophelia, that her performance was "interesting"; the other is to say that it was "adequate".

The third newspaper waited for the second performance a few nights later before making its comments. It found this much superior to the first, with Knowles as Hamlet "very perfect, very effective, and very deserving the applause he received". It also disliked the King and Polonius, found Mrs. Taylor looked too young for the Queen, and didn't mention Ophelia at all.

In June this year Knowles again became manager, and though by no means an alcoholic he found that under the increased burden it was necessary to take more and more alcohol each night to keep himself going. Early the next year he announced that he was leaving for England, and by June 1837 the newspapers which had had so much to say about his real or supposed failings were regretting his loss. "The best if not the only tragedian that ever trod the Sydney boards, although at the same time the most careless", said one. And at the same time a writer in the *Gazette* attacked the "drama" in Sydney, attributing all its failings to the poor leadership of Barnett Levey. At once an anonymous correspondent came to his defence in a long letter in another newspaper, in which it was denied that Levey was the cause of the so-called decline in the drama in Sydney.

The first writer accused Levey of having "purged" the theatre of all its talent, to which the second replied that he had done nothing of the kind. They had purged themselves. The cause of their disunion had always been their jealousy of each other. Meredith, Simmons, and Knowles "were stars which it were impossible could shine in the same hemisphere, and so eventually they have ceased to shine at all". Knowles, this writer hinted, had also got rid of his only real rival, the dissolute young Mackay, in an underhand way. When this was written Meredith was conducting a small theatre in Tasmania, Simmons' name was being mentioned in connection with the managership of the Theatre Royal's rival, the Victoria, and Knowles was in England.

About fifteen months after Knowles had left Sydney the first news of him filtered through to the Sydney press. It was said he had abandoned the stage, and was serving the remainder of his apprenticeship with his brother, a London solicitor. Only five days after this appeared another newspaper announced that Knowles was on his way back to Sydney. Two months later still, he and Mrs. Jones (they had travelled together as Mr. and Mrs.

161

Knowles) arrived, and Knowles was greeted by such newspaper effusions as: "The Sydney public we are sure will hail Mr. Knowles's return with joy, for his place on the stage has never been supplied since he left the colony, and miserable, *miserable* were the substitutes they had to put up with", and a retrospective comment on his Hamlet as "one of the very few Shakespearian characters to which justice has been done in this colony".

The press "puffs" about Knowles's activities in London can be discounted as a smokescreen to hide the fact that neither he nor Mrs. Jones had been able to obtain a theatrical engagement in England, and that they had decided to return to Sydney where they could at least earn a good living. It is highly unlikely that either Knowles or his brother would favour a return by Knowles to his position of some eight to ten years before, all the more unlikely as Knowles had a "wife" to support, which an articled clerk could not do in London except in conditions of direst poverty. Nor is it at all likely that Knowles, vain, arrogant, and the recipient for some years of the adulation of almost nightly audiences at the theatre, would have been content to throw everything overboard to take an "inferior" position in a dingy London solicitor's office. It is far more likely that his and Mrs. Jones's undoubted success in the Sydney theatre had led them to believe they could do even better in London. A very short stay in that city, however, must have been enough to show them that not even in a provincial theatre of any standing could either of them obtain a place without a hard and, for some time at least, unrewarding struggle. They must also have had to face the cold economic realities of their situation. Between them they must have had just enough money for a brief stay in London, and their return fare. An immediate engagement would have tided them over until possibilities for the future could be assessed, but when this was not forthcoming they chose the more prudent course of returning to Sydney and security.

But although he had been away only about seventeen months, Knowles found that he had returned to a Sydney that was,

162

theatrically, quite changed. A number of new rivals had taken to the boards to woo the fickle public, including at least one who was to prove superior to him as an actor and as a "draw" with the public. And the public had changed, too, for Knowles found a large and enthusiastic audience to greet him on his first night at the Victoria Theatre, and then, as though to tell him he no longer had what the public wanted, a very poor one for his second.

To open the new season at the Victoria the proprietor engaged Knowles to play *Hamlet*. With him in the cast were his old rivals, Meredith as the Gravedigger, Simmons as Laertes, and Spencer as the Ghost. There was a new Queen, Mrs. Cameron, and Ophelia, Miss Winstanley. The critics' chief complaint against the latter was that she was not a singer, and therefore should not have been chosen for "a singing part".

As they so often do with *Hamlet,* the critics found the performance like the curate's egg. Knowles was much surer in his words than he had ever been, said one, and must have made good use of his time during his trip to England. "We have always admired his performance of Hamlet, and we admire it more than ever now." His playing was much more subdued than formerly, he wrote, with none of the rant of the old days. The speech to the players was admirably delivered, and the scene with Ophelia well sustained.

A second critic thought there was some good acting by Knowles in the play, but that many points were either overlooked or mishandled. He advised Knowles that a soliloquy was meant to be a self-communion, not an address to the audience. "Taken as a whole, it may be deemed a very fair piece of acting", he concluded.

For a third critic the performance "did not altogether fail", but was at times tame and uninteresting.

Hamlet was repeated three nights later to a beggarly audience. It was as small and unenthusiastic as the first had been full and vociferous in its welcome. Was the play the trouble, or the actor? A fourth critic, who was at both performances, decided the lack of public interest gave a "melancholy view of the state of dramatic taste in New South Wales. The colonists seem to be as low in

163

their taste in this respect as they are in their religion and patrio-
tism." This writer said the "getting up" of the play was good
as to the dresses and scenery. "All appeared according to *rule,*
and the effect was highly creditable. . ." He found the second
performance to be better in many ways than the first, and was
sure that in Knowles "we can boast of a first-rate actor, second
only to the first actors in London". This assessment irritated
one reader so much that he wrote a long anti-Knowles letter to
another newspaper in which he concluded that "everybody
acquainted with London Theatricals must know that the third
and fourth rate performers on the London stage are superior to
him in every respect". The true Knowles must have stood somewhere between these two extremes.

Knowles remained at the Victoria for some months, playing
much the same roles as he had always played, with fellow actors
from his Theatre Royal days and with newcomers from England.
But he was a man consumed with an ambition which could no
longer be satisfied in Sydney. In 1842 Simmons succeeded
Knowles as manager at the Victoria (the old see-saw again) and
Knowles and Mrs. Jones transferred to the newly-opened Olympic
Theatre in Hunter Street. It had a life of only a few weeks before
its owner finished up in the insolvency court. Then Knowles
went back to the Victoria until, in May 1843, Simmons opened
his own theatre in Market Street, the City Theatre. Here, where
there were again a large percentage of Theatre Royal "originals",
Knowles played in much the same programmes as those given in
the Theatre Royal's palmiest days. This theatre, too, soon proved
a failure, and after a brief visit to Tasmania Knowles and Mrs.
Jones went to Melbourne, where he tried to bring life to the moribund theatre attached to an hotel in Bourke Street, opened the
year before by another Sydney Theatre Royal "original", George
Buckingham. The effort was too much for him, and the man who
had gained the distinction of being Australia's first Hamlet and
first Othello died in Melbourne after a short illness on 19 May
1844.

14

The Mrs. Siddons of Sydney

Of the many actresses in Levey's company, only one was able to achieve a wide following over a number of years in Australia. She was also the only member of his company trained by him and her fellow players to move successfully from the Australian to the overseas stage. Reviewing a performance of Kotzebue's *The Stranger,* a writer in the *Gazette* of 15 March 1842 said ". . .the part of Mrs. Haller was well sustained by Mrs. O'Flaherty, the Mrs. Siddons of Sydney". The woman he thus likened, somewhat over-enthusiastically, to the great eighteenth century tragedienne, was Eliza Winstanley.

Eliza has often been referred to as the first Australian-born actress. In fact, she was born in England and did not come to Australia until she was fifteen, in 1833. She seems to have retired from the stage some time towards the middle of the sixties, but before that she had established her name in another sphere — as a writer. In 1859, the year in which Charles Kean completed his tenure of the Princess's Theatre in London, Messrs. Routledge, Warne, and Routledge published her first novel, *Shifting Scenes in Theatrical Life,* "by Mrs. Winstanley, comedian" [*sic*]. She followed this through the succeeding years with more novels, and with stories and articles for magazines, for some of which she drew on her knowledge of and experiences in Australia. "In 1865 she became editress of the weekly *Fiction for Family Reading,* a subsidiary of *Bow Bells"*, an article in the *Australian Dictionary of Biography* tells us.

Shifting Scenes in Theatrical Life, Eliza Winstanley said in the preface, is founded on facts and "the characters figuring in these 'Shifting Scenes' are also equally real, but sufficiently disguised in their portraiture, it is hoped, to avoid the charge of ill-natured personality". It is a book unaccountably overlooked by theatre historians, which is a pity, for in its pages are to be found cleverly limned portraits of theatrical characters; descriptions of booth, provincial, and London theatres; greenrooms, theatre-managers, and call-boys — all recognizably true portraits of men and women with whom she had worked. As a novel it does not rise above the mediocre in plot, but it is when she does not have to worry about pushing the plot along that the book comes marvellously alive. Her description of the Manchester Theatre manageress and her many idiosyncracies, obviously a "photograph" of a living person, though not necessarily one connected with the Manchester Theatre, is one only of many fascinating pen-portraits in this book.

The basis for the study of Eliza Winstanley's life has been, in the past, an article which appeared on 21 December 1864 in *Bow Bells.* Lacking evidence, it may be assumed either that she wrote this herself, or that it was written by somebody else using details supplied by her — that it was the result of an interview. The latter seems the more likely, and a slipshod job the article turns out to be. It leaves today's reader with the conviction that either the facts were deliberately misrepresented, or that her memory was failing. As she was only forty-six and at the peak of her powers as a writer in 1864, the failure of her memory does not seem a very strong possibility.

The writer of the *Bow Bells* article said that Eliza was born at Blackburn in Lancashire, but no date — women and actresses being what they are — was given. He or she then said that Eliza came to Australia at the age of ten, made her stage debut in Sydney at the age of fifteen, and when she was eighteen married "the eldest son of Captain George Sterling Offlahertie of Galway" in Sydney. "Soon after this," the writer claimed, "in 1848 she came to England", where she appeared first at the theatre at

166

Manchester, and then at Newcastle-on-Tyne. He added that her husband had "died about ten years since", that is, in 1854 or thereabouts.

It does not require much searching to discover that these statements are, in the main, a farrago of nonsense, published for some reason which today escapes us. Eliza Winstanley died in Sydney, where the members of her family had remained, and was buried in Waverley Cemetery on 3 December 1882. Her death certificate, signed by her brother Robert, shows her age at death was sixty-four, which means 1818 was the year of her birth. The certificate also shows that she was married in Sydney to H.C.O' Flaherty at the age of twenty-three, which is to say in 1841. The *Bow Bells* article must therefore have been written by somebody with a poor grasp of the facts, for it is difficult to believe that Eliza Winstanley would have wished to establish herself as the first woman in history to forget the date of her wedding.

As to her stage debut, this was made in Sydney at Barnett Levey's Theatre Royal on 31 October 1834, when she was sixteen years of age. Furthermore, she returned to England in 1846, not 1848, and made her English debut at Manchester. In 1848 she was playing on the New York stage.

Although Eliza made her stage debut in Sydney, and gained the bulk of her theatrical training and experience in the Royal, Victoria, Olympic, and City Theatres in Sydney, never in her publicity while overseas did she refer to herself as an Australian actress, or as an actress trained in Australia. This is not surprising. The fact would carry no cachet in the London or New York theatres of the time — rather the opposite. Which makes it the more remarkable that she was able to break in as she did. In New York she was billed as "from the Princess's Theatre, London". But D.G.C. Odell in his *Annals of the New York Stage*, although he did not say that she had come originally from Australia, showed he knew she was not a London "original" when he wrote of her and others in the Broadway Theatre company of 1847–48,

". . . yet I suppose the Broadway management would have resented a natural inference that many of the new players were provincial, in that they hailed from the provinces in their native country".

The true dates concerning Eliza Winstanley's arrival in Australia, her stage debut, marriage, and return to England are as follows. On 3 May 1833 the barque "Adventure" arrived in Sydney from Liverpool, among the passengers being the Winstanley family consisting of William Winstanley, described as a painter; his wife, Elizabeth; and their children (the passenger list supplying the age of each), Eliza 15, Edward 11, Ann 8, Robert 6, Mary 3, and Henry, an infant. Soon after the family's arrival in Sydney, William Winstanley was employed as scenepainter at the Theatre Royal. The life he and his family had led in England is not known.

On 9 October 1834 an advertisement in the *Gazette* announced that a benefit for Mr. Winstanley would be held at the Theatre Royal, when Shakespeare's tragedy of *Romeo and Juliet* would be performed, with Conrad Knowles as Romeo and Miss Winstanley, "her first appearance on any stage", as Juliet. The performance would conclude, the advertisement said, with Bickerstaffe's farce, *The Spoiled Child,* in which Eliza's sister, Miss Ann Winstanley, would play the part of Little Pickle.

The date of Eliza's marriage may be obtained from the parish register of St. James's Church in Sydney, where it is recorded that she married Henry Charles O'Flaherty on 6 February 1841. There was no press record of her marriage, apart from a cryptic paragraph which appeared a week later in *The Free Press and Commercial Journal.*

Matrimony — We understand that a young lady, who has long been in the habit of receiving vows from lovers old and lovers young, on the boards of the Sydney theatre, fatigued at length with imagination, stole a march on her watchful guardians a few days ago, and perpetrated matrimony in good earnest; the successful suitor has had most favourable opportunities for furthering his suit at the footlights.

Finally, the *Australian Journal* of 2 April 1846 carried in its "Shipping Intelligence" column the news that, the day before, the barque "Kinnear" had left Sydney for London with Mr. and Mrs. O'Flaherty among the passengers.

The two Winstanley girls apparently showed theatrical aptitude, and were taken in hand by Barnett Levey and Conrad Knowles. The extravagant if not impossible idea of presenting the sixteen-year-old inexperienced Eliza as Juliet sounds very much like Barnett Levey at his most optimistic and impractical. But the part must have been beyond her, for on 31 October 1834 Eliza made her stage debut, not as Juliet but in the title role of John Howard Payne and Henry Bishop's semi-opera, *Clari, the Maid of Milan,* which was presented as a straight play without the music. It seems obvious that no matter who hit upon the idea of presenting Eliza on the stage, it was Conrad Knowles who gave her her initial training. On 28 October 1834 Barnett Levey left Sydney for Tasmania, in search of new actors. Up to this time he would have been too busy conducting his theatre to keep more than a fatherly eye on Eliza's progress, and to agree with Knowles, perhaps, that she could not manage Juliet. That Eliza had kind thoughts of Conrad Knowles for many years afterwards is evident from the fact that he appears in her first novel, where he is named Craggsbridge and, like Knowles, is said to have been a former Methodist preacher. Eliza also throws a new light on the charge consistently made against Knowles that he did not know his words, that he was not "up in his part". She wrote of her fictional character: "He was not without talent; yet, at times, his readings were so very mysterious and ridiculous, you were almost tempted to regard the reader as either a madman or a fool."

The *Sydney Herald* account of Eliza's debut was generally full of praise for her voice, intonation, reading, and the considerable skill she displayed "in the development of the various passions". Its major criticism of her acting revealed Knowles to have been her mentor. "She has natural powers, and must not be carried away by ranting into a kind of bombastic style. . ." The writer added that her acting in the last scene of the play "reached the sublime, and in fact many of the fair visitors were in tears, and the scene was received with rapturous applause".

The *Australian* found that in the part of Clari, Eliza, "considering the many disadvantages under which she laboured (than which none was more serious than the interruptions thrown in her way by some of the old performers) she surpassed what even the most sanguine of her friends could have expected". This critic also listed what he considered to be her bad points, and the necessity for constant study on her part to overcome them. Both newspapers mentioned the attempts made by jealous older members of the company to turn the success of the sixteen-year-old into a fiasco. No doubt the lessons Eliza learned in this theatrical "in-fighting" at Sydney's Theatre Royal proved of value to her when she entered the fiercer competition of the London and New York stages.

For the five years or so before her marriage in 1841 Eliza played every conceivable role, from Cora in Sheridan's *Pizarro* to Ophelia in *Hamlet,* as a typical "maid-of-all-work" of the early nineteenth century theatre. She must have been a hard and conscientious worker, for although she had more often than not to appear in six different plays a week, the charge of not being "up in the part" levelled so often against other members of the company was rarely made against her. She had many rivals for public favour — Mrs. Mackay, Mrs. Maria Taylor, Mrs. Harriet Jones, Miss Douglass, and, later, Mrs. Chester and Mrs. Cameron — but she managed over the years to create a firm place for herself and, up to the time of her departure for England, to win the approval of the critics.

She must also have been a good mimic as well as a fair actress in her own right, for she seems from time to time to have reflected the mannerisms of all the more "important" players with whom she came into contact, including Knowles, Mrs. Taylor, Mrs. Cameron, and, in later years, Mrs. Charles Kean. One of the existing engravings of her shows her in a typical Ellen Kean pose as Mistress Quickly in *The Merry Wives of Windsor.*

170

During her first five years in Sydney Eliza received a great variety of Press comment on her acting, from the blatantly adulatory to the fiercely caustic. In February 1835 she was praised for the way in which she played Cora in *Pizarro* at short notice, because of the indisposition of Mrs. Mackay, who was to have played the part. "Her absence was not in the least regretted, for Miss Winstanley's performance was far beyond Mrs Mackay's . . ." one report said. But in April she was told that "her action on the stage (was) not good by any means", and in May that as the love-sick Harriet in the farce *The Duel; or, My Two Nephews* she looked interesting, but was too affected, and made use of the letter "h" improperly. After this she seems to have kept, or to have been kept, in the background for a while. All the "plum" parts went to Mrs. Taylor, Mrs. Jones, and Miss Douglass for a time.

In June 1836 good parts and good reports began to come her way again, so that in September she was playing Lady Anne in *Richard III,* and earning the comment that not only did the part suit her but that her acting went some way towards redeeming a play which was close to being an utter failure as a performance.

In 1838, when the Victoria Theatre opened, Eliza was among the company engaged. Here she appeared in *Othello, Hamlet,* and the usual dramas, melodramas, comedies, and farces of the day. In this year Mr. and Mrs. Samson Cameron came over from Tasmania, and Mrs. Cameron, said to be a trained English actress, inevitably took the leading parts. In *Hamlet* she played the Queen to Eliza's Ophelia. Of the latter one critic wrote:

. . . Ophelia was sustained by Miss Winstanley with tolerable success, although there is a very great drawback in her personation of this character, in the circumstances of her not being a singer. The strains in this character throw a peculiar charm over Ophelia, and considerably enhance the sympathy for her mournful condition. From the outset, Miss Winstanley was too gay — Ophelia in her happiest moments is cheerful, but not jaunty — forced smiles are by no means necessary to indicate contentment or happiness. This young lady is a promising actress, and possessing talent, we desire to see her exercise it with justice to herself. . .

She had been reminded that even after four years success was not to be too easily won. But she persisted, and improved, despite many instances of the blatant miscasting which was one of the hazards of the theatre of her time. After her marriage she began to mature, and to "work up" those parts in which she later made a success overseas. It was unfortunate that within a few years this "maturing" included putting on a great deal of weight.

Between 1841 and 1846 Eliza moved from one of Sydney's three theatres to the other, first to the Victoria, then to the rival "tent" theatre in Hunter Street, the Olympic; then to Simmons' Royal City, and back to the Victoria, with occasional sorties to Tasmania and Melbourne. At this time she preferred to be known as Mrs. O'Flaherty. From the time she left Australia she called herself, on the stage and in her writings, Mrs. and sometimes Miss Winstanley. Her husband, Henry Charles O'Flaherty, was a theatre musician. Sometimes, possibly at the prodding of his ambitious wife, he also took to the boards. He was apparently not a success as an actor, or perhaps he really did not want to be an actor, and soon went back to his violin.

The Olympic Theatre was opened for equestrian and gymnastic performances on 26 January 1842, the forty-fourth anniversary of the foundation of the Colony of New South Wales. Within a few weeks it was converted to a theatre, where among others from the Victoria Theatre company appeared Mr. and Mrs. O'Flaherty. As the stage was small, at first only short dramas and farces were produced, such as *The Two Friends* (1828), *The Wedding Day* (1794), *The Rival Queans* (1764), *Love in Humble Life* (1822), and others. Then Mrs. O'Flaherty appeared in *The Stranger*, that perennial favourite in which she had seen Mrs. Cameron and other "leaders" of the Sydney stage perform. One critic said she played Mrs. Haller "in the most exquisite manner", while another found that only her acting in the last act was

172

faultless. During this act, he said, she "exhibited her great powers as a tragic actress". Next she appeared as Belvidera in *Venice Preserved* (1682) with (surprisingly, in view of the presence in the company of the experienced Knowles) her husband as Jaffier. Her acting in this was said to be "as usual, excellent", and her husband was let off very lightly with the statement that Jaffier was "too arduous a character for so young an actor as O'Flaherty, though he will no doubt make a good actor with time and study".

But the Olympic Theatre lasted only a few months, and then its owner went insolvent. Not long afterwards most of the company were again back at the Victoria, and Eliza was playing Isabel, Queen of Spain, in the play Conrad Knowles was said to have written for his wife, *Salathiel; or, The Jewish Chieftain.* Not surprisingly, Mr. O'Flaherty emulated Conrad Knowles in writing a play for *his* wife, *Isabel of Valois; or, The Tyrant Queen.* On the night this was given Eliza appeared first in *Isabel of Valois,* then as Lady Macbeth in a scene from the last act of *Macbeth,* and then as Mad Mabel in the afterpiece, *Mabel's Curse* (1837).

And so the years passed, with Eliza appearing fairly consistently at the Victoria in a wide variety of parts, earning sometimes the highest praise and sometimes the mere mention that she was among those in the cast. It is not known what made her decide to try her fortunes in England, but ambition must have played its part in this as in all her other moves. Perhaps her husband was behind it; perhaps Simmons, said to have played at the Manchester theatre, had promised her introductions, or perhaps she felt her useful days in Sydney were over. A slow but steady influx of actors from England was changing the once restricted Sydney scene. Perhaps she felt this was only the first trickle of what was to be a flood, and that it could only mean more people to seek a share in whatever profits were available. Whatever the reason, in due course one of Sydney's several newspapers, *The Atlas,* carried a brief report on 17 April 1847 that Eliza had made a successful debut at Manchester Theatre Royal the previous

173

December, adding: "The English papers speak of her in very flattering terms."

This proud announcement made it look as though finding theatrical employment in the England of 1846 was delightfully easy. What actually happened to Eliza and her husband? They left Sydney on 1 April 1846, so they would have arrived in London by at least the following September, but probably a great deal earlier. Little is known about Henry O'Flaherty but that he was not a successful man is fairly obvious. Was he one of those well-connected, "dead loss, send him to the colonies" sons with which this period in Australia's history abounds? The pair could not have had much money between them, and obviously they had a serious unemployment gap between the time of their arrival in London and Eliza's Manchester debut. Was he the husband she had in mind when she wrote in *Shifting Scenes*:

> Among those itinerant actors there was a woman whose beauty and talents ought long ago to have been rewarded by a high position in the theatrical world, had she not sacrificed herself to a selfish worthless husband, who neither appreciated her affection nor understood the motives which kept her slaving in obscurity, when she might have been at the "top of the tree." Alice Thorn was a proud woman, who felt that her husband was her inferior in every respect. She *would* not climb the ladder of fame, because her pride forbade her leaving her husband at the foot of it; therefore, she preferred to continue a nameless stroller rather than enter a theatre where he could not follow her.

Either instinct or necessity, or perhaps a recommendation from someone at the Theatre Royal in Sydney was responsible for her visit to Manchester, and it is possible that she arrived there at the tail-end of Macready's visit, and watched him backstage and from the front of the house while she was waiting for an engagement. Macready played at Manchester from 23 August to 4 September 1846, but that he did not impress her either as a man or an actor is made quite clear in her novel, where he appears thinly disguised as "Mr. Maverstone". Eliza made her

174

first appearance at the Theatre Royal, Manchester, not in December 1846 as the *Atlas* had claimed, but on 2 November, playing Constance in *King John*. Billed as "Miss Winstanley", she played the following parts at Manchester between 2 November and 8 December inclusive, making a total of seventeen appearances: Constance, Lady Macbeth, Volumnia (a part she first played in Sydney at the Victoria Theatre on 11 November 1844, the first Australian production of *Coriolanus*), Mrs. Haller, the title role in David Garrick's *Isabella* (1757), Queen Katharine in *Henry VIII*, Elizabeth in *Richard III*, Paulina in *The Winter's Tale*, Mrs. Woodville in Cumberland's *The Wheel of Fortune* (1795), Alicia in *Jane Shore* (1714) and the Baroness de Serigny in the farce *Ask No Questions* (1838).

Her acting did not always please the Manchester critics. The *Manchester Examiner* (21 November 1846) said of her Queen Katharine that it "became in Miss Winstanley's hands, rather soporific than pathetic". The same writer said of her Constance that she "rated friend and foe with considerable vigour but no great tragic skill". Only the *Manchester Guardian* (7 November 1846), writing of her Lady Macbeth, found some good points among the bad. It said her

> . . . conception appears to us hardly equal to the character, and her bearing wants dignity and earnestness. Her delivery is clear and neat, and her voice agreeable in quality. Her manner was too quiet in the banquet scene, it partook more of indifference than of suppressed, powerful emotion. . .

By the time the Manchester Theatre Royal closed later in December to prepare for the Christmas pantomime, Eliza had left, having learned the hard way what she must do to improve her acting. And she did learn it, and apply it.

We now arrive at a period in her life which, because of lack of material, can only be described in fits and starts. After Manchester she secured an engagement at Newcastle-on-Tyne, and then moved on to other provincial theatres, carefully noting personalities and situations which were later incorporated in her novel. When, in the

175

novel, the scene moves to the theatre at Newcastle-on-Tyne, for instance, she gives an amusing pen-picture of the besotted manageress and the rest of the company, and then continues with her plot. In this, one of her characters, an actress, is fatally shot by a rejected suitor while she is on stage. In a footnote Eliza Winstanley adds: "The tragic event here described is no fiction — save as respects the scene of its occurrence."

What does stand out clearly throughout as much of her life history as it is possible to discover, is that whatever else she may have been Eliza was an indomitable battler, one of those extraordinary women of the Victorian period who, while still playing the expected role of the weak woman subservient to the all-powerful male, yet managed to achieve what she had set out to achieve entirely by her own efforts. If what she wanted could not be had in one place, she moved on to another. Putting what is known of her character together with her description of the vicissitudes of the strolling booth players and the theatricals who moved from one provincial theatre to another, we get the impression that she lived through as a child what she describes in her novel. Certainly, once she reached England she seemed to be perfectly at home, not only geographically but also in the world of the theatre. And all the while those shrewd eyes were sizing up opportunities, and sorting out the character and personality of all those with whom she came into contact. That her assessments were occasionally tinged with malice, or even envy, is a failing it is easy to forgive her.

Her provincial stint over, she then (truly an exceptional step for one so little known in England's theatrical world) secured a brief engagement at the Princess's Theatre in London, some three or four years before Charles Kean inaugurated his famous management. Here she appeared during the management of J.M. Maddox, and during the seasons given by William Macready and Madame Vestris. There is no evidence that she ever acted *with* either, though she did act with Charles Mathews. She may have had "walk on" or crowd parts in those plays in which her

name is not featured in the theatre's advertisements. During her
stay at this theatre in 1847 she called herself Miss Winstanley.
Whether Mr. O'Flaherty had by this time dropped by the wayside
or been given his marching orders can only be a matter for con-
jecture. Eliza appeared first at the Princess's as Hippolyta in
A Midsummer Night's Dream. Later she played Regan in *King
Lear.* She also appeared as the Countess Wintersen in *The
Stranger* to Mrs. Warner's Mrs. Haller; as Meg Merrilees in
Guy Mannering (1816); as Miss Lucretia McTab in *The Poor
Gentleman* (1801); as Lady Clutterbuck in *Used Up* (1844) to
Charles Mathews's Sir Charles Coldstream, and as Becky Morgan
in *He Would be An Actor* (1836).

While she was at the Princess's Theatre, George H. Barrett,
American actor and just-appointed acting-manager of the new
Broadway Theatre in New York, came to London in search of
actors for the opening season at that theatre. He persuaded Lester
Wallack (later to become famous in American theatre history),
Rose Telbin (sister of the famous scenepainter, William Telbin),
two or three other actors from the Liverpool and Manchester
theatres, and Mrs. Winstanley "from the Princess's Theatre,
London", to return to New York with him.

The new theatre opened on 27 September 1847 with *The School
for Scandal,* in which Eliza played Mrs. Candour, and *Used Up.* The
opening performances, as a whole, were not very highly praised,
though one critic said of Mrs. Winstanley that she would prove a
favourite. A later writer said of her performance as Mrs. Candour:
"Mrs. Winstanley, also a new-comer, was a fine-looking, portly
woman, of sound judgment and discretion, and every way competent to fill the station in which she was placed".

On 30 September she played Lady Beauchamp in the comedy
Ladies Beware! (1847); and then, on 1 October, Madame Des-
chapelles in *The Lady of Lyons* (1838). As the highly successful
season continued, Eliza appeared in such plays as *The Rivals, The
Jacobite* (1847), and *The Prisoner of War* (1842). On 4 November
she played Lady Franklin in *Money* (1840), on 20 November Mrs.

Rackett in *The Belle's Stratagem* (1780), and on 3 December Widow Green in *The Love Chase* (1837).

The next year Eliza, with other actors from the Broadway Theatre, transferred to the Park Theatre in New York, where she first appeared on 4 September 1848 as the Queen in *Hamlet,* with the American actor-manager Thomas Hamblin in the name part, and then in the afterpiece *Ladies Beware!* There seems to be no foundation in fact for the claim made in the *Australian Dictionary of Biography* that when she reached New York in 1848 she played Mistress Quickly to James Hackett's Falstaff at the Astor Theatre. Odell, who missed remarkably little, makes no mention of this, though he does mention with care her other appearances.

At the Park Theatre, the most famous in the history of the early nineteenth century American theatre, she played in *Lucius Junius Brutus* (1792), *Othello, Macbeth* (as Lady Macbeth), *Virginius* (1820), *Pizarro,* and *Coriolanus* (as Volumnia again). As late as 7 December she was again playing Mrs. Candour in *The School for Scandal.*

Towards the end of this year the Park Theatre was destroyed by fire, and Eliza moved on to Philadelphia. Here she appeared at both the Walnut and Arch Theatres. In May 1848 she played Barbara in *Romance and Reality* (1847) for an eight-day engagement at the Walnut Theatre, with John Brougham as Jack and Mrs. Brougham as Blossom. Later, in 1849, she became a regular stock player at the Arch Theatre. Among the parts she played were Beatrice in R.B. Peake's *Three Wives of Madrid* (1844) on 23 May, Pink Patter in *Chloroform* on 11 June, and Wardock in *Wardock Kennilson* (1824) on 8 September. Perhaps as a result of her experience and "contacts" in Philadelphia, towards the end of the year she was engaged at William E. Burton's newly opened New York theatre, Burton's Chambers Street Theatre, opening there on 19 November for a brief season before returning to England. Here she again played in *Romance and Reality* and in *Ask No Questions,* as well as *A Bird of Passage* (1849) and *Mammon and Gammon* (1848).

We can discount the statement in the *Bow Bells* article that she returned to England because the management of the Drury Lane Theatre was clamouring for her services. They were not, but she did play there. James Anderson became lessee of Drury Lane Theatre in 1849, and his company gave its final performance on 4 May 1850. Only once is Mrs. Winstanley's name listed in the casts in the daily advertisements for this theatre which appeared in the *Times* — on 16 February 1850, when she played Miss Pickle in *The Spoiled Child,* a play in which she had first appeared in Sydney. Anderson's lesseeship of Drury Lane was a disaster for him, and he lost all his money. His leading lady for a period was Mrs. Nisbett, referred to frequently with real affection by Eliza Winstanley in her *Shifting Scenes* as "the bright-eyed, fascinating N – b – t".

Whatever the real reason for Eliza's return to England, she was back in London in time to join the company which Robert Keeley and Charles Kean formed in partnership to open the Princess's Theatre in 1850. Their first season opened on 28 September, and by the time it closed on 17 October the following year they had made a profit of £7,000. Keeley retired, leaving the Princess's to Kean, who at once set about organizing the series of Shakespearian productions he had long had in mind, which were to set a new standard for the London theatre. Eliza appeared in a great many of them throughout the following eight years, and they were the proudest years in her theatrical life. She has left detailed descriptions of the Keans and of various aspects of the Princess's Theatre in her novel.

When the second season opened on 22 November 1851, Eliza played Mistress Quickly in *The Merry Wives of Windsor* to the Mistress Ford of Mrs. Kean and the Mistress Page of Mrs. Keeley. Sitting in a box at the theatre that night was the novelist George Eliot, with George Henry Lewes, the man she lived with for twenty-four years ("I ended the day in a godless manner, seeing *The Merry Wives of Windsor. . .*" she wrote in a letter to a friend two days later.) Lewes occasionally wrote dramatic criticism for

179

The *Leader,* and his account of this Kean production was, as was usual with his comments on Kean and his theatre, not complimentary. He admitted from the start the play was one he did not like ("the wit for the most part is dreary or foolish; the tone is coarse and farcical"), and he liked least of all the way it was presented at the Princess's. He found the dresses and scenery were excellent. "I saw everywhere *intention* (an excellent thing in management), but the effect ill–responded to the labour," he wrote. He said there was too much striving after effect, too much "business". Dealing with the "wives", Lewes said Mrs. Kean tried too hard, Mrs. Keeley (a favourite of his) was quietly and irresistibly comic, and Mrs. Winstanley *"laughed* her part, and *emphasised* it; *act* it she certainly did not".

Lewes was no doubt right in his criticism, given that this particular production did not supply whatever it was he was looking for; but it was wrong for its time. As so often happens with critics, the tide of public opinion was against him. Kean's production ran for twenty-five performances, quite a long run at that period in the history of the theatre. Shortly after it concluded Mr. Lewes found, with some surprise and chagrin, that Kean had cut him off the free list because of what Kean considered to be his consistently unsympathetic criticism. Perhaps the *Times* notice of the same performance was nearer the reality of its general tone (at least as far as Eliza was concerned) in finding that ". . . Mrs. Winstanley looked magnificent as Mrs. Quickly, coaxing the knight with that broad cajolery which belonged to an old school of acting. . ."

During the second season Eliza appeared many times in productions of such favourites of the day as *The Duke's Wager* (1851), *Love in a Maze* (1851), and *Town and Country* (1807), having her name featured with the Keans' in the *Times* advertisements, a favour not extended to lesser members of the company. And through the years that followed the critics proved much kinder than Lewes had been, even if only in intention. In 1853 she appeared in the first English production of *The Lancers; or, The*

Gentleman's Son from the the French of Bayard's *Un Fils de Famille,* and was greeted by the *Illustrated London News* with the syntactically ambiguous remark that "Mr. Ryder, as the Colonel, is a disciplinarian, but a gentleman; Mrs. Winstanley, his veritable lady-sister — not a comic and eccentric parody of military tastes and phrases." In 1854 she played in a version of the Faust story from the French of Michael Carre, *Faust and Marguerite.* Said one critic of her performance in this: "Mrs. Winstanley's Martha was a thorough impersonation of a part which required remarkable excellence in the acting to reconcile the audience to the character."

It was while Eliza was with Kean's company, a company favoured by Queen Victoria and the Prince Consort, that she appeared, over a period of five years, in the Court Theatricals at Windsor Castle. Her debut there was made on 16 January 1852, when she played in *Not a Bad Judge* (1848) and *The Lottery Ticket; or The Lawyer's Clerk.* The following year she appeared twice, first on 14 January in *The Captain of the Watch* (1841) and *The Windmill* (1842), and then on 28 January in *Paul Pry* and *A Lucky Friday* (1852). On 12 January 1854 she played at Windsor in Lytton's *Money,* and the following year, on 21 November, she took the part of Mrs. Malaprop in *The Rivals.* In 1856 she again appeared twice, on 17 January in *The Jealous Wife* (1761) and on 28 January in *Still Waters Run Deep* (1855) and *A Game of Romps* (1855).

In these plays she acted with such "favourites of the day" as Harley, Mathews, Webster, Bartley, Keeley, Cooper, Buckstone, Wigan, Vining, Meadows, and others, and such actresses as Agnes Robertson, Mrs. Keeley, Mrs. Walter Lacey, Miss Woolgar, and Miss Le Clercq. Sometimes for these Windsor appearances, when she was the leader of the female contingent, she received £10 per performance, at other times £5.

In 1858, at the Princess's, Eliza played Lady Beauchamp in *Ladies Beware!* and Mrs. Peckham in *Samuel in Search of Himself* (1858). In his report of the latter one critic wrote: "Mrs. Peckham (Mrs. Winstanley), the aunt of the lady, and Sir Paul Prince (Mr. Harley) . . . were both very amusing."

181

On 29 August 1859 Charles Kean made his farewell at the Princess's Theatre, closing a long, successful, but not very prosperous reign. Soon afterwards, hoping to boost his savings for his retirement, he embarked on, of all things, a theatrical tour of Australia, but Eliza stayed on in London. She went to the Lyceum Theatre and, as the *Bow Bells* article correctly states, was "still engaged there" in 1864, during the management of another famous nineteenth century tragedian, Charles Albert Fechter (January 1863 to November 1867). During 1864 she was named as a member of the Lyceum Theatre company which presented *Playing with Fire* (1861) and *Ruy Blas* (1860). But that hers was not a permanent or sustained engagement seems likely from the fact that the years 1860 to 1876 were her most prolific as a writer.

It seems that by the late sixties Eliza, like so many members of her profession who could not reach top rank, had outlived her real usefulness to the theatre. She was by this, theatrically at least, old. She was also stout, and the occasional part which came her way no doubt proved enough, with her writing, to support her. In 1880 she returned to Australia where, according to "Old Chum" (J.M. Ford) in Sydney *Truth,* 13 February 1921, she finished up as directress of a dyeing establishment in Clarence Street. Here she died, of "diabetes and exhaustion", on 2 December 1882, and was buried in Waverley Cemetery the following day.

Her return to Australia, where she had had her training and success in the theatre, and was for a long time a "favourite" with the public, was unheralded, and largely unnoticed by theatregoers. In the thirty-four years since she had left Sydney, and forty-six years since she had made her theatrical debut, a new generation had grown up which knew nothing of her or the first Sydney Theatre Royal. One ironic exception was F.C. Brewer, theatre reporter for the *Herald,* who wrote in his book published ten years after her death: "On the close of her theatrical career in England some years ago, Mrs. O'Flaherty returned to Australia, and, though past the ordinary length of even a long life, is still in possession of all her faculties and remembrances of the days of old."

15

Patriarch of the Drama

When Levey and Mrs. Taylor aired their "one pound a night" dispute in the newspapers, Mrs. Taylor ironically referred to him in one of her advertisements as the "patriarch of the drama". This was a reference to his constantly voiced, though quite true, claim that he had founded the drama in New South Wales.

On Levey's retirement from the theatre in favour of the six lessees the *Gazette* grasped the opportunity to tell its readers, all of whom were surely by now sated with such information, why the theatre had "failed" under his management. Into this word "failed", however, more must not be read than was meant. The financial success of Levey's theatre was never in doubt. The failure, if such, was that it was not the kind of theatre the critics and newspaper proprietors, the scornful moralist and the churchman said the public wanted or needed. The only protests ever made against it by the audiences seem to have been those deliberately incited by dissatisfied actors, and the odd demonstration induced by the carelessness or ineptitude of the actors. Only rarely did the theatre have a poor attendance. It could have been a better theatre than it was, in that it was lacking in the control and supervision of the players and the audience, but so were the theatres in London, Dublin, and other world centres at the time.

Now others were to be given the opportunity to conduct Levey's theatre, if not according to the best precepts (whatever they might be) at least, it was hoped, better than Levey had conducted it.

Like Levey, they were not to want for advice on how to do this. Meantime the *Gazette* went out of its way to bid a kind-hearted and knowing farewell to Levey, and to become the first to advise the lessees what they must do to save the drama in Sydney. Levey, it said, had been ironically designated "the patriarch of the drama in New South Wales, but the irony loses it point when it is known that he *is* so". No one, least of all the *Gazette,* would deny him his meed of praise for this, and for the long fight he fought to establish his theatre. "Here, however, we stop." In his theatre there really was no head — no controlling power — the favourite of today was denounced by him tomorrow — there was always a *party* behind the curtain, and with a *party* the proprietor was inevitably linked. Yet this was not a fault on his part so much as an omission. "From a knowledge of Mr. Levey for several years, we unhesitatingly declare, despite of all that may be said to the contrary, that he is a good natured man — ever ready to do an act of kindness; but he is weak, easily led, and as easily imposed upon."

Turning to the new management and its likely future, the *Gazette* could see little to cheer about. The lessees, though respectable, were not qualified to conduct the theatre as it ought to be conducted. There were too many of them, and consequently it required little foresight to anticipate divisions. The *Gazette* wished them success, though it doubted they would attain it. If there was any hope for them at all it lay in their not interfering with the backstage management of Mr. Simmons.

In the same issue of the newspaper in which Levey announced his farewell performance there appeared an advertisement by the lessees stating that they would take over direction of the theatre the next day. They said they would keep the house open for a fortnight, presenting plays as usual, and then after a short recess their real management would start. As Levey had his players under a contract which made it necessary to give them a fortnight's notice before closing the theatre, the new lessees had no other choice. The programme for this first night under the new management would be *Luke the Labourer; or, The Lost Son,* and *The Irishman in London.* Correctly gauging his popularity with audiences, the new management announced that Simmons would be back in his post as manager, and the company would consist of Simes, Peat, Knowles, Meredith, Dyball, Buckingham, Palmer, Mackie, and Mrs. Meredith, Mrs. Taylor, Mrs. Jones, and Miss Winstanley.

There was a full audience for this performance, which was generally pronounced to be very good. No doubt every member of the company was on his best behaviour because of the new management. Four days later there was another new programme, and the first criticisms began to appear. On the same night a man involved in a fight in the upper tier of boxes overbalanced and fell into the pit, being badly injured.

Soon after this the promised recess was held, and then on 2 May 1835 the lessees announced that the theatre would reopen on 4 May. The stage had been entirely altered, they said, and the scenery and machinery so constructed as to work on the same principles as had been recently adopted on the London stage. Mr. Phillips the machinist had apparently been displaced, for now the whole was to be under the direction of Mr. Belmore, "late of the London theatres".

The proscenium had been re-designed and painted by Mr. Winstanley, the seats were newly carpeted, and the ceiling had been raised to better the sound and make the house cooler. The upper circle had been completely repaired, and the seats raised and carpeted. Most important of all, a private entrance had been made to the dress circle, thus doing away with the necessity for ladies to pass through the hotel saloon on their way to their seats.

Not all of these improvements, the announcement said, would be completed by the opening night. It was not possible to keep the theatre closed too long, for there were "upwards of 120 persons whose livelihood depends on the theatre". Doors would be opened at half-past five, and the performances would start at seven o'clock with an overture by the orchestra. Children in

185

arms would not be admitted, nor would bonnets be allowed in the dress circle. Mr. Simmons was to be both acting and stage manager, the two offices thus being combined for the first time.

The programme consisted of one of the many stage versions of *Jane Shore,* and the farce of *The Duel; or, My Two Nephews.* Among the improvements noted by the large first night audience was, of course, the private entrance to the dress boxes, which made it possible for the ladies "to visit the theatre without having to run the gauntlet through a string of moustachioed puppies". The house had been plainly but neatly painted; the partitions at the back of the boxes had been cut down, making it impossible now for people to get behind them and create a nuisance; a number of new stage scenes had been painted, and money had been spent on a theatrical wardrobe.

The performance was praised by the critics, and for a time things went swimmingly with the new management, apart from the fact that the police who had been stationed in the theatre to keep order were apparently unable to prevent several gentlemen in the upper boxes from being robbed by pickpockets.

By June the praise began to turn a little sour. The pit was said to be dirty and disorderly. Its occupants had adopted the habit not only of standing so that they could see, but of standing on the seats, despite the efforts of the police to stop them. As a result those in the lower or dress circle tier of boxes were prevented from seeing the stage at the most crucial moments of the play. One actor was told to stop his habit of ranting at the top of his voice, another, not to use so many tragic "starts". The orchestra was said to be so bad it was beyond hope.

But in July the Governor made his annual visit to the theatre, and everybody was again on his best behaviour. For this performance the orchestra was ousted and replaced by the band of the 17th Regiment.

Meantime, Levey occupied himself as a land agent, advertising that he would receive landed property for public or private sale, and soliciting patronage.

186

By September the benefit season had come around again, Simmons and Knowles being first on the list and drawing over-flowing houses. But there had been an even graver deterioration in the behaviour of the police constables who were present at each performance, ostensibly to keep order. They had tired of trying to discourage the pit-ites from standing on the seats, and had joined them in this practice. A correspondent in the *Australian* complained that they were called *peace* officers with more truth than had been realised, for "a more peaceful, quiet set could not be. They let everyone have his way, and looked on unconsciously during fighting and annoyance of every description."

Knowles announced his benefit as his "farewell" performance. He said he was quitting the stage, and for his farewell played Shylock in *The Merchant of Venice*. His performance earned him high praise, the *Herald* adding that "it is paying him no compli-ment to say he has no competition on the Sydney boards". But the *Gazette* called the "farewell" part of his performance "all fudge". It hinted that Knowles was being petulant because he had tried to get the stage manager's post for himself and had failed, even though he had been promised "the influence of some of those more particularly concerned". Whatever the truth, Knowles was away from the theatre for only a few weeks.

At this time Mrs. Taylor, who had long been the theatre's leading actress and singer, was forced to take a back seat for a while. She had made her first stage appearance at the opening of the Hobart theatre on 17 December 1833, with "Mr. Taylor". Not long afterwards she had come to Sydney and joined Levey's company. Although apparently a competent and gifted self-taught actress, and a great favourite with the public, she had soon proved to be every bit as capricious and unreliable as the other members of the company. She was attractive, if not beautiful, and, as the *Gazette* noted, "with a little more elegancy, and the omission of one or two expressions which for the sake of decorum might well be spared, she would really be a very fascinating comic actress".

But decorum was something for which Mrs. Taylor cared

187

nothing. If a Mr. Taylor ever really existed his permanent role must have been that of the complaisant husband, for she made no secret of her many liaisons, and was wont to exchange signals from the stage in the course of a play with her latest "gentleman" in the boxes.

To compete with this lady towards the end of 1835 there came a Mrs. Chester, said to be late of Drury Lane and Covent Garden, who arrived in Sydney from Hobart where she had "made a great noise". That Mrs. Chester was no inexperienced beginner soon became evident. Having arrived in Sydney, she did not ask for a position but stated the terms on which she would appear at the Theatre Royal. This was something entirely new to Sydney and the theatre. Nor did she fail to let it be known publicly that the offers she did receive were below her expectations, if not her due, and were therefore refused. She did, however, with feminine sweetness, offer to sing at Mrs. Taylor's benefit without charge, by way of a trial. Hers was undoubtedly the voice of theatrical experience advising Mrs. Taylor and the other members of the company that if they wanted to start anything they might as well know she was prepared for it. The lessees, tactfully enough, refused her kind offer, stating that they "thought they could not consistently sanction it". The result was that Mrs. Chester got whatever it was she held out for, the lessees later being described as "out of pocket by their bargain".

That Mrs. Chester was able, after all this, to appear successfully and without incident at the Theatre Royal is another reason for believing this lady knew all the stage tricks of the time. She first appeared on 1 October 1835 in the tried and true *Clari; or, The Maid of Milan* before a "highly respectable" audience which was at a high pitch of expectation. Was she as good as, or better than, Mrs. Taylor? Her reception was enthusiastic, and although there were many differing opinions about her abilities the general one seemed to be that she was undoubtedly a better singer than Mrs. Taylor, but not as good an actress.

Mrs. Chester continued to be a drawcard at the theatre for a while, but evidently not a money-making one for the lessees. In November they decided to farm out their lease to Simmons, who now became sole lessee and manager. The six lessees had had enough. There was too much worry for them; too much time wasted in conducting the theatre in addition to their other business. Whether they also lost money is not recorded, but certainly they had not made as much as they had expected to make or they would not have sub-let their lease so quickly and unexpectedly. Nor had they been able to show that they could run the theatre better than Levey had run it.

In April 1836 Barnett Levey again came before the public notice, first with the notification that he had become one of the directors of the newly-formed Australian Gaslight Company, and then, towards the end of the month, in a brief, unexpected, and not altogether glorious appearance on the stage of the Theatre Royal. Either he was not satisified with Simmons as lessee, or Simmons had found that he had bitten off more than he could chew. Whatever the reason, Levey must have visited the theatre and had a meeting with Simmons. The next thing was that he appeared on stage that night in a high state of intoxication and sang one of his comic songs. The *Gazette,* satirizing his love for and mispronunciation of Latin tags, and his performance, reported that "his reception was worthy of so old a stage veteran, who is the father of the *legittimy dramme*". The newspaper added that he sang "The *Rum* Old Commodore" in a *spirited* style, "at least so we should judge from his singing the first verse over three successive times".

It seems that Levey, knowing that Simmons' lease was to expire on 15 May, had gone to the theatre to arrange either for his own reinstatement or in the hope of having Simmons refused a renewal of his sub-lease. In this he was more successful than he had hoped. Although the lessees still hung on to their lease, possibly because its terms could not be altered and no other takers were in sight, they offered Levey £30 a week to manage the theatre for them. This precipitated an upheaval of domestic politics

189

in which Levey, Simmons, Knowles, and the only two known members of the syndicate of six, Wyatt and Knight, were involved, and whose repercussions were to be felt for the next few years.

Simmons was dismissed, and immediately retaliated by inserting an advertisement in the newspapers detailing his wrongs, in the course of which he said "that Mr. Levey had consented to receive £30 per week as manager of the theatre, and that any dog who breakfasted upon his, Levey's, generosity, would not be liable to choke upon it". Levey, not to be outdone in invective, at once wrote an advertisement of his own which Simes was asked to put into English for him. Levey planned to have it printed as a handbill and distributed by the town bellman. But it was so "strong" the printer refused to print it. Instead, he maliciously gave it to Simmons, who handed it to his solicitor. The public and private quarrels which then ensued did nobody any good. Simmons went off to that mecca of the rejected or thwarted Sydney actor, Tasmania; and Levey, confident in victory, prepared to take over management of his theatre, for which he had longed for months.

Levey advertised that having viewed the management of the theatre by others with much regret, and being the founder of the drama "in this part of the world", he "is induced to resume the management". But his advertisement and his arrangements proved premature. Levey himself had often promised one thing and performed another, had often played "politics" before and behind the curtain. Now he was to fall victim to this kind of thing practised by others. The lessees backed out of their promise of the managership. It is possible they had had second thoughts about having a man so unpredictable in a position where he could do little real harm to himself but a great deal, financially, to them. But perhaps the truth is that by this time they had grown heartily sick of the theatre, and were only too eager to grasp an unexpected opportunity which came their way. An "angel" appeared and paid them the rights to the remainder of the lease; an "angel" inimical to Levey, for the first thing he did was to make Knowles manager, and Levey was left to insert yet another advertisement in the newspapers stating that despite the wonderful plans he had formed for *his* theatre under *his* management, it was not his "intention" to resume management until the expiration of the present lease. In the same newspaper in which this appeared was another for the Theatre Royal carrying Knowles's signature, in which he announced that the theatre would reopen on 6 June with *Isabelle ; or, Woman's Life,* and the farce *Everybody's Husband.*

The new lessee, or sub-lessee, was Joseph Wyatt, who had apparently bought in the remainder of the lease from the other five lessees. Very astutely, this theatre-struck ex-haberdasher of Pitt Street had seen his opportunity to gain more experience in the workings and management of a theatre. But he did not interfere in any obvious way. Knowles, with the assistance of Knight, seems to have had things more or less to himself in the conduct of the theatre.

For the reopening under the new management the theatre was again repainted and decorated, and again the planned improvements were incomplete. The result was that as the weeks of the new season progressed the scenery was gradually improved, and the fronts of the boxes were painted with the various national emblems — rose, shamrock, thistle — enclosed in wreaths. Knowles had also introduced and persisted in prompt starting time and much briefer pauses between the acts. He had also made additions to the orchestra, "the good effect of which is too obvious to need pointing out".

By July a rumour which had been circulating, on and off, since the middle of 1835—that a second theatre was to be built in Sydney — had grown stronger. Pitt Street was named as its location. The next month rumour became fact with the publication of some of the details of the appearance of the proposed theatre. The front elevation was to consist of two shops, with the entrance to the boxes being by a 17 feet wide passage between them. Over the whole would be a pediment supported by five handsome

191

columns. The building would be 17 feet wider than Levey's Theatre Royal, which besides giving more room on the stage would allow a lobby nearly 6 feet wide behind the boxes. The body of the house would also be much higher than that of the Theatre Royal. The estimated cost of the new theatre was said to be £5,000.

Soon after this it was revealed that the man behind the new theatre, who had been planning it for some time, was the wealthy ex-haberdasher, Mr. Joseph Wyatt. It was to be built in Pitt Street with its back parallel to the back of Levey's theatre, but slightly north of it. The foundation stone of this building was laid on 7 September 1836.

Meantime the Royal continued on its way under the management of Knowles, presenting a wide range of classics and comedies, melodramas and farces, and introducing a number of amateur aspirants to stage fame, some of whom earned praise and success, and some of whom were prevented by the jealous "regulars" from attaining either.

Mrs. Taylor had again left the theatre, this time no doubt because of a *cause celebre* in which she and a worthy Sydney ironmonger were involved. It all began at the end of March, when one of the seven newspapers with which Sydney was then being served, the *Colonist,* from what it called a sense of "public duty", published a little verse which it called *The Family Man.* The *Colonist* was founded in 1835 by that rabid Presbyterian divine, Dr. John Dunmore Lang.

> John Thomas was a Shropshire man,
> And eke a worthy nailer;
> He had a stout-built portly frame,
> And his flame she was a *Taylor.*
> Who, though she tried to fasten John
> In Hymen's pleasant noose,
> Found to her cost, alas! that he
> Was not a *Taylor's* goose.
>
> She bound him with a silken cord,
> And then a cord of cotton;

192

But silk and cotton, flax and tow,
Snapped as if each were rotten!
She took to pouting then and vowed
"She'd sooner die of hunger,
Than ere be bound with *bullock* chains,
Or wed an *Ironmonger!*"

"What is't you say?" said he, as she
Stood bolt upon *the boards*;
"You're tenfold happier than if *kept*
By half a dozen lords.
There's not a showroom in the place
Can be compared with mine;
There's not a woman in the town
Has such a lot as thine.

"Why, there's the Sydney Theatre,
Its owners wish to let it;
'Twould be the noblest spec of all,
If we could only get it.
We'd take it either by the week,
Or by the month or year;
And there's my good friend B——n,
Will back us out, my dear."

Said Parson H—— one day as they
Were riding in their carriage,
"Why, you'll disgrace us all, friend John,
If you don't make this a marriage.
The thing has got about the town
In fearful notoriety;
And mind, we'll turn you out of each
Religious society."

John Thomas blushed, and said " 'twas strange
How idle people CAVILL,
But he would tell him all the truth
And the whole case unravel.
He would have married long ago;
(He's one of the marrying kidney:)
But when one has a wife at home,
He can't have one in Sydney."

In a town where lawsuits were breakfast, dinner, and tea to the inhabitants, the inevitable horsewhipping of the editor of the *Colonist* by an irate John Thomas Wilson, and the long-drawn-out suits and counter-suits which followed proved highly enjoyable. The *Colonist* raged for weeks afterwards in its columns about the "injustice" of the emancipists' jury award of five pounds to the paper's editor as compensation for his sufferings under the horsewhip. But while Mr. Wilson, unable to bear the notoriety, sold up his profitable business and returned to England, Mrs. Taylor eventually returned to the Sydney stage, where she continued to earn the inky wrath of the *Colonist* with the sly, disrespectful digs at Dr. John Dunmore Lang which she interpolated in her lines. The whole affair left a nasty taste in a great many mouths, but nasty as it was it had an unexpectedly humorous twist at its end, a twist which even the *Colonist* itself seemed to enjoy. To help defray his legal costs the editor had placed public subscription lists in the various banks and other public places. One of them was even placed on the cabin table of the steam packet "Ceres", "to afford our friends at the Hunter an opportunity to come forward to our assistance". Among the contributors to this particular list, the *Colonist* reported, "was that distinguished member of society and ornament to our colonial bar, Edward Joseph Keith, Esq." Mr. Keith, "with that liberality which has ever characterised his actions", signed himself "A Friend to Concubines", and donated five shillings. The *Colonist* explained that it thought it as well to erase both his name and his donation from the list of subscriptions.

> We felt at a loss whether to admire most Mr. Keith's liberality or his honesty, for although all the world knows that Mr. K.'s description of himself is literally true, yet there are few who would have supposed that he possessed sufficient candour to avow it, and his liberality the more astonished us, as it came from one of the very sources which had rendered the establishment of our journal necessary.

Nor were there lacking, this year, other court cases of interest connected with the theatre, all of which were duly attended and discussed. There was Knowles's successful action against Levey for, among other things, recovery of payment for the theatrical address he had written for the opening of the theatre nearly three years before. And there was Simmons' return from Hobart, where he had given a series of "At Homes", to sue Levey for libel, claiming £500 over the fracas the previous May. Simmons was awarded a farthing damages, but the heavy costs went against Levey. And the Supreme Court, now that Simmons was back in Sydney, took the opportunity of fining him five pounds for not answering an earlier jury call.

Because the court costs were a burden to Levey, Wyatt and the performers at the theatre immediately offered, respectively, free use of the theatre and free use of their services to Levey for a benefit night. Said the *Gazette* in spiteful glee:

Mr. Simmons has not therefore much cause to triumph in his *farthing* verdict. The disposition of all of the profession he formerly followed being too in favour of assisting Mr. Levey defray expenses put to by Mr. Simmons does not say much for his popularity behind the scenes at any rate.

16

The Juvenile Drama

On 1 October 1836 Mrs. Chester gave her farewell performance before leaving for India. She chose, appropriately enough, the opera in which she had made such a success at the beginning of the year, *No Song, No Supper.* Sydney could no longer hold her, for it could not or would not meet the high price she set on her abilities. One newspaper explained:

> Although Mrs. Chester does not possess any great degree of talent as an actress, still as a vocalist she was unrivalled on the Sydney stage, where, we think, she certainly excels, and it is much to be regretted that the proprietor of the theatre could not come to terms with this lady.

By way of replacement, in the almost continuous shuffle and re-shuffle between Hobart and Sydney which had now become commonplace, came Mr. and Mrs. Samson Cameron from the Hobart theatre. Mrs. Cameron, "the celebrated Tasmanian actress", was described as being a "regularly educated English actress". She chose for her Sydney debut the difficult but rewarding part of the unchaste but ultimately repentant Mrs. Haller in Kotzebue's *The Stranger.*

In Mrs. Haller the English stage received, via Germany, the first of a long line of erring heroines who were still holding the boards in the hey-day of such plays as *East Lynne,* and to whom even *The Second Mrs. Tanqueray* owes something. When August von Kotzebue wrote *Menschenhass und Reue* in 1790 he could not have known that he had written a play which would appear on the world's stages for something like eighty years. It took immediately, and before long was translated into French, Spanish, Dutch, Russian, Italian, and English. First produced in Sydney on 16 October 1834, under its English title of *The Stranger,* with Mrs. Taylor in the part of Mrs. Haller, it was still holding the stage in Melbourne in 1864, where it was presented by Charles and Ellen Kean. In the first Sydney performance Knowles played the Stranger to Mrs. Taylor's Mrs. Haller, both receiving high praise for their performances.

Mrs. Cameron's portrayal of Mrs. Haller held her audience riveted to the character.

> So intense was the interest she excited that the most trifling noise was easily discernible... The effect of her acting in the fourth and fifth scenes was electric, and the audience paid homage to the truth of the delineation, if we may judge of the numerous pocket handkerchiefs that were in requisition wiping away the starting tears from many a fair eye.

To the audience of this time there was something strangely affecting in this story of a Magdalen who was also a wife and a mother, and who returns to the home she had deserted.

Mr. Cameron, it was said, was every bit as good in his way as his wife was in hers. His style of acting and treading the stage was gentlemanly and "devoid of that redundancy of action but too often witnessed".

The Camerons stayed on for some time, attracting good houses and appearing in such diverse plays as *Othello, Clari,* and Kotzebue's *Die Spanier in Peru,* which Richard Brinsley Sheridan translated as *Pizarro* and so improved that his version was immediately translated back into German, and has since been described as having said the first word for nineteenth century melodrama.

The undoubted success of the Camerons, achieved in a matter of days compared with the long fight Knowles had had for recognition, annoyed him intensely, and he did nothing to assist any plans they might have had for joining the theatre permanently. It was said, in fact, that he did everything in his power to discourage them. As a result they announced, early in 1837, that they had obtained a licence to perform dramatic and other entertainments at the Pulteney Hotel for a month. They gave their first on 4 January, which was so poorly patronized that for a short term they returned to Hobart.

Soon after this Wyatt saw fit to forbid the theatre to the *Gazette* reporter, William Kerr. It seems Kerr had been overheard boasting that "be the performance what it might, good or bad, he would *show* all the performers *up,* as he had a *down* upon them". He was apparently not the only one with a down on the theatre, for the paid and the unpaid critics began to concentrate their attention on the theatre interior. Nothing was overlooked, from the dirty chandeliers to the "filthy state" of the canopies over the theatre's two most important boxes. As to the orchestra, Wyatt was advised to dispense with it and install a barrel-organ instead. But although at least one of the plays, *The Somnambulist; or, The Phantom of the Village,* was heavily criticized because the actors did not know their parts, the great majority of the plays presented by Knowles during his managership earned him and the theatre high praise and regular audiences.

Knowles, the "gentleman" of the Sydney stage, was also the one with the most dedicated interest in and knowledge of the theatre. He introduced in 1837, for instance, something which one puzzled critic thought violated "nature, theatrical custom, and the good taste of our Sydney audience" — the "picture" or "tableau" at the end of each act or strong scene of a play. To gain the strong dramatic effect this tableau was said to achieve, just before the curtain fell to denote the end of an act the actors "froze" into their particular attitudes or positions at the moment, so that the effect was that of a painting or a three-dimensional model. "We never saw this attempt at stage effect practised either in London or the provincial theatres, and we should have been surprised if we had", summed up the only critic to mention the novelty. But not even in this was the Sydney theatre an innovator. Though the tableau or picture was to be used much more frequently in the next twenty years, it seems that its first use in the English theatre was in Buckstone's *Isabelle; or, Woman's Life*, in 1834, though quite possibly it had been used even before this.

But while Knowles seems to have had few troubles with the actors (or few that were publicized), he had more with his audiences than any of his predecessors had had. This was particularly so towards the end of his term as manager, when he was losing interest and had let it be known that it was his intention to seek theatrical fame in England.

He was finding the task of managing the actors, learning new parts two and three times a week, memorizing the old ones, and apologizing to the audience for the various theatrical mishaps and minor misdemeanours increasingly hard to bear. He was sincerely interested in acting, and willing to work himself to death in his efforts at self-improvement, but the majority of his supporting actors and their audiences wanted laughs and thrills, with the necessary leavening of artificial sentiment, rather than drama or "art". *King Lear,* for instance, was beyond their taste and understanding. When Knowles played it, with Mrs. Cameron, Mrs. Taylor, and Miss Douglass as the three daughters, a full house turned up for the performance, only to ignore it in the interests of gossip and laughter and a great deal of the usual noises with which an audience indicates its disinterest in what is happening on the stage. Said the *Monitor* regretfully: "Whenever our Sydney theatre is *full,* the vulgarity of the people breaks forth, turns all the pathetic scenes into ridicule, and the tragic into burlesque." From which it can be concluded that Sydney audiences, like those in London, treated the play with indifference whenever they felt like it. Visits were paid between boxes; conversations were held; there was constant movement, laughter, chattering, and arguments all through the play, punctuated by the click and slam of box doors being opened and shut.

By 1 April Knowles had left for England, and Simes was installed as manager. It was said he was to hold the appointment until Meredith arrived back from Hobart, but in fact he held it for many more months than expected. Meredith had spread his wings too wide in Hobart town and was unable to leave until he had satisfied his creditors.

Wyatt's lesseeship was now drawing to a close. By 6 April there were only three performances to go, all of them benefits, at one of which (not her own) Mrs. Taylor was showered by the enthusiastic audience with half-crowns, shillings, and sixpences for her singing of "The Broom Girl". On 10 April the theatre closed after an unusually long season of ten months, and there was again a hurried and not fully successful attempt to paint and redecorate it for its reopening on 21 April for the new season under Levey's ownership and direction.

All this time, of course, Levey had been going through one of the most frustrating and unproductive periods in his life, a period not one whit alleviated by the frequent trips he made on the calmer reaches of Sydney Harbour in his boat, ingeniously propelled by paddles worked with a crank by an obliging convict servant. At one period, towards the end of 1836, Levey was so carried away with the splendours of his little boat that, with his usual mixture of exuberance and vainglory, he challenged a steamer to a race to Parramatta. No record exists to show whether anything ever came of this challenge.

But these side issues, these forays into public life by means of bets and wagers, and by attendance at Gas Company and Bank of New South Wales meetings, could not make up for the real need he felt to be back once again on the stage and at the controls of his beloved theatre. This was not a time for inaction, for the future of his theatre was threatened. The approaching opening of the new theatre; the nagging, time-wasting period he had had to spend in waiting for Wyatt's lease to expire; the knowledge that the man who was about to open a palatial replacement for the Theatre Royal was learning the ropes at *his* expense and in *his* theatre; his growing alcoholism and the physical toll it was taking,

200

combined to induce in him a feeling of desperation. There would soon be competition for the first time in the Royal's career, and it would come from a theatre larger, better planned, and better situated than his own. Inevitably he began to think back to the theatres of his youth — Sadler's Wells, the Coburg, the Lyceum.

Towards the end of 1836, although it would be still some months before he regained control of his theatre, he announced that he would install a mirror curtain to replace the traditional green baize curtain, and that he had signed a contract for the installation of gas-lighting in the theatre. Both were again dreams impossible of complete or immediate realization. Mirror curtains had been installed in English theatres, had lasted a short while because of their novelty, and had then been discarded because their enormous weight put too great a strain on the building fabric. One was installed at the Coburg in 1822, and at the Queen's Theatre, Manchester in the early 1830's.

As for gas-lighting, although it was planned for Sydney and Levey was a shareholder in the company, all the plant had to come from England. It was 1840 before it arrived, and gas was not turned on in Sydney (in a restricted area only) until 24 May 1841.

Even the mirror curtain, when finally revealed to Levey's audience, turned out to be nothing of the kind. It consisted of a cloth or baize curtain with a number of small mirrors glued or hung all over on much the same principle as sequins on a costume. The newspapers contemptuously dismissed it as something made of "children's penny looking-glasses", and "penny shaving glasses".

Levey was never given the benefit so fulsomely promised him by Wyatt and the theatre company as compensation for the cost of his legal involvement with Simmons, so the first thing he did was to advertise that on 17 April, four days before the season proper was due to open under his management, there would be a benefit for the newly-returned proprietor for which splendours previously unheard of were being prepared. The band of the 4th

Regiment was to be called into requisition to provide the music, and Major England of that regiment had kindly given his permission for forty of the privates to be used on the stage as supernumeraries to provide the necessary "bulk" for the stage processions and crowd scenes.

The programme was to include, Levey announced, *Napoleon Buonaparte; or, The General, Consul, and Emperor,* followed by *The Infernal Secret; or, The Invulnerable,* and *The Mock Doctor.* In between these three dramatic items were to be interspersed songs and dances, and the reappearance of Master Quinn with his stage-to-gallery-and-back tightrope walk, giving the public overflowing measure so far as novelty and length of performance were concerned. This *Napoleon* was really M.R. Lacy's dramatic spectacle (or Levey's version of it) *Napoleon Buonaparte, Captain of Artillery, General and First Consul, Emperor and Exile,* noted more for its spectacle than its dramatic content. In his advertisement for this Levey named eighteen of the principal characters but did not reveal who was to play them. He promised such delights as a grand march, the entrance of the French troops, Napoleon on his white charger, the attempted assassination of Lucien Joseph Buonaparte, a levée at the palace of St. Cloud, Napoleon on the throne — "the whole of the splendid costumes in the above pageant are entirely new, and of the most superb and appropriate description".

On the night that this long and arduous programme was presented the theatre was packed to the doors. Whatever Levey's faults, or whatever the newspapers said were his faults, they seemed to make no difference to the public, which still stood solidly behind him. To them he was still "the inimitable Barnett Levey", the man who had given Sydney its first theatre, and they attended in strength to welcome him back. Unfortunately, as this was a benefit performance, the newspapers, as usual, did not detail the performers or comment on the success or failure of the night's plays. Typical of the usual "notice" of a benefit was the *Australian*'s — "The Theatre. This place of entertainment was

202

opened on Monday night last for the benefit of Mr. Levey, the proprietor, and the house was crammed to the ceiling." Perhaps Levey relied on this custom of the laconic paragraph when he decided on the form two of the main attractions were to take, and hoped that his subterfuge would escape, if not unnoticed at least unmentioned. But the splenetic *Gazette,* three days after the benefit, and the *Monitor* six days after the *Gazette* saw fit to play the role of faithful watchdogs of the public.

The theatre was in the very blood of the people of the early nineteenth century. It was the only form of public amusement cheaply and easily available, and favourite plays and actors, favourite scenes and sensations were on everyone's tongue. There was an immense trade in theatrical handbills, books of the play at one penny each, likenesses of actors and scenes from popular plays, and toy cardboard theatres or stages which could be assembled by child or adult. These toy theatres featured the scenes and characters of most of the plays of the day — to say nothing of the accompanying "book", from which theatre enthusiasts of all ages could read aloud the parts as they moved the characters on the stage. Skelton, Hodgson, Pollock — these were the names of the principal magicians who thus made available to every nursery and drawing room the wonders and terrors, the pains and pleasures of the offerings of the principal London theatres. And it was on Hodgson, not Lacy, that Levey drew for his presentation of *Napoleon,* and also for Amherst's *The Infernal Secret.* The book of the play which accompanied toy theatres left out a great deal of the dialogue in the original plays, and all but the most spectacular or telling scenes, so that Levey's audience saw a considerably curtailed version of the original plays. But he is not entirely to be blamed. He once again demonstrated that he knew more than the newspaper critics about the tastes and wishes of his audience. He had no highfalutin ideas about art or culture; his aim was to entertain. That he again succeeded is evident from the fact that there were no riots or demonstrations against what was, to a large extent, Hodgson's night.

Giving the game away, the *Gazette* left Levey to deny its charges, which he couldn't, or admit them, which he wouldn't. He would have been able to ignore its disclosures, perhaps, if the *Monitor* had not only made a great fuss about his attempt to foist the *juvenile* drama on the public with an astute but nevertheless shabby trick, but also attacked him on other matters. It made all kinds of unsupported allegations about his handling of and payment to his actors.

"We have now lying before us", said the *Monitor*, "Hodgson's *juvenile* drama", by which it meant the book of the play which accompanied Hodgson's toy theatre. "From this baby's book did Mr. Levey play off his *Napoleon Buonaparte* the other night." In its leading article, the newspaper then accused Levey of underpaying or reducing his actors' salaries, trotted out the old familiar complaints against the theatre, told Levey how he should run his theatre, and then attacked the actors.

Levey replied to the *Monitor's* attacks in a paid letter in the *Gazette* under a pseudonym, in which all charges about his "squeezing" the actors were denied. The letter claimed all salaries had been increased an average of one third more than was paid when theatricals were first established in Sydney. As for Hodgson's juvenile drama —

> I willingly allow (this) was one of the most absurd acts Mr. Levey could have committed — that it *was* one, he candidly admits, while at the same time he pledges himself it shall never be repeated. All men are liable to err in judgment, then surely for one fault (committed when all things connected with the theatre were in a state of confusion) poor Mr. Levey may claim forgiveness?

The writer also claimed that he had every reason to believe the *Monitor* had been misled and misinformed, "knowing as I do, that certain parties are at this moment plotting and striving by every means in their power to injure Mr. Levey and his prospects".

At some stage in this furore the newspapers might have asked themselves was it reasonable to expect any theatre to be able to

204

present on one night the *full* dramatic spectacle of *Napoleon,* the *full* melodrama of *The Infernal Secret,* the afterpiece of *The Mock Doctor,* and half a dozen divertissements? If they did expect it they were as gullible as Levey took them to be; if not, their frequently paraded knowledge of *real* theatre was a sham. Levey had once again achieved his purpose — a full house — and confronted his critics with a fait accompli, which the *Gazette* admitted a few days later with its statement that: "Everyone knows that on benefit nights it is quite customary to get up the vilest gaudy trash imaginable, and this Levey certainly did for his benefit."

The audience at this benefit saw for the first time the changes made in the auditorium during the brief time the theatre had been closed. Though incomplete, the planned scheme was evident. The house had been repainted, and to match the so-called mirror curtain there was a large star of mirror glass in the centre of the ceiling. From this depended a cut glass chandelier which the *Gazette* unkindly described as being, with its no more than twelve candles, admirably suited for a gentleman's drawing-room but useless in a theatre. But then nothing about the transformed theatre pleased this newspaper. It was too dark, "and even the stairs from the saloon to the upper boxes had the usual light taken away, admitting scope for highly improper conduct". The fronts of the lower tier of boxes had been ornamented with painted vignettes of marine victories, but the *Gazette* thought the money this cost would have been better spent re-covering the seats and re-stuffing the fronts, or armrests, of the boxes. "Mr. Levey has also stationed throughout the theatre a set of animals called Special Constables. We call them a special nuisance, getting drunk, annoying and insulting the audience, and vociferating applause, as in duty bound, to the vilest buffoonery." The house needed more lights, the writer said, and a purer oil was needed for the oil lamps, not the stuff now in use, which nearly suffocated and blinded the audience each night with its smoke and fumes.

Patently, nothing would please the *Gazette,* but nevertheless

Levey bought another and larger chandelier, this time of gilt. If he had thought this would earn the gratitude of the *Gazette* he soon found out his mistake. The newspaper acknowledged that the chandelier was new and elegant, but complained that it had nearly burnt out before the end of the first play. Further, "by a strange perversity it has been exalted in the front of the house, where it is not required, instead of the back which is in almost total darkness".

After his benefit Levey announced that the new season under his control would open on 29 April with the performance of *The Soldier's Daughter* and *The Seven Clerks; or, The Three Thieves and the Dreamer*. The theatre would be open four nights a week — Monday, Wednesday, Thursday, and Saturday — and prices would be as usual. His company for this first night's performance was advertised as Simes, Spencer, Peat, Collins, White, Buckingham, Winters, Wheatley, Riley, Fitzgerald, Master Quinn (as an actor), and Miss Douglass, Mrs. Downes, Miss Jones, Mrs. Larra, Miss Winstanley, and Miss Bliss. Simes was acting-manager, and Buckingham, the first actor to walk on the stage when the Theatre Royal curtain was first raised in 1832, was stage manager.

Almost from the moment this announcement appeared the campaign by the *Gazette* reporter, William Kerr, against Levey, became fiercer, with the newspaper from now on taking every opportunity it could to denigrate the Theatre Royal. Kerr was a protégé of Dr. John Dunmore Lang. Before going to the *Gazette* he had been employed on the *Colonist*. He was a bitter, twisted man who got on with nobody, and he made no secret of the fact that he was full of hatred for Mrs. Taylor, Barnett Levey, and the Theatre Royal. In 1839 he went to Victoria, and his subsequent inglorious career in that colony may be traced in the *Australian Dictionary of Biography*.

Throughout the seaon the *Gazette* followed its long diatribes against Levey and his theatre with equally long periods when it ignored the theatre altogether, considering its contempt the most powerful form of criticism. It was as if the newspaper, pinning its hopes on the probability of the new theatre being more in conformity with its idea of things theatrical, was determined to do its best first to kill the old. Levey was baited at every opportunity, and he, despite his illness and inebriety, did what he could to counter the attacks, the first step again being to refuse Kerr admittance to his theatre.

The first few performances of the new season were uneventful, but they failed to gain full houses. This was attributed to various causes, and was once again the occasion for the familiar pronouncements by sections of the Press on the iniquity of the Sydney stage. But all critics were agreed on one point: with the departure of Knowles the theatre was without a leading actor worthy of the name, and was also in need of Mrs. Taylor to bolster the "feminine department".

Meantime Levey, always amenable to suggestions, withdrew first the offending mirror curtain and then the tinsel ribbons which he had strung from all points of the theatre to meet at the centre chandelier, and had hung in festoons in front of the boxes. The *Gazette* critic had professed to find this tinsel particularly annoying because of the habit people had of fingering it and setting it swinging during a performance, thereby creating a disturbing noise.

In mid-May the Theatre Royal, short for so long of a leading actor, was granted a reprieve. Sydney was advised by advertisement on 16 May that two days later "the admired play in five acts called *The Merchant of Venice*" would be presented, "in which Mr. Lazar, from the Theatres Royal Drury Lane and Covent Garden will make his first appearance at this theatre as Shylock". This "from the Theatres Royal Drury Lane and Covent Garden" claim was received with a tongue-in-cheek attitude by the *Gazette* and the *Herald*. The former contented itself with reporting that he was from those theatres "as the bills state". Not so the *Herald*. This newspaper flatly denied that Lazar had been a *prominent* performer at either theatre, "for the names of all the performers are as well known in this Colony as in London". But both agreed that in Lazar a suitable replacement for Knowles had at last been found.

Lazar, before he moved into the usual melodramas and comedies which filled most of the bills, played first Shylock in *The Merchant of Venice,* and then *Othello.* He was said to be superior to Knowles in the one, but inferior in the other. His chief defects, it appears, were his habit of dropping aitches, and a lisp. As Shylock both these were admitted to be an advantage. As Othello the effect was said to be catastrophic. But whatever the critics had to say for or against him, they all had to admit that Lazar's performances drew the wildest enthusiasm from the packed audiences that witnessed them.

Said the *Gazette:*

> When we saw him in the Jew, we gave him much credit for adapting his voice to the Jewish style, not supposing he was playing in his usual tone. We, however, find that Mr. Lazar not only personates the Jew on the stage, but that he is a Jew off it, so that when playing the Moor he was unable to disguise his being a true son of Israel, which is a considerable drawback to his personification of such characters as Othello.

But apart from some speech defects all the critics agreed that Lazar was a "find". He was "rather tall and well-proportioned"; his figure and face were said to be "adapted to the stage"; his voice was powerful and good, he was letter perfect in his part and was well dressed.

The idiosyncratic *Herald* reviewed Lazar's performance of 18 May almost a month later, on 16 June, pleading "want of space" for the delay. It found that generally he had failed in the important characters he had undertaken, but had appeared with tolerable success in others. "He will be a useful addition to the company — besides which, he is said to be a very decent man, having lately arrived in the Colony with his wife and family." Lazar's daughter, a child of ten or twelve years, also appeared on the stage, as a dancer, and her dancing was said to be a big improvement on anything previously seen on the Sydney boards. She also played child characters in such plays as *One O'Clock*, and *The Spoiled Child*.

Meanwhile Levey, constantly reminded of the progress being made in the construction of the rival theatre, began to plan his "answer" to the threat it represented. In July he announced that his theatre would be widened thirty feet, and, once again, that the whole house would be lighted with gas. He also said the Royal's stage would be reconstructed on the lines of the stage at Sadler's Wells Theatre in London, and that in several scenes "*real* water would be introduced". While the Royal was undergoing these radical changes the company would transfer to the saloon of the Royal Hotel, which would be fitted up as a theatre in much the same way as it had been nearly six years before.

17

Levey at Bay

It is significant that in his attempt to find some way of enabling the old theatre to compete with the new, Levey's thoughts should go back to the aqua-dramas at Sadler's Wells, which he no doubt saw as a boy. Sadler's Wells, built alongside the New River, was having a lean time in 1803 and was threatened with closure. Finally the lessee, Charles Dibdin, hit on the idea of using the unlimited supply of water close at hand and presenting shows on real water. Throughout the winter of 1803 work was carried out day and night on the installation of a huge tank beneath the stage. The new "water" season opened in 1804 with *The Siege of Gibraltar,* in which 117 model ships were used, manoeuvred in the water by a corps of young boys who were dosed with brandy before they entered the water and provided with towels and a fire when they came out. These naval battles in miniature were followed later in the season, and up to as late as 1824, by real aqua-dramas in which every known plot and side-plot of melodrama was "wedded" to a watery locale or background, with burning castles, dogs rescuing babies and despairing maidens who had fallen or been thrown into the water, and fierce combats between individuals and groups on board ship and in the water.

That Levey should be thinking in terms of this kind of theatrical spectacle indicates many things, not least of them being that he must have felt the drama alone was not sufficient to hold the public interest, and that novelty was the answer to any threat the

210

Victoria represented. On the other hand, it could also indicate that he was at his wit's end, worried, harrassed, and sick, and that in this condition his thoughts turned more and more to the theatre of his youth in London, and to his first Sydney theatrical success in the saloon theatre in 1832. How often must he have recalled how he had fought to establish his theatre, how he had trained and guided the bunch of raw recruits which made up his first company, and how they had turned on him once their conception of success had been achieved.

In truth, Levey's announced plans were plans in name only. He made no move to carry them out. Rather, he tried to keep the inevitable at bay with an increasing recourse to drink. The *Gazette,* which for some time now had disdained to notice the existence of the Theatre Royal, must have got wind of what was happening, for on 5 August it broke a long silence to record with disgust that Levey had played the part of Francisco in *A Tale of Mystery* "in such a 'flow of spirits' as scarcely to be able to keep his feet. . ."

The *Australian,* on the other hand, saw nothing unusual in Levey's movements or appearance, no hint that he was under the influence, and had nothing but praise for his performance. His part called for pantomime only, as Francisco was dumb. The *Australian*'s notice drew from the *Gazette* the acid comment that "we suspect the writer was not in a much better condition himself". Of Levey's performance and the reaction of the audience the *Australian* wrote:

> On Wednesday evening last Mr. Barnett Levey appeared in the character of Francisco in *The* [*sic*] *Tale of Mystery,* being his first appearance in that part for these two years. As might have been expected the house was well filled to witness the exertions of the Patriarch of the Drama, and if we may judge from the vociferous marks of approbation expressed on the occasion, Mr. Levey succeeded in pleasing his admirers and friends. . . The pantomimic action of Mr. Levey was elegant and chaste, and it was truly surprising to witness the command he had on the working of his countenance, — for the various feelings of surprise, sorrow, and

211

conscious innocence, with which this arduous character is wrought, were beautifully delineated; indeed, his representation of Francisco may, without fear of contradiction, be called a masterpiece of dumb eloquence. We are sure we need not say more to convince the public of the superior performance of Mr. Levey than that, at the fall of the curtain, he was loudly called for by the audience to sing "'Rum' Old Commodore".

The *Herald,* in a later comment on the comments, said it did not deny the truth of the assertion that Levey was in a "flow of spirits" on the night. It also said it believed the *Australian's* view of the performance was deliberate satire. The truth of the matter at this distance is almost impossible to unravel. All that can said is that there seems to be nothing at all satirical about the *Australian's* straightforward report, with the possible exception of the quoted "Rum" in "Rum Old Commodore". If this report was indeed deliberate satire it was so subtly couched as to defeat its supposed ends.

Five days later the *Gazette* again mounted an attack against Levey, this time because he had announced that in a few days "Levey's night" would be held at the theatre. "What claims the proprietor of a theatre has to *two* benefits in *one* season — and such a proprietor as Mr. Levey, too, we are yet to learn", it thundered. And it raked up the earlier benefit with its juvenile drama, which it now chose to regard as "disgraceful". It raked up, also, his "recent exhibition" in the part of Franciso. "Really the man's impudence is only equalled by his consummate ignorance, to presume he could meet with anything like respectable patronage on his *second* benefit night. A benefit indeed, what next will be attempted, we wonder."

Levey held his benefit, obviously planned to raise some of the money needed to enlarge and reconstruct his theatre, on 14 August. He was bewildered and hurt by these attacks by the press, but not so bewildered that he was unable to seek redress. He decided to sue the *Gazette* for libel in stating that he had been drunk on stage and had insulted his audience. And then caution

asserted itself, and he allowed his friends to talk him into with-
drawing the case. The *Gazette* said it was glad he had done so,
for he had thus made sure his wife and children were not deprived
of the £100 such a case would have cost him. But Levey did the
next best thing. He gave instructions once again that the *Gazette*
reporter, William Kerr, was not to be admitted to the theatre.
Kerr thought he would get over this by paying for his ticket as
an ordinary member of the public, but Levey's staff had had their
orders, and Kerr was refused admission with or without a ticket.
He went to the theatre, put down his money, and sought
to go to a seat, but was stopped by Henry Jones, the ticket-
taker at the theatre. On Kerr insisting on his right to enter,
Jones "assaulted" him "with as little violence as was compatible
with effecting his object". Kerr then sued Jones for assault, but
the court ruled that as the ticket-taker had to be given a ticket
before he could allow anyone to enter the theatre, and Kerr had
no ticket, Jones was in the right. The court also ruled that the
real question involved — whether Levey had the right to refuse
anyone admission to his theatre — was not for it to decide.

The *Gazette*, reporting the hearing, delivered a "ruling" of its
own. "If a principle be good its converse must be true, and Mr.
Kerr, judging from appearances, is as capable of maintaining his
own part in an assault as either Mr. Jones or his drunken employer." So that only two days after this the same parties were
again before the Bench, with their roles reversed. This time Jones,
through Barnett Levey, was suing Kerr for assault; or, as the
Gazette chose to put it, in the earlier case Jones had exerted his
presumed right to keep out Mr. Kerr, while in this Mr. Kerr
had used his presumed right to obtain admittance. This newspaper
then reported, with more than a hint of parody, what it said was
Levey's special pleading in this case, not forgetting to imply once
more that he was in a drunken state. It *did* forget to mention
that the *Gazette* was represented in court by its owner, who did
a little special pleading of his own until he, too, was silenced by
the court. This case was dismissed on the same grounds as the

first — that the right of entry to a theatre was a civil matter.

Some few weeks after this the *Gazette* used a visit its representative had made to inspect the new theatre to strike still further blows at the Royal. A long article listed everything the *Gazette* said was wrong with this theatre, including "the filthy state of the house, the ruinous state of the scenery, and the dilapidated condition of the machinery". The theatre's frequenters were the lowest of the low, the article claimed. Disgusting language was allowed unchecked in the gallery and pit, and disgraceful conduct among the blackguard portion of the audience. "It was but the other night we saw a *convict* dance a sailor's jig till he was weary on the middle of the pit benches, amid the clamorous applause of the gods, and no attempt whatever was made to restore order in the house." The *Gazette*, not for the first time, looked forward to the brighter prospect offered by the new theatre, for "competition is good for every description of trade, and we have no doubt it will be found particularly so in theatrical affairs".

This article must have been the last straw for Barnett Levey. These vindictive and planned attacks, which dated from that night early in the year when Wyatt had first forbidden Kerr the theatre, were something against which he was not only powerless but also more vulnerable than he had been in the past.

Then at last someone whose patience had been tried to the limit by the *Gazette*'s attacks came to Levey's defence in the *Australian*. Signing himself "Fair Play", he accused the *Gazette* of indulging personal antipathy against Levey in its "evident intention . . . to effect the total annihilation of that gentleman's establishment". "Fair Play" said it was useless and unfair to blame Levey for faults in the theatre which had persisted under a succession of managements. Nor was he to be blamed because his theatre was now without a Meredith, Knowles, Simmons, or Mackay, a Mrs. Chester or Mrs. Jones. These were all out of the theatre because of their inability to fit in except as absolute top dog. Meredith, Knowles, and Simmons were jealous of each other. "Each wanted to be monarch of all; none would bear a rival near

214

his theatrical throne, and they pursued this conduct until they had wormed one another out of both management and performing."

Mackay (the original "Mackie"), a clever but dissipated actor of great promise, of whom "Fair Play" said Knowles had been intensely jealous, gave Knowles the opportunity he needed to drive him from the stage and the colony. Mrs. Chester, "her vanity alarmed because she had to become second where she thought she had an undoubted right to lead, quitted our shores". Mrs. Jones followed the fortunes of her paramour. All this had happened when Levey was no longer manager of his theatre. As for Simmons, "Fair Play" advised him in future to avoid that course of conduct which, at the Royal, had caused him to raise up against himself a competitor (Knowles) who had ultimately driven him from the stage to pursue "activities less congenial to his taste and genius".

"Fair Play" was equally impatient with the *Gazette's* claim that the attendance of the "respectable" at the theatre was not possible because of the low company to be found there. The pit and the gods in every theatre will have their fun, he said; that was expected. But if the company in the dress circle was not always to the taste of the "holier than thou", what difference did that make? Surely their main reason for going to the theatre was to enjoy the play, not their neighbours? If it was good enough for the Governor's daughter and the daughters of the colony's judges and other leaders to sit next to people in the theatre without first inquiring about their character and antecedents, it was certainly good enough for anyone the *Gazette* could nominate. Again, as to the indecency or indelicacy of the women players, and particularly Mrs. Taylor, why, he asked, did the *Gazette* not come forward with exactly the same charges when, as it knew, Knowles and Mrs. Jones while they were in the colony were living together as man and wife? It did not do so, "Fair Play" claimed, because Knowles and Mrs. Jones were *Gazette* favourites, and had even dined with the editor.

Point by point "Fair Play" demolished the fabrication he said

215

the *Gazette* had piled up against the Theatre Royal merely "to write down the old theatre in favour of the new one", and because of a pique and antipathy it felt towards "poor Barnett". His arguments and facts could not have been immediately answerable. Ultimately, the week's silence which followed the publication of his letter in the *Australian* of 22 September became permanent, not because anything he had written had sent Levey's enemies scuttling for cover, but because of a development no one had expected.

Kerr and his employers had to wait but a little while longer for the final result towards which they had both contributed their share. On 23 September the *Gazette* was able to announce that the stage manager at the Theatre Royal had found it

> absolutely necessary ... to enable him to conduct the business of the house with anything like propriety, to stipulate for the entire exclusion of Mr. Barnett Levey, the proprietor, from behind the scenes, it being found that his presence and interference is anything but conducive to the prosperity of the drama.

The *Gazette* professed to see in this a "hope that brighter days are about to dawn in the Thespian hemisphere". But this staid beginning to its report soon degenerated into the usual abuse against Levey, and revealed the real purpose behind the *Gazette*'s attacks. The last sentence laid bare its true hopes. "With these alterations we may expect the present theatre to live till the new one is opened; then, of course, it must finally close."

Through all this Simes and the rest of the company went on with the business of the theatre as best they could. Plays were produced regularly, sometimes to full, sometimes to scant houses. Lazar continued to prove an acquisition, and so did little Miss Lazar. Mr. and Mrs. Cameron again joined the company, and while the *Gazette* indulged in its deliberate campaign of denigration, the other newspapers contented themselves with reporting the success or failure of the plays presented and the parts played by individual actors, with an occasional afterthought on the

216

general failings of the moment. There were no more attempts during the year to present the "classics" or Shakespeare, the repertoire consisting entirely of contemporary plays geared to contemporary taste. That there was a surprising range of these is evident from the fact that although 1837 was a difficult year for the theatre in many ways, the Royal still managed to present eighty-three new plays — plays not presented in Sydney before — as well as repeat performances of some of the old favourites presented since the theatre first opened in 1832.

On 30 September 1837 a triple bill was again presented. Mrs. Cameron played the lead in the favourite *Clari, the Maid of Milan,* the other two plays being *Is He Jealous?* and one advertised as *Benjamin Bowbell; or, The Illustrious Stranger.* The correct title of this play is *The Illustrious Stranger; or, Married and Buried,* the Royal calling it *Benjamin Bowbell* because of the popularity of the sailor of that name who is the play's chief character. Sydney's newspaper readers on Monday, 2 October, opening their *Monitor* (the first newspaper to be published that week) were disappointed if they were looking for a report of the Saturday night's performances at the theatre. There was not the usual page two article headed "The Theatre", but, tucked away among the "Local Intelligence" was a small paragraph which said: "In consequence of the death of Mr. Barnett Levey, the theatre will be closed for one week..."

Apart from the *Herald,* which made no mention of the fact at all, with one exception the newspapers contented themselves with noting that Barnett Levey had died, leaving it at that. In fact, they could not agree on when he had died, some saying the first and some the second of October, while the same disagreement on his age showed it as having been both thirty-nine and forty. It was almost as if they felt he had moved beyond blame or praise, that anything they might have to say would be addressed to an empty house, and was therefore not worth saying. The exception was the *Sydney Times.* Some twenty days after Levey's death this newspaper devoted a leading article to him, written by someone who had obviously known the private as well as the public figure. His death was seen as yet another example of "thousands of other anti-temperance-principle men who are bringing themselves to a premature grave and about to convert their wives into widows and their children into orphans by the dreadful *mania for drink* which pervades and is desolating this fine country". It was not its wish to censure the deceased, the *Times* said, but to warn and thereby benefit the living. Barnett Levey had been one of those persons justly described as "nobody's foe but their own", the newspaper said. Good humoured, fond of fun and laughter, able to sing a "capital" comic song, his exuberance led him into the sort of company by which nine people out of ten are introduced to the drink habit. Further, the profession to which he had so wholeheartedly devoted himself, to which, indeed, he had devoted his life in the colony, was calculated to induce rather than repel a habit of dissipation. "In fact he was, and everybody knows it, a hard drinker." He had long been in a very bad state of health, his constitution shattered by the over-use of ardent spirits.

The article then listed the details of his life which it said the "old hands" well remembered and which colonists who had arrived within the last four years would be surprised to hear — his massive building with the windmill on top, his theatre, which for so long could not be used because of Governor Darling's ban, and the Royal Hotel, which was all he had left of any use from the huge fortune he had sunk in his ill-advised or ill-timed enterprises, until it, too, went under the hammer.

"Although Levey and his family have been the sacrifice of his enterprise, yet *to his spirit and perseverance* are the public *indebted* for the introduction of theatricals into New South Wales." Levey had had both faults and enemies, the article concluded, but it was hoped that in gratitude for the benefit he had rendered the colony by providing it with its first permanent theatre the public would liberally support his widow and "four orphaned children" by continuing their patronage of the Theatre Royal.

218

Thus one individual out of the 23,000 in Sydney publicly paid his last respects to a man who had had vision enough to build an empire but not enough skill to construct a weatherproof shed. Like so many of the uneducated people of his day Levey dearly loved the Latin tag and the resounding phrase, which he often used, always mispronounced, and rarely understood. He would have savoured without being able to apply the one which best describes him: *Qui nimis notus omnibus ignotus moritur subi* — he who is too well known to all, dies without knowing himself.

Following Levey's death the theatre was closed for a week, and was then reopened under the proprietorship of Mrs. Levey. The public, touched by the plight of a woman with four children suddenly widowed, packed the theatre, and it began to look as though under her control things would be better than they had been for a long time. Even the Governor promised to attend the performance on 10 October. But in that week the news arrived in Sydney of another unexpected death. King William IV of England had died on 20 June, and th eVictorian era had arrived. Governor Bourke sent a note of apology to Mrs. Levey, regretting that for obvious reasons he would not be able to attend the performance, and his letter was read from the stage at the rise of the curtain. With the note the Governor had enclosed ten pounds.

But the *Gazette* made sure peace did not endure for long. Simes was still manager, or, as the *Gazette* put it in yet another article a week later attacking everything about the theatre, "uncontrolled in his management". The *Gazette* said it had expected a change for the better with the "new" proprietorship, but regretted to find it had been mistaken. It recommended the entire suppression of "that abominable nest of pollution, now nicknamed the Theatre Royal". The article was a savage attack without the saving grace of one fair comment, and although it was patently aimed at Simes rather than Mrs. Levey, it was certainly not designed to aid her in her efforts to carry on where her husband had left off. Simes helped to increase the revenue of the *Australian* by replying to the article in a lengthy "advertisement".

219

In this he made two errors, first in attributing the article to the vindictive *Gazette* reporter, Kerr, and then in indulging in vulgar abuse of the writer. His letter was hysterical in tone on the matter of unspecified people behind the curtain who were supposedly anxious to wrest the theatre management from him. Whereupon another "advertisement" was published, this time in the *Gazette,* as a reply to the reply. The writer of this, William Kerr, said Simes was right in believing he wished to oust him from his situation. "It *is* my wish, as it *is* my intention that Mrs. Levey shall be set free from the trammels of such heartless sycophants as himself. . . I take upon myself to prophesy that the management of the Theatre Royal, George Street, shall not six months hence be in such feeble hands as now. . ." To Simes's claim that the writer's enmity to the theatre had largely been responsible for Levey's death, Kerr replied that if he really was responsible for "a consummation so devoutly wished" then he considered he was richly entitled to a free benefit from all connected with the Theatre Royal. But he denied that he had written the original attack on Simes and the theatre which had initiated this correspondence.

Perhaps Kerr knew more about the theatre's politics than he had revealed, for he proved right in his prognostication. Within a few weeks of the newspaper "battle" involving Simes that gentleman had been replaced as manager by Lazar.

But still Mrs. Levey needed a strong arm to lean upon, and it was not long in offering. The Mr. Knight who had been with Knowles during his management, and who seems to have been one of the original six who leased the theatre from Barnett Levey, now offered to lease it from Mrs. Levey. On 28 November she announced that Mr. W. Knight had become the lessee of the theatre. Eleven days later this was denied, one report being that Mr. Knight had gone back on his agreement to pay £15 a week for a year, another simply stating that Mr. Knight had not become the lessee of the theatre "as erroneously stated". The management of the theatre, this report said, would be continued by Mrs. Levey.

Five months were to pass before it was revealed that Mrs. Levey and not Mr. Knight had been the defaulter. She had agreed to give the lease to Knight, but apparently at the last minute Levey's old friend-enemy, Joseph Simmons, dropped his commercial interests long enough to secure from her the "part lease" of the theatre. So that by the middle of November 1837 Mrs. Levey had Jacob Josephson (variously described as her father and her step-father) and Joseph Simmons to guide her in the conduct of the theatre.

On 5 December Sir Richard Bourke ceased to be Governor of New South Wales. Before this date the Theatre Royal company, remembering that he had made their existence possible, determined to join in the almost universal praise of his administration and to add their quota to the mass of addresses of farewell with which he was presented before leaving Australia. They accordingly sent him the following:

We, the undersigned, connected with the first theatrical establishment raised in the Colony of New South Wales, request permission respectfully to approach your Excellency with our sincere expressions of esteem and veneration for your person and Government prior to your relinquishment of the important trust confided to you, as Our Most Gracious Sovereign's representative in this distant part of the British Empire.

While the many beneficial and munificent public acts which have adorned your Excellency's administration of the Government of the Colony of New South Wales, have justly called forth the tribute of grateful praise (in which we heartily join) from the great body of the colonists, as well as from some of our Public Institutions, it may perhaps be permitted to us, who as a body have been raised into existence under your Excellency's gracious favour, especially to advert to that for which we feel our most grateful acknowledgements are more particularly due to your Excellency.

It is to your Excellency that the public of Australia is indebted for the first introduction of dramatic, as well as other social public amusements, among them; and we, who under your permission, have been made the first to aspire

221

to theatrical fame here, have doubly reason to be grateful for your Excellency's condescension displayed in your several personal visits to the theatre to witness our humble efforts to cultivate a taste for the drama in this remote part of the globe. By this act on the part of your Excellency we feel that you have done much to advance the moral as well as intellectual improvement of this rising community, for it can be no less conducive to the well government of society in general in this colony, than in that of the parent state, —

> To hold, as' twere, the mirror up to nature;
> To show Virtue her own feature,
> Scorn her own image,
> And the very age and body of Time
> His form and pressure.

We now respectfully take our leave of your Excellency, with the sincere and earnest wish that your Excellency may experience a safe and speedy passage to your native land; and that you may enjoy in the social circle which awaits your return there with fond expectation, the calm and peaceful retrospect of an useful and honourable career, to which your eminent talents and exalted VIRTUES, long exercised in the service of your country, so highly entitle you.

Sarah Emma Levey, sole proprietor of the Sydney Theatre, and widow of the late Barnett Levey, first proprietor thereof.

John Lazar, manager, and on behalf of the performers of the Sydney Theatre.

W. Deane and G. Sippe, for the orchestra of the Sydney Theatre.

Joseph Simmons, late manager and part lessee of the theatre.

To this address and its accompanying letter Mrs. Levey received the following reply from the Governor's private secretary, dated at Government House 3 December 1837.

I have the honour to acknowledge the receipt of a letter, enclosing a copy of an Address and requesting to know when it would be convenient to His Excellency the Governor to receive a deputation to present the same, from those connected with the Drama in this country.

Having submitted both the letter and the Address to His

Excellency, he has directed me to say in reply to the former, that he regrets not being able to name a time for the reception of the deputation, as every spare moment between the present and his departure is already engaged. In reply to the latter, His Excellency takes this opportunity of saying, through me, how gratified he feels for the extremely gratifying Address which you have been good enough to forward to him, coupled as it is with some highly flattering allusions to the part which he has taken in forwarding the interests of the Drama.

His Excellency moreover is sensible of the many and important benefits which have accrued to the community at large, from the introduction of Dramatic exhibitions, and directs me, in conclusion, to express his conviction, that regarding the hands into which the dramatic representations have now fallen, he has no doubt that they will continue to increase in interest, and in the moral effect which, when well regulated, they are calculated to exercise upon society. I have the honour to be, Gentlemen, your most obedient humble servant, H.F. Gisborne, private secretary.

All this was printed in the *Sydney Times,* together with a report that the address was subsequently presented to the Governor by Mrs. Levey and her father, Mr. Josephson, "and received with that gratifying urbanity for which His Excellency was remarkable".

That the Governor should not only receive an address from the players but, in the face of everything the newspapers had said to the contrary, should also express a favourable opinion about "the hands into which the dramatic representations have now fallen" outraged the Sydney newspaper proprietors. The "effrontery" of this address and the publication by one of their number of all the details appertaining to it brought an immediate newspaper storm about the heads of the grateful theatricals. The shopkeeper-sheepfarmer "aristocracy", the civil servants, the army, the moralists, and the churchmen were aghast, and the newspapers faithfully echoed their snorts of disgust. The *Gazette* was amazed, pained, shocked, even wounded by the impertinence of the players in presenting such an address.

Of what possible value, for instance, in the eyes of the poorest inhabitants of Britain, can a certificate of character be, of a description such as that furnished to Sir Richard Bourke by the graceless "unwashed" rabble who had the impudence to designate themselves his *friends*?

this newspaper asked. The *Herald* said it had *heard* that the players had attempted to intrude upon the Governor and *"insult* him by presenting him with an 'Address'". So horrified did the *Herald* profess to be that it refused to believe the events related had taken place. For the sake of the reputation of Sir Richard it hoped that the letter from his secretary signed "H.F. Gisborne" was a forgery. "Notwithstanding all our opposition to much of the administration of Sir Richard Bourke, we would be glad indeed had he been spared the insult of an Address from the Sydney players", the *Herald* article concluded, giving away in its final sentence the sham behind its talk of hearsay and forgery. It was a little late to be playing the sanctimonious ostrich, for the players had had their little hour; they had thanked the man who had given his permission for a theatre to be established, and no one could take that from them.

By January 1838 the Royal was continuing on its usual way, with unpunctual starts being punished by the audience with hisses and groans on the eventual rise of the curtain, and with the "regulars" among the actors doing their best, or worst, to discourage newcomers to stage fame. The imminent opening of the new theatre, which was at first also to have been called the Theatre Royal, but was ultimately called the Royal Victoria, was a source of constant concern to Mrs. Levey and the players, but perhaps most of all to Mrs. Levey. She knew that once it opened Wyatt would be able to take his pick of her actors, for they would desert without compunction if given the chance. Among the players themselves the new theatre was already a source of heartburning and envy, for they knew that once it opened there would be room for only a few, not all, and without exception they all believed they should be among the chosen.

Wyatt finally announced that his theatre would open on 26 March 1838 with a performance of *Othello,* a Mr. Arabin from Hobart to play the name part. Now the "execution" date had been announced there was the utmost confusion of gossip and recrimination in the Royal company. There was a new story every minute of the day about how this member of the Royal had been chosen by Wyatt for the Victoria, and this one had been ignored. There was not, and everyone knew it, room for two theatres in Sydney. The newest and most palatial would attract the crowd as surely as light attracts the moth. Obviously guided by Josephson and Simmons, Mrs. Levey guarded as well as she could against wholesale desertion by her actors. Quite early in the year she had a clause put in their contracts that they were to forfeit twenty pounds if they left her within a specified period without her consent. There was also a clause making her responsible in the sum of ten pounds if the actors were dismissed without cause.

Nor was the anxiety all on one side. Wyatt felt sure his theatre would affect attendances at the Royal once the two theatres were operating, but there was no certainty about this. Suppose that for some reason the public, notoriously fickle, crowded his theatre for its opening week, and deserted it from then on for the familiar Royal? Such a thing was not impossible, for the Royal had been established about six years and had a fairly consistent following. The threat did exist, and Wyatt had to do something about it. He went to see a far from confident Mrs. Levey who nevertheless (possibly on advice) had done nothing to meet the threat of competition. Between them all a lease was drawn up in Wyatt's favour which effectively closed the Theatre Royal.

One newspaper found that the "whole proceedings had been marked with the foulest duplicity". Not only had Mrs. Levey rid herself of an almost certain liability at a pleasant profit, she had also managed to do so just before her actors were due to receive their benefits. The *Gazette* calculated that despite the apathy Mrs. Levey invariably showed towards conducting the theatre properly, for the season which ended with the lease to

Wyatt she had made a profit of at least £400. But with all their strictures, not one of the critics bothered to suggest what else she could do, or what they would have done in her situation.

Wyatt now had no competition, but, as he was to find, the threat of it still remained.

Among the company which opened the Victoria were the following "regulars" from the Theatre Royal: Morton, Lane, Smith, Spencer, Simes, Grove, Harvey, Collins, Miss Winstanley, Mrs. Grove, and Mrs. Simes. By the end of March it was noted that Meredith, Simmons, Buckingham, Lee, Winters, Mrs. Taylor, Mrs. Meredith, Mrs. Larra, and Mrs. Downes were still theatrically unemployed. These were the troublemakers, and so they had possibly been "overlooked" by Wyatt on purpose. But they were also the pick of Sydney's acting talent, and he was not able to ignore them for long.

For a few months there were desultory attempts by various individuals to obtain use of the empty Theatre Royal and open it again, which for Wyatt meant the threat to his Victoria Theatre still existed, and would become real once his lease expired. Either because he felt he had to (as the only way of controlling its future use) or because he could not get a renewal of his lease, towards the end of October 1838 Wyatt bought the George Street property — the Royal Hotel and the Theatre Royal — for £9,500. But if he congratulated himself on this deal he was not allowed much time to indulge his feelings. He was soon to find himself no better served by the actors, the public, or the press than Barnett Levey had been. He had a new building, but theatrically he had no more than Barnett Levey's theatre transferred to his. Wyatt's was a larger and more commodious building, but it was the "toy" of a man who had no real theatrical knowledge or experience. After each of the first three seasons it was found that radical constructional changes were necessary backstage and in the auditorium to make the theatre a workable "machine". And for its first five years at least, if not for longer, the Victoria was the scene of many of the excesses and shortcomings for years said by the newspapers to be solely due to Levey's mismanagement of his Theatre Royal. Not until the Victoria had, with the Colony itself, passed the difficult period of change from Georgian adolescence to early Victorian young manhood was it able to settle down to its remaining thirty-odd years as Sydney's oldest if not always leading theatre.

Under Wyatt's ownership the Theatre Royal fell into disuse. Although, at one stage, it was suggested that it should be used by the Roman Catholics (who were looking for a building suitable for use as a chapel), nothing came of this idea. Various people also tried to lease the building for theatrical use, but without success. Like the Theatre Royal at Richmond in England, it was used for some time as a storehouse and repository for all kinds of unwanted furniture and fittings from the Royal Hotel and other buildings. Unlike the Richmond Theatre Royal, it was never reopened. On 18 March 1840 a drunken stablehand upset a candle in the hayloft at the Royal Hotel, and in the course of only a couple of hours everything for which Levey had worked, suffered, and finally killed himself was reduced to ashes and rubble.

18

Epilogue

Neither time nor the historians have dealt kindly with Barnett Levey and his theatre. Brewer was fair enough, but, writing in 1892 as he was, his facts rather than his intentions were at fault. The same could be said for W. J. Lawrence, who, in his life of G.V. Brooke, made the unsupported claim that Brooke had been "mainly instrumental in the production for the first time in the colonies of a third of the Master's (Shakespeare's) works". Subsequent writers, with the rich store of material in the Mitchell Library in Sydney to draw upon, have largely been content to shirk the necessary research in favour of repeating or elaborating on the mistakes of these and other early writers. It has also been the fashion to denigrate Levey's as a "convict" theatre, and therefore unworthy of notice: this by writers who do not know and make no attempt to find out what the theatre was and what it did. As recently as 1965 there appeared a book called *Coppin the Great: The Father of the Australian Theatre*. The subject, George Coppin, an English low comedian from the provincial theatres, arrived in Australia in 1843. The author of this book does not explain how he is able to present Coppin as fathering something which was in existence ten years before Coppin's arrival in Australia.

Not surprisingly, in *Coppin the Great* neither Levey nor his theatre is mentioned by name. To mention Levey, of course, would be to produce two fathers for one and the same child. But the commissions in this book are every bit as surprising as its omissions. The introduction tells the reader: "It is true enough that it was he (i.e. Coppin) who really established Shakespeare as an integral part of Australian theatre." Barnett Levey's company presented first performances of nine Shakespeare plays at the Theatre Royal. When the company moved over to the Victoria Theatre they presented, up to the end of 1843, a further five performances of Shakespeare's plays, so that in a ten-year period a total of fourteen different Shakespearean plays were given their first Sydney performances, with repeat performances of all of them throughout these years. Coppin himself never touched Shakespeare. The highest he ever reached in the dramatic canon was the part of Sir Peter Teazle in *The School for Scandal* which, as a low comedian, he quite misinterpreted. G.V. Brooke did produce a number of Shakespeare's plays in Sydney and Melbourne, but they had all been done before him, by Sydney's original players and by the many American actors who visited Sydney and Melbourne in the early fifties.

Levey's Theatre Royal, as a reference to the Appendix to this book will show, presented an amazingly wide variety of plays during its short life. Here were seen first Australian performances of Shakespeare, early eighteenth and nineteenth century "classics", operas, semi-operas (plays with songs and music), and early nineteenth century melodramas. Most of the performances of Shakespeare's plays earned well merited applause from their audiences and literally columns of comment in the newspapers.

Turning to opera, it is found that in 1833 alone the Theatre Royal produced at least seven operas or semi-operas, all reported by the newspapers with the usual mixture of praise and blame, with an occasional singer, such as Grove, being singled out for adverse comment. Of a song sung by this singer it was said: "To countenance such a departure from musical propriety as is displayed in this gentleman's view and style of singing, is to encourage vicious taste, extremely offensive to a judicious ear, and tending to depress the value of real talent." In 1835 the

Theatre Royal presented one of the first and most successful of the semi-operas written by Isaac Nathan. This was *The Illustrious Stranger; or, Married and Buried. The Illustrious Stranger,* and another semi-opera, *Sweethearts and Wives,* received several performances. *Sweethearts and Wives,* first performed at London's Haymarket Theatre on 7 July 1823, with music by Whitaker, Isaac Nathan, T. Cooke, and Perry, was first given at the Victoria Theatre in Sydney on 23 December 1844, and was still "on the boards" at that theatre in 1854. *The Illustrious Stranger* was given at a benefit performance for Nathan in 1847, and for a benefit for the ageing Joseph Simmons in 1879, in which he played again the part he made famous in 1835, Benjamin Bowbell.

On 26 December 1836 the Royal presented *Oberon; or, The Charmed Horn.* This was obviously a pale shadow of Weber's *Oberon* of 1826, with the music "composed and arranged by Mr. Sippe", a former army bandmaster who stayed on in Sydney after completing his military service. He was at various times during the theatre's life conductor of the Theatre Royal orchestra. The *Gazette* was caustic in its remarks on this production, although it proved popular enough with the public to run to five well-supported performances. Each of the main characters and his or her faults was mentioned, culminating with Mr. Collins, who, as Prince Badekan, "reminded us of a huge crayfish dressed up in a white furbelowed dimitty petticoat". The music was described as "a dead failure; a barrel organ, or a hurdy gurdy for us in preference".

With the opening of the Victoria and, in the early 1840's, the arrival of such singers as John and Frank Howson and Mrs. Guerin (later to become the mother of the popular Australian actress and singer, Nellie Stewart) more ambitious operas were given their first Australian performance, including *The Barber of Seville, La Sonnambula, La Cenerentola, Der Freischutz, The Bohemian Girl,* and, only eleven months after its London première, *The Night Dancers,* an operatic version of the ballet *Giselle.* John and Frank Howson were brothers of the mezzo-soprano Emma

Albertazzi, who was largely responsible for the London success of this opera.

As already noted, the Victoria Theatre was opened as a direct competitor to Levey's theatre. In time, it too had its competitors. Just as Wyatt had felt he could conduct a theatre better than Levey had conducted his, so there were people who believed they could do better than Wyatt, or who wished to break what they considered to be the Victoria's monopoly. In 1841 a Signor Della Case presented a series of gymnastic entertainments at the Victoria Theatre. His reception was so good that he formed the idea of opening his own theatre. This was opened in Hunter Street on 26 January 1842, and closed in September the same year.

The Royal Victoria's next competitor, the Royal City Theatre, was built in Market Street by Barnett Levey's former partner, the popular actor Joseph Simmons, and opened on 20 May 1843. This was a beautifully appointed "perfect little bandbox of a theatre", but it was never a financial success. The larger dramas of the period could not be performed there because of the smallness of the stage and its restricted facilities, and this theatre had a history of intermittent performances before it was finally turned into a furniture warehouse in 1850. In the same year the Royal Australian Equestrian Circus was opened at the rear of the Adelphi Hotel in York Street, and on 19 September 1851 Noble's Olympic Circus was opened at the rear of the Painter's Arms Hotel in Castlereagh Street. It was not long before the novelty of circus and equestrian performances palled on the public, and both establishments had to turn to the drama. Noble's had the shorter life of the two. It was used intermittently for circus and equestrian performances, then for a brief period in 1854 dramatic performances were given, the building being renamed the Royal Albert Theatre. It was not a success, and closed that year.

The Royal Australian Equestrian Circus was a different matter. Early in 1851 it was renamed Malcom's Royal Australian Amphitheatre, and on 23 August that year it was reopened with a stage, dramatic and equestrian performances being given. The stage was enlarged for the opening of a new season on 5 November 1852. In 1854 the theatre was taken over by the American actor Charles R. Thorne, and renamed the Royal Lyceum. On 14 July 1856 it was reopened as Our Lyceum Theatre with a season by the Shakespearian actor, Gustavus Vaughan Brooke. It subsequently had a career up to the 1880's as the Queen's Theatre.

Meantime, in 1854 Joseph Wyatt lost the lease on the land on which his Royal Victoria Theatre stood. He sold the Victoria and built a new theatre, the Prince of Wales, in Castlereagh Street (on the site occupied today by the Theatre Royal), which was opened on 12 March 1855 with the American actors D. Wilmarth Waller and his wife, Emma, as the principal attractions. The Prince of Wales was destroyed by fire in 1860, rebuilt in 1863, destroyed by fire again in 1872, and rebuilt and reopened as the Theatre Royal in 1875. This, with many modifications over the years, is the theatre which occupies the site today.

That the standard of acting in these early Sydney theatres was far from negligible is attested by evidence left behind by overseas actors who had them in support in Sydney and Melbourne. In some instances it was as high as, and in others higher than, the actors they supported, and in almost all instances the pay the local players received was better than that received by their equivalents in England. As late as 1853 George Coppin wrote from Australia to an actor friend in England:

> This country would be a good place for anyone to come to that is in the position I was in at home receiving about thirty shillings per week in the country. They would get from £4 to £5 a week here with good benefits (living is double) but it is *no place* for anyone that is in the receipt of £4 or £5 in England. There is no room to Star it, and none of the managers will give more than £6 per week here.

In the remaining years of this decade Coppin was to be proved hopelessly wrong in the matter of payment and "starring it".

None of the early actors equalled Eliza Winstanley's overseas success, but they did play an important part in the establishment of the Australian theatre. The only other member to leave Australia was Mrs. Taylor who, no longer as successful in Sydney as she had been, in 1840 followed Mrs. Chester to India (possibly at her suggestion). The fun-loving, talented, unpredictable Mrs. Taylor died there the following year.

George Buckingham, the first actor to walk on to the Sydney stage at the opening of Barnett Levey's theatre in 1832, was also the first member of Levey's company to give theatrical performances in Melbourne and Adelaide. He also formed what must have been the first touring theatrical company in Australia — with his own family of wife and four children, presenting a program of songs, recitations, and instrumental solos. Occasionally, on his inland tours, he added one or two actors to his troupe, and plays were presented. As late as 1859 the Buckingham Family, as they were billed, were performing at such inland towns as Wagga Wagga in New South Wales and also in towns in Victoria.

Simmons, Meredith, Lazar, Grove, Simes — all are long-lived names in the annals of the early Autralian theatre. They set the foundations and the style which was to be followed right up to the middle of the 1850's.

With the discovery of gold at this period in Australia's history a sudden fillip was given to theatrical life. Not only did diggers come to Australia from all over the world in search of gold (and entertainment), but American actors who had been entertaining the diggers on the Californian goldfields also came in search of theatrical gold — and proved more successful in their search than most of the diggers.

Mr. and Mrs. James Stark, who arrived in June 1853, were the first of these American visitors to take Sydney by storm. Their financial success may have been equalled by those who followed them, but it was never bettered. The Starks presented a repertoire of six plays by Shakespeare and the usual round of melodramas such as *The Lady of Lyons, Richelieu, The Corsican Brothers, Ingomar,* and many others. Next came, in 1854, Emma and D. Wilmarth Waller, he American, she English. They had both played at Sadler's Wells in London before setting out for Australia. They had a season of only thirteen days in Sydney, then moved on to Melbourne and Tasmania. They were brought back to Sydney in March 1855 to open the new Prince of Wales Theatre, and stayed there until May. After another visit to Melbourne and Tasmania they returned to Sydney's Victoria Theatre for a season of about two months. Their Australian repertoire included six of Shakespeare's plays and the usual melodramas. The Wallers also gave the first Australian performance of Webster's *The Duchess of Malfi,* in a version prepared some years earlier for Sadler's Wells Theatre by R. Hengist ("Orion") Horne, who at this time (1855) was living in Melbourne.

Soon after the Wallers left Sydney at the conclusion of their first season in 1854 they were followed by Laura Keene and Edwin Booth, she English and he American. Both were to become famous in American theatrical history, Booth as the leading Hamlet of the late nineteenth century. These two clever but temperamental actors gave a brief season of about a fortnight in which they presented four of Shakespeare's plays and a number of melodramas.

Towards the end of 1854 Charles Thorne arrived with his company and, as already described, opened the Royal Lyceum Theatre. In 1856 the Starks paid a return visit to Australia, with a repertoire of six of Shakespeare's plays and many melodramas, including (first Australian performance) *Camille.* Subsequent American actors to prove successful in Sydney were Marie Duret, Mrs. C.N. Sinclair (the former Mrs. Edwin Forrest), Charles Kemble Mason, Joey and Adelaide Gougenheim, and McKean Buchanan. The Starks' second season was not a success. They were of the old, ranting, "tear a passion to tatters" school of acting, and in the brief period between their first and last Australian seasons audiences had seen, in the performances of the Wallers, Laura Keene and Edwin Booth, the Gougenheims and others, the newer, quieter form of acting, which placed a new emphasis on teamwork, settings, costumes, and unity of production. The theatre in Australia was beginning to grow up.

APPENDIX

List of Plays, Pantomimes, and Ballets Performed at Barnett Levey's Theatre Royal, Sydney 1832–38.

The dates in this list are of first performances only; most of the plays were given many repeat performances. The manuscript work by an unknown hand, "Plays in Sydney", in the Mitchell Library, though incomplete and sometimes incorrect, has been of assistance in the compilation of this list. For basic information and background on the plays of the period Professor Allardyce Nicoll's standard work, *A History of English Drama 1660–1900,* has been the main guide.

The following plan has been adopted in listing the plays: First, title and author; next, in brackets, the London or other theatre at which it was first performed, and date, followed by the date of the first performance at Sydney's Theatre Royal. Abbreviations of London theatre names used are: A. Adelphi; B. Brunswick; C. City; Co. Coburg; C.G. Covent Garden; D.G. Dorset Garden; D.L. Drury Lane; E.O.H. English Opera House; G. Goodman's Fields; Ga. Garrick; H. Haymarket; L. Lincoln's Inn Fields; Ly. Lyceum; O. Olympic; Q. Queen's; R. Royalty; R.A. Royal Amphitheatre; R.C. Royal Circus; R.P. Royal Pavilion; St. Strand; S.W. Sadler's Wells; S.P. Sans Pareil; S. Surrey; V. Victoria (former Coburg); W.L. New Royal West London.

Angelo; or, The Tyrant of Padua, by F.F. Cooper (V. 1835), 13.3.1837.
Abu Hassan; or, The Living Dead, by W. Dimond (D.L. 1825), 16.10. 1835.

The Actress of All Work; or, My Country Cousin, by W.H. Oxberry (O. 1819), 12.10.1837.

The Adopted Child, by S. Birch (D.L. 1795), 11.6.1833.

Agnes de Vere; or, The Broken Heart, by J.B. Buckstone, (A. 1834), 15.5.1837.

Aladdin; or, The Wonderful Lamp, by Soane (D.L. 1826), 26.12.1837.

Ali Baba; or, The Forty Thieves, by G. Colman the Younger (D.L. 1806), 19.10.1835.

All at Coventry; or, Love and Laugh, by W.T. Moncrieff (O. 1816), 6.2.1837.

All Hallows' Even; or, The Brownie of the Brig (author unknown), (Co. 1831), 23.10.1837.

All the World's a Stage, by I. Jackman (D.L. 1777), 23.1.1834.

Alonzo the Brave, by H.M. Milner (Co. 1826), 26.8.1835.

Amateurs and Actors, by R.B. Peake (E.O.H. 1818), 29.10.1834.

Ambrose Gwinett; or, A Sea-Side Story, by D.W. Jerrold (Co. 1828), 9.5.1836.

Animal Magnetism, by Elizabeth Inchbald (C.G. 1788), 21.3.1835.

The Apprentice, by A. Murphy (D.L. 1756), 8.10.1834.

Bampfylde Moore Carew, by D.W. Jerrold (S. 1824), 21.4.1836.

The Banks of the Hudson; or, The Congress Trooper, by T.J. Dibdin (Co. 1829), 5.6.1837.

The Bear Hunters; or, The Fatal Ravine, by J.B. Buckstone (C. 1825), 16.10.1837.

Benjamin Bowbell (see *The Illustrious Stranger*).

Billy Taylor; or, The Gay Young Fellow, by J.B. Buckstone (A. 1829), 23.11.1837.

Black Ey'd Susan; or, All in the Downs, by D.W. Jerrold (S. 1829), 26.12.1832.

The Blind Boy, by J. Kenney (C.G. 1807), 2.7.1834.

Blue Beard; or, Female Curiosity, by G. Colman the Younger (D.L. 1798), 25.8.1836.

A Bold Stroke for a Wife, by Mrs. S. Centlivre (L. 1717), 7.3.1836.

Bombastes Furioso, by W.B. Rhodes (H. 1810), 20.3.1833.

The Brave Irishman; or, Captain O'Blunder, by T. Sheridan (G. 1746), 21.10.1836.

The Bride of Ludgate, by D.W. Jerrold (D.L. 1831), 20.11.1837.

The Brigand, by J.R. Planche (D.L. 1829), 12.6.1834.

The Captain Is Not A-Miss, by T. Egerton (E.O.H. 1836), 25.9.1837.

Captain Stevens, by C. Selby (C. 1832), 3.6.1837.

The Castle of Andalusia, by J. O'Keefe (C.G. 1782), 19.10.1837.

The Castle Spectre, by M.G. Lewis (D.L. 1797), 16.2.1833.

Catherine and Petruchio, by D. Garrick (D.L. 1756), 22.2. 1834.

Catching an Heiress, by C. Selby (Q. 1835), 4.9.1837.

The Cedar Chest; or, The Lord Mayor's Daughter, by G. Almar (S.W. 1834), 3.8.1835.

The Chain of Guilt; or The Inn on the Heath, by T.P. Taylor (S.W. 1836), 28.8.1837.

The Charcoal Burner; or, The Dropping Well of Knaresborough, by G. Almar (S. 1832), 5.3.1838.

Charles the Second; or, The Merry Monarch, by J.H. Payne (C.G. 1824), 19.1.1833.

Charles XII; or, The Siege of Stralsund, by J.R. Planche (D.L. 1828), 4.9.1837.

The Chelsea and Greenwich Pensioners, by C. Dibdin (C.G. 1779), 6.4.1837.

Cherry Bounce, by R.J. Raymond (S.W. 1821), 25.2.1837.

The Child of Nature, by Mrs. E. Inchbald (C.G. 1788), 6.7.1833.

The Children in the Wood, by T. Morton (H. 1793), 5.12.1833.

The Tragedy of Chrononhotonthologos, by H. Carey (H. 1734), 10.10. 1833.

Cinderella; or, The Fairy and the Little Glass Slipper (ballet), 12.10.1837.

The Citizen, by A. Murphy (D.L. 1761), 20.10.1834.

Clari; or, The Maid of Milan, by J.H. Payne, music by H. Bishop (C.G. 1823), 31.10.1834.

Crossing the Line; or, The Boat Builders of Brugen, by G. Almar (S.W. 1833), 27.7.1837.

A Cure for the Heart-Ache, by T.Morton (C.G. 1797), 5.10.1835.

Darkness Visible, by T. Hook (H. 1811), 27.5.1833.

The Day after the Fair; or, The Roadside Cottage, by C.A. Somerset (O. 1829), 11.4.1836.

The Day after the Wedding; or, A Wife's First Lesson, by Marie-Therese Kemble (C.G. 1808), 6.2.1836.

A Dead Shot, by J.B. Buckstone (A. 1827), 6.6.1835.

Deaf and Dumb; or, The Orphan Protected, by T. Holcroft (D.L. 1801), 28.3.1835.

The Demon; or, The Magic Rose (pantomime), 22.10.1834.

Demon's Dice (probably J. Oxenford's *The Dice of Death,* E.O.H. 1835), 9.1.1837.

The Devil's Ducat; or, the Gift of Mammon, by D.W. Jerrold (A. 1830), 22.9.1834.

The Devil's Elixir; or, The Shadowless Man, by E. Fitzball (C.G. 1829), 4.4.1836.

The Devil to Pay; or, The Wives Metamorphosed, by C. Coffey (D.L. 1731), 20.4.1833.

The Dog of Montargis; or, The Forest of Bondy, by W. Barrymore (C.G. 1814), 20.2.1837.

Don Juan; or, The Libertine Destroyed (ballet), 21.8.1837.

Douglas, by the Rev. J. Home (Edinburgh 1756), 23.10.1834.

The Dream at Sea, by J.B. Buckstone (A. 1835), 8.5.1837.

The Duel; or, My Two Nephews, by R.B. Peake (C.G. 1823), 4.5.1835.

The Dumb Maid of Genoa (see *The Maid of Genoa*).

The Early Days of Richard III (see *The Peerless Pool*).

Edda; or, The Hermit of Warkworth, by E. Fitzball (S. 1820), 25.6.1834.

Eily O'Connor; or The Foster Brother, by J.T. Haines (C. 1831), 2.11.1837.

The Elbow Shakers; or, Thirty Years of a Rattler's Life, by F.F. Cooper (A. 1827), 10.1.1835.

Ella Rosenberg, by J. Kenny (D.L. 1807), 24.3.1834.

Ellen Wareham, by J.B. Buckstone (H. 1833), 22.6.1837.

Elshie the Wizard of the Moor (see *The Wizard of the Moor*).

Eugene Aram; or, St. Robert's Cave, by W.T. Moncrieff (S. 1832), 5.12.1836.

Everybody's Husband, by R. Ryan (Q. 1831), 6.6.1836.

The Evil Eye, by R.B. Peake (A. 1831), 14.9.1837.

Exchange No Robbery; or, The Diamond Ring, by T.E. Hook (H. 1820), 1.1.1834.

The Exile; or, The Deserts of Siberia, by F.R. Reynolds (C.G. 1808), 2.5.1836.

Fair Rosamond, by J.S. Faucit (W.L. 1821), 21.9.1837.

The Falls of Clyde, by G. Soane (D.L. 1817), 20.7.1835.

The Farmer's Story, by W.B. Bernard (E.O.H. 1836), 30.10.1837.

The Farmer's Wife, by C.I.M. Dibdin (C.G. 1814), 12.6.1837.

Father and Son; or, The Rock of La Charbonnière, by E. Fitzball

(C.G. 1825), 8.2.1836.

The Fire Raiser; or, The Haunted Tower, by G. Almar (S. 1831), 14.11.1836.

Fire and Water; or, A Critical Hour, by S. Beazley, Jnr. (E.O.H. 1817), 11.1.1838.

The First of April, by Caroline Boaden (H. 1830), 24.3.1836.

The First Floor, by J. Cobb (D.L. 1787), 9.11.1833.

The First Night; or, My Own Ghost, by T. Parry (A. 1834), 28.8.1837.

The Floating Beacon; or The Norwegian Wreckers, by E. Fitzball (S. 1824), 20.8.1835.

The Flying Dutchman; or, The Phantom Ship, by E. Fitzball (A. 1827), 14.9.1835.

Fortune's Frolic, by J.T. Allingham (C.G. 1799), 31.12.1832.

The Forty Thieves, by G. Colman the Younger (D.L. 1806), 21.9.1837.

The Foundling of the Forest, by W. Dimond (H. 1809), 6.8.1834.

The Gambler's Fate (see *The Hut of the Red Mountains*).

The Gamester, by E. Moore (D.L. 1753), 18.1.1836.

George Barnwell (see *The London Merchant*).

Gilderoy; or, The Bonny Boy, by W. Barrymore (Co. 1822), 1.8.1836.

Giovanni in London; or, The Libertine Reclaimed, by W.T. Moncrieff (O. 1817), 4.9.1834.

The Golden Axe; or, Harlequin and the Fairy Lake, by W. Barrymore (D.L. 1823), 8.10.1834.

The Green-Eyed Monster, by J.R. Planche (H. 1828), 8.10.1835.

Gustavus III; or, The Masked Ball, by J.R. Planche (C.G. 1833), 29.1.1838.

Gustavus Vasa; or, The Hero of the North, by W. Dimond (D.L. 1803), 4.4.1835.

Guy Fawkes; or, The Gunpowder Treason, by G. Macfarren (Co. 1822), 29.10.1834.

Guy Mannering; or, The Gipsy's Prophecy, by D. Terry (C.G. 1816), 25.9.1834.

Hamlet (Shakespeare), 18.8.1834.

Harlequin and Cinderella (pantomime, author unknown), 26.12.1834.

Harlequin Sailor (pantomime, author unknown), 26.12.1833.

The Haunted Inn, by R.B. Peake (D.L. 1828), 10.12.1835.

The Heart of Midlothian; or, The Lily of St. Leonard's, by T.J. Dibdin (R.C. 1819), 11.5.1835.

The Heir at Law, by G. Colman the Younger (H. 1797), 9.2.1833.
The Heiress of Bruges, by C. Selby (Co. 1834), 10.7.1837.
Henry IV Part 1 (Shakespeare), 14.4.1836.
Henry VIII (Shakespeare), 7.1.1836.
The Highland Reel, by J. O'Keefe (C.G. 1788), 18.4.1836.
High Life below Stairs, by the Rev. J. Townley (D.L. 1759), 14.10.1833.
Highways and Byways, by B.N. Webster (D.L. 1831), 21.9.1835.
Hit or Miss!, by I. Pocock (H. 1808), 26.12.1837.
Hofer; or, The Tell of the Tyrol, by J.R. Planche (D.L. 1830), 18.7.1836.
The Honest Thieves, by T. Knight (C.G. 1797), 27.4.1833.
The Honey Moon, by J. Tobin (D.L. 1805), 15.5.1833.
Humphrey Clinker, by J.T. Dibdin (R.C. 1818), 11.8.1835.
A Hundred-Pound Note, by R.B. Peake (C.G. 1827), 9.1.1837.
Hunting a Turtle, by C. Selby (Q. 1835), 20.11.1837.
A Husband at Sight, by J.B. Buckstone (H. 1830), 18.4.1836.
The Hut of the Red Mountains; or, Thirty Years of a Gambler's Life, by H.M. Milner (Co. 1827), 17.2.1834.
The Hypocrite, by I. Bickerstaffe (D.L. 1768), 26.10.1835.
The Idiot Witness; or, A Tale of Blood, by J.T. Haines (Co. 1823), 17.3.1836.
The Illustrious Stranger; or, Married and Buried, by J. Kenny (D.L. 1827), 28.5.1835.
The Inchcape Bell; or, The Dumb Sailor Boy, by E. Fitzball (S. 1828), 12.10.1835.
The Indian Maid (ballet), 9.2.1835.
The Infernal Secret; or, The Invulnerable, by J.H. Amherst (S. 1822), 17.4.1837.
The Innkeeper of Abbeville; or, The Ostler and the Robber, by E. Fitzball (S. 1822), 25.1.1834.
Inkle and Yarico, by G. Colman the Younger (H. 1787), 22.5.1833.
The Intrigue; or, The Road to Bath, by J. Poole (D.L. 1814), 14.5.1835.
The Invincibles, by T. Morton (C.G. 1828), 27.11.1837.
The Irishman in London; or, The Happy African, by W. Macready (C.G. 1792), 5.10.1833.
The Irish Tutor; or, New Lights, by R. Butler (C.G. 1822), 27.10.1834.
The Iron Chest, by G. Colman the Younger (D.L. 1796), 30.1.1837.
Isabelle; or, Woman's Life, by J.B. Buckstone (A. 1834), 6.6.1836.
Is He Jealous?, by S. Beazley, Junior (E.O.H. 1816), 31.10.1836.

Is She a Woman?, by W. Collier (Q. 1835), 27.11.1837.

Ivanhoe; or, The Knight Templar, by S. Beazley, Junior (C.G. 1820), 30.4.1836.

Jane Shore, by N. Rowe (D.L. 1714), 4.5.1835.

Jessie, the Flower of Dumblane; or, "Weel May the Keel Row", by Capt. H.R. Addison (A. 1833), 9.10.1837.

The Jew and the Doctor, by T.J. Dibdin (C.G. 1798), 15.12.1836.

The Jew of Lubeck; or, The Heart of a Father, by H.M. Milner (D.L. 1819), 27.2.1834.

The Jewess; or, The Council of Constance, by W.T. Moncrieff, (V. 1835), 4.12.1837.

Joan of Arc, Maid of Orleans (author unknown), (Co. 1826), 20.10.1834.

John Bull; or, An Englishman's Fireside, by G. Colman the Younger (C.G. 1803), 9.3.1833.

Jonathan Bradford; or, The Murder at the Roadside Inn, by E. Fitzball (S. 1833), 26.12.1834.

John of Paris, by I. Pocock (C.G. 1814), 21.9.1835.

Killing No Murder, by T.E. Hook (H. 1809), 12.12.1836.

The King of the Beggars (see *Bampfylde Moore Carew*).

King Lear (Shakespeare), 23.1.1837.

The Knights of St. John; or, The Fire Banner, by G. Almar (S.W. 1833), 3.7.1837.

The Lady and the Devil, by W. Dimond (D.L. 1820), 19.2.1838.

The Lancers, by J.H. Payne (D.L. 1827), 26.2.1835.

The Lear of Private Life; or, Father and Daughter, by W.T. Moncrieff (Co. 1820), 21.11.1835.

The Liar, by S. Foote (C.G. 1762), 25.3.1835.

Lyieushee Lovel; or, The Gipsy of Ashburnham Dell, by A.L. Campbell (S.W. 1828), 25.3.1837.

Lodoiska, by T.J. Dibdin (S. 1811), 18.9.1834.

The London Merchant; or, The Tragedy of George Barnwell, by G. Lillo (D.L. 1731), 28.12.1833.

The Lord of the Manor, by C.I.M. Dibdin (C.G. 1812), 19.6.1833.

The Lottery Ticket; or, The Lawyer's Clerk, by S. Beazley, Junior (D.L. 1826), 29.12.1836.

Love in a Village, by I. Bickerstaffe (C.G. 1762), 22.2.1836.

Love in Humble Life, by J.H. Payne (D.L. 1822), 16.10.1837.

Love, Law and Physic, by J. Kenney (C.G. 1812), 13.4.1833.

Lover's Quarrels; or, Like Master Like Man (author unknown, but adapted from J. Vanbrugh's *The Mistake,* 1705), (C.G. 1790), 23.2.1833.

Lover's Vows, by Mrs. Elizabeth Inchbald (C.G. 1798), 31.10.1836.

Luke the Labourer; or, The Lost Son, by J.B. Buckstone (A. 1826), 6.3.1834.

The Lying Valet, by D. Garrick (G. 1741), 25.11.1833.

Macbeth (Shakespeare), 7.9.1835.

The Maid and the Magpie; or, Which Is the Thief?, by S.J. Arnold (Ly. 1815), 11.4.1836.

The Maid of Genoa; or, The Bandit Merchant, by J. Farrell (Co. 1820), 8.10.1835.

Maid or Wife; or, The Deceiver Deceived, by B. Livius (D.L. 1821), 21.7.1836.

Management; or, The Prompter Puzzled, by J. Lunn (H. 1828), 4.10.1834.

The Man and the Marquis; or, The Three Spectres of the Castle of St. Valori, by T. J. Dibdin (S.W. 1825), 5.12.1836.

The Marriage of Figaro, by T. Holcroft (C.G. 1819), 11.5.1833.

Married and Buried (see *The Illustrious Stranger*).

The Married Bachelor; or, Master and Man, by P.P. O'Callaghan (A. 1821), 6.10.1834.

Married Life, by J.B. Buckstone (H. 1834), 22.1.1838.

The Married Rake, by C. Selby (Q. 1835), 19.6.1837.

Massaroni (see *The Brigand*).

The Master's Rival; or, A Day at Boulogne, by R.B. Peake (D.L. 1829), 2.10.1834.

Maurice the Woodcutter; or, The Prince and the Peasant, by C.A. Somerset (S.W. 1835), 26.2.1838.

The May Queen, by J.B. Buckstone (A. 1828), 11.6.1836.

The Mayor of Garret, by S. Foote (H. 1763), 26.1.1833.

Melmoth the Wanderer, and Walburg the Victim, by B. West (Co. 1823), 12.2.1838.

The Merchant of Venice (Shakespeare), 17.9.1835.

The Midnight Hour; or, War of Wits, by Mrs. Elizabeth Inchbald, (C.G. 1787), 21.11.1833.

The Miller and His Men, by I. Pocock (C.G. 1813), 5.10.1833.

The Miller's Maid, by J.S. Faucit (E.O.H. 1821), 4.6.1833.

Mischief Making, by J.S. Buckstone (S. 1828), 18.6.1835.

The Miser, by H. Fielding (D.L. 1732), 16.3.1833.

Miss in Her Teens; or, The Medley of Lovers, by David Garrick (C.G. 1747), 28.3.1833.

Mr. and Mrs. Pringle, by J.T. de Trueba (D.L. 1832), 4.7.1835.

Mrs. Wiggins, by J.T. Allingham (H. 1803), 20.8.1836.

The Mistletoe Bough; or, The Fatal Chest, by C.A. Somerset (Ga. 1834), 26.10.1837.

A Mogul Tale, by Mrs. Elizabeth Inchbald (H. 1784), 28.2.1835.

Monsieur Tonson, by W.T. Moncrieff (D.L. 1821), 26.12.1833.

More Frightened than Hurt, by D.W. Jerrold (S.W. 1821), 28.9.1837.

The Mountaineers, by G. Colman the Younger (H. 1793), 22.6.1833.

The Mutiny at the Nore; or, British Sailors in 1797, by D.W. Jerrold (R.P. 1830), 10.10.1833.

My Husband's Ghost, by J. M. Morton (H. 1836), 26.10.1837.

My Poll and My Partner Joe, by J.T. Haines (S. 1835), 3.4.1837.

Napoleon Buonaparte, Captain of Artillery, General and First Consul, Emperor and Exile, by M.R. Lacy (C.G. 1831), 17.4.1837.

Nettlewig Hall; or, Ten to One, by C.M. Westmacott (D.L. 1831), 17.7.1837.

A New Way to Pay Old Debts, by P. Massinger (1633), 5.5.1836.

No!, by F. Reynolds (Bath 1828), 8.2.1834.

The Nobleman at Home (probably *The Nobleman; or, The Family Quarrel,* by Mrs. Elizabeth Cooper, 1736), 4.8.1836.

No Song, No Supper, by P. Hoare (D.L. 1790), 23.1.1836.

No. 23 John Street (probably *No. 2; or, The Old Figure,* by C.I.M. Dibdin) (S.W. 1817), 15.8.1835.

Nothing Superfluous, by C.I.M. Dibdin (Hull 1829), 2.3.1837.

Oberon; or, The Elf King's Oath, by J.R. Planche (C.G. 1826), 26.12.1836.

Obi; or, Three-Fingered Jack, by J. Fawcett (H. 1800), 30.4.1836.

The Old Oak Chest; or, The Smuggler's Sons and the Robber's Daughter, by Jane M. Scott (S.P. 1816), 6.3.1837.

Old and Young, by J. Poole (D.L. 1822), 28.11.1835.

One O'Clock!; or, The Knight and the Wood Daemon, by M.G. Lewis (Ly. 1811), 20.10.1836.

One, Two, Three, Four, Five by Advertisement (author unknown) (E.O.H. 1819), 14.9.1835.

Othello (Shakespeare), 26.7.1834.

Othello Travestie, by M.G. Dowling (Liverpool 1834), 20.3.1837.

The Padlock, by I. Bickerstaffe (D.L. 1768), 11.9.1837.

Paul Jones; or, The Solway Mariner, by T.J. Dibdin (A. 1827), 23.4.1836.

Paul Pry, by C.I.M. Dibdin (S. 1826), 29.10.1835.

Pedlar's Acre; or, The Wife of Seven Husbands, by G. Almar (S. 1831), 24.8.1835.

Peeping Tom of Coventry, by J. O'Keefe (H. 1784), 25.4.1836.

The Peerless Pool; or, The Early Days of Richard III, by G. Almar (S.W. 1833), 9.10.1837.

The Pet of the Petticoats, by J.B. Buckstone (R.P. 1833), 8.1.1838.

The Pilot: A Tale of the Sea, by W.B. Bernard (Co. 1826), 15.9.1834.

The Pirate; or, The Wild Woman of Zetland, by T.J. Dibdin (S. 1822), 3.11.1834.

Pizarro, by R.B. Sheridan (D.L. 1799), 19.1.1835.

The Point of Honour, by C. Kemble (H. 1800), 11.1.1834.

The Poor Gentleman, by G. Colman the Younger (C.G. 1801), 27.10.1834.

Popping the Question, by J.B. Buckstone (D.L. 1830), 9.10.1834.

The Prompter Puzzled (see *Management*).

The Prophet of the Moor (see *The Fire Raiser*).

"P.S. Come to Dinner", by R.J. Raymond (S. 1830), 22.5.1837.

The Purse; or, The Benevolent Tar, by J.C. Cross (H. 1794), 7.12.1833.

A Race for a Dinner, by T.G. Rodwell (C.G. 1828), 25.4.1833.

Raising the Wind, by J. Kenney (C.G. 1803), 19.4.1834.

The Rake's Progress, by C.I.M. Dibdin (S. 1826), 13.2.1837.

Raymond and Agnes, by M.G. Lewis (Norwich 1809), 4.10.1834.

The Recluse; or, Elshie of the Moor (author unknown), (Edinburgh 1825), 8.4.1837.

The Red Indian; or, The Shipwrecked Mariner and His Faithful Dogs (author unknown), (S. 1824), 25.9.1837.

The Red Rover; or, The Mutiny of the Dolphin, by E. Fitzball (A. 1829), 29.6.1835.

The Rendezvous, by R. Ayton (E.O.H. 1818), 15.2.1834.

The Rent Day, by D.W. Jerrold (D.L. 1832), 8.9.1836.

The Review; or, The Wags of Windsor, by G. Colman the Younger (H. 1800), 12.6.1833.

Richard III (Shakespeare), 26.12.1833.

Rinaldo Rinaldini; or, The Secret Avengers, by T.E. Wilks (S.W. 1836), 20.7.1837.

The Rivals, by R.B. Sheridan (C.G. 1775), 14.11.1833.

The Rival Lovers (ballet), 17.1.1835.

The Road to Ruin, by T. Holcroft (C.G. 1792), 27.8.1834.

The Robber's Wife (author unknown), (C. 1831), 24.4.1834.

Robert le Diable, by E. Fitzball (A. 1832), 9.1.1836.

Rob Roy, by I. Pocock (C.G. 1818), 13.10.1834.

Robinson Crusoe; or, The Bold Bucaniers, by I. Pocock (C.G. 1817), 2.11.1835.

A Roland for an Oliver, by T. Morton (C.G. 1819), 12.10.1837.

Romeo and Juliet (Shakespeare), 28.9.1835.

The Romp, by ——— Lloyd (C.G. 1778), 27.2.1837.

Rosina, by Frances Brooke (C.G. 1782), 15.9.1834.

The Rover's Bride; or, The Bittern's Swamp, by G. Almar (S. 1830), 9.7.1834.

The Ruffian Boy, by T.J. Dibdin (R.C. 1819), 6.2.1837.

Rugantino; or, The Bravo of Venice, by M.G. Lewis (C.G. 1805), 10.10.1836.

The Russian of Bohemia (see *The Ruffian Boy*).

St. Patrick's Day; or, The Scheming Lieutenant, by R.B. Sheridan (C.G. 1775), 18.3.1835.

Salamagundi; or, The Clown's Dish of All Sorts, by C.I.M. Dibdin (S.W. 1818), 20.2.1837.

Sally in Our Alley, by D.W. Jerrold (S. 1830), 28.2.1835.

The Scape-Goat, by J. Poole (C.G. 1825), 13.10.1834.

The Scapegrace, by S. Beazely, Junior (S.W. 1832), 30.11.1835.

The School of Reform; or, How to Rule a Husband, by T. Morton (C.G. 1805), 19.5.1834.

The School for Scandal, by R.B. Sheridan (D.L. 1777), 26.1.1835.

The Sea; or, The Ocean Child (provenance unknown), 28.4.1836.

The Seven Clerks; or, The Three Thieves and the Dreamer, by T.E. Wilks (S. 1834), 29.4.1837.

The Shade; or, Blood for Blood, by C.P. Thompson (S. 1829), 2.10.1834.

Shakespeare's Festival; or, The New Comedy of Errors, by W.T. Moncrieff (S. 1830), 11.3.1837.

She Stoops to Conquer, by O. Goldsmith (C.G. 1773), 26.6.1833.

The Slave, by T. Morton (C.G. 1816), 29.9.1834.

The Sleeping Draught, by S. Penley (D.L. 1818), 26.11.1835.

The Sleep-Walker; or, Which Is the Lady?, by W.C. Oulton (H. 1812), 25.9.1834.

The Soldier's Daughter, by A. Cherry (D.L. 1804), 29.4.1837.

The Somnambulist; or, The Phantom of the Village, by W.T. Moncrieff (C.G. 1828), 20.6.1835.

The Spectre Bridegroom; or, A Ghost in Spite of Himself, by W.T. Moncrieff (D.L. 1821), 22.5.1833.

Speed the Plough, by T. Morton (C.G. 1800), 17.7.1834.

The Spoiled Child, by I. Bickerstaffe (D.L. 1790), 17.6.1833.

The Stranger, by B. Thompson (D.L. 1798), 16.10.1834.

The Sultan; or, A Peep into the Seraglio, by I. Bickerstaffe (D.L. 1775), 16.1.1837.

A Tale of Mystery, by T. Holcroft (C.G. 1802), 3.1.1833.

The Taming of the Shrew (see *Catherine and Petruchio*).

Teddy the Tiler, by G.H. Rodwell (C.G. 1830), 28.4.1834.

Tekeli; or, The Siege of Montgatz, by T.E. Hook (D.L. 1806), 31.3.1834.

Therese; or, the Orphan of Geneva, by J. Kerr (Co. 1821), 5.1.1838.

The Three and the Deuce, by P. Hoare (H. 1795), 6.10.1834.

The Three Hunchbacks, by E. Fitzball (Edinburgh 1826), 31.12.1835.

Three Weeks after Marriage; or, What We Must All Come to, by A. Murphy (C.G. 1776), 2.2.1833.

The Three Wishes; or, Harlequin and Funny Island (pantomime, author unknown), (R.A. 1819), 15.7.1833.

Timour the Tartar, by M.G. Lewis (C.G. 1811), 26.12.1835.

Tom and Jerry; or, Life in London, by W.T. Moncrieff (A. 1821), 4.6.1834.

Tom Bowling, by A.V. Campbell (S.W. 1830), 25.7.1836.

Tom Thumb, by H. Fielding (H. 1730), 29.5.1834.

The Tower of Lochlain; or, The Idiot Son, by D.W. Jerrold (Co.1828), 24.8.1837.

The Tower of Nesle, by G. Almar (S. 1832), 11.7.1835.

Trial by Battle; or, Heaven Defend the Right, by W. Barrymore (Co. 1818), 13.11.1837.

Turning the Tables, by J. Poole (D.L. 1830), 23.4.1836.

The Turnpike Gate; A Musical Entertainment, by T. Knight (C.G. 1799), 25.7.1835

The Two Drovers, by W.H. Murray (Edinburgh 1828), 23.6.1836.

The Two Galley Slaves; or, The Mill of St. Aldervan, by J.H. Payne (D.L. 1822), 19.4.1834.

The Two Gregories; or, Where Did the Money Come from?, by T.J. Dibdin (S. 1821), 4.1.1834.

Two Strings to Your Bow, by A. Cherry (D.L. 1814), 3.5.1834.

An Uncle Too Many, by J. Thomson (B. 1828), 12.1.1834.

The Unfortunate Miss Bailey, by G.A. A'Beckett (S. 1835), 6.11.1837.

Valentine and Orson; or, The Wild Man of Orleans, by T.J. Dibdin (C.G. 1804), 3.11.1834.

The Vampire, by W.T. Moncrieff (Co. 1820), 16.4.1836.

Venice Preserved, by T. Otway (D.G. 1682), 18.10.1834.

Verona and Angelo (see *Angelo; or, The Tyrant of Padua*).

Victorine; or, The Maid of Paris, by C.Z. Barnett (R.P. 1831), 15.1.1838.

The Village Lawyer, by W. Macready (H. 1787), 12.1.1833.

Wallace, by C.E. Walker (C.G. 1820), 21.8.1837.

The Wandering Boys, by J. Kerr (S.W. 1830), 4.6.1835.

Wardock Kennilson; or, The Outcast Mother and Her Son, by E. Fitzball (S. 1824), 16.1.1837.

The Warlock of the Glen (author unknown), (S. 1827), 21.5.1835.

The Waterman; or, The First of August, by C. Dibdin (H. 1774), 24.5.1834.

The Weathercock, by J.T. Allingham (D.L. 1805), 22.9.1834.

What Next?, by C. Dibdin, Junior (D.L. 1816), 23.3.1833.

Whittington and His Cat, by S. Davy (Dublin 1739), 23.2.1835.

Wild Oats; or, The Strolling Gentleman, by J. O'Keefe (C.G. 1791), 19.6.1834.

Will Watch, by J.H. Amherst (R. 1825), 6.11.1837.

William Tell; or, The Origin of Swiss Liberty, by J.S. Knowles (D.L. 1825), 7.5.1836.

William Thompson; or, Which Is He?, by Caroline Boaden (H. 1829), 1.2.1834.

Winning a Husband; or, Seven's the Main, by G. Macfarren (Co. 1819), 23.11.1837.

Wives by Advertisement; or, Courting in the Newspapers, by D.W. Jerrold (Co. 1828), 6.3.1837.

The Wizard of the Moor (see *The Recluse*).

The Wonder: A Woman Keeps a Secret, by Mrs. Susannah Centlivre (D.L. 1714), 26.9.1836.

The Wraith of the Lake (see *All Hallows' Even*).

The Wreck Ashore; or, A Bridegroom from the Sea, by J.B. Buckstone (A. 1830), 9.7.1834.

The Wrecked Mariner and His Dogs (see *The Red Indian*).

X.Y.Z., by G. Colman the Younger (C.G. 1810), 16.10.1834.

Yes or No?, by I. Pocock (H. 1808), 4.5.1833.

The Young Reefer, by G. Soane (Q. 1835), 15.10.1836.

The Youthful Queen, Christine of Sweden, by C. Shannon (D.L. 1828), 9.2.1835.

Zara (or *The Tragedy of Zara*), by A. Hill (D.L. 1735), 27.2.1837.

BIBLIOGRAPHY

1. Manuscripts

The Elyard Papers (MS in Mitchell Library).
ELLIS, GEORGE CRESSALL, "Account Book", (MS in Kean Collection, Folger Shakespeare Library, Washington, U.S.A.)
Governor Darling's Despatches (MS in Mitchell Library).
Plays in Sydney, Vol. I, 1789 to 1840 (MS in Mitchell Library).
Reports of Vessels Arrived, 1833. Vol. I (5204), (MS in Archives Office of New South Wales).

2. Newspapers

(In Sydney's Mitchell and Public Libraries)
The Atlas
The Australian
The Australian Journal
Bent's News
The Blossom
The Colonist
The Currency Lad
The Examiner
The Free Press and Commercial Journal
The Gleaner
Hill's Life in N.S.W.
Illustrated Sydney News
Sydney Gazette
Sydney Herald

Sydney Monitor
Sydney Times
Weekly Observer
The Australian Builder and Land Advertiser (Melbourne)
The Art Journal (London)
Illustrated London News
The Times (London)

3. Books and Articles

ARUNDELL, DENNIS. *The Story of Sadler's Wells 1683-1964.* London: Hamish Hamilton, 1965.

Australian Dictionary of Biography. Vol. II. Melbourne: Melbourne University Press, 1967.

BAGOT, ALEC. *Coppin the Great.* Melbourne: Melbourne University Press, 1965.

BATESON, CHARLES. *The Convict Ships 1787–1868.* Glasgow: Brown, Son & Ferguson, 1959.

BENNETT, GEORGE. *Wanderings in New South Wales.* London: Bentley, 1834.

BERGMAN, G.F.J. "Solomon Levey in Sydney: From Convict to Merchant Prince", *Royal Australian Historical Society Journal and Proceedings,* Vol. XLIX, Pt. 6, March 1964.

BERTIE, CHARLES H. *The Story of the Royal Hotel and the Theatre Royal Sydney.* Sydney: Simmons Limited, 1927.

BLIGH, N.M. "Mirror Curtains", *Theatre Notebook,* Vol. XV, 1960–61.

BOOTH, MICHAEL. *English Melodrama.* London: Herbert Jenkins, 1965.

"BOZ" (Charles Dickens). *Memoirs of Grimaldi.* London: George Routledge and Sons, 1838.

BRERETON, AUSTIN. *The Lyceum and Henry Irving.* London: Lawrence and Bullen Limited, 1903.

BREWER, F.C. *The Drama and Music in New South Wales.* Sydney: Government Printer, 1892.

BROWN, T. ALLSTON. *A History of the New York Stage.* New York: 1903. Reissued Blom, 1964.

BUTLER, E.M. (ed.) *A Regency Visitor. The English Tour of Prince Puckler-Muskau. Described in His Letters 1826–1828.* Translated by Sarah Austin. London: Collins, 1957.

BYRNE, M. ST. CLARE. "Early Multiple Settings in England", *Theatre Notebook*, Vol. VIII, 1953–54.

CLARK, WILLIAM SMITH. *The Irish Stage in the County Towns 1720–1800*. London: Oxford University Press, 1965.

CLINTON-BADDELEY, V. *All Right on the Night*. London: Putnam, 1954.

COLE, J.W. *The Life and Theatrical Times of Charles Kean*. Vol. I. 2nd ed.; London: Richard Bentley, 1859.

CORRY, PERCY. "Richmond Preserved", *Tabs,* Vol. XX, No. 2, 1962.

DISHER, MAURICE W. *Blood and Thunder*. London: Frederick Muller Ltd., 1949.

———. *Melodrama Plots That Thrilled*. London: Rockliff, 1954.

———. *Victorian Song*. London: Phoenix House, 1955.

DOWD, B.T., and FOSTER, WILLIAM. *The History of the Waverley Municipal District*. Waverley Municipal Council, 1959.

DUCHARTE, PIERRE LOUIS. *The Italian Comedy*. Translated by Randolph T. Weaver. London: George G. Harrap & Co. Ltd., 1929.

DUNCAN, BARRY. *The St. James's Theatre*. London: Barrie and Rockliff, 1964.

EDDISON, ROBERT. "Souvenirs du Théâtre Anglais à Paris", *Theatre Notebook,* Vol. IX, 1954–55.

FOWLES, J. *Sydney in 1848*. Sydney: D. Wall, 1848.

GASCOYNE, BAMBER. *World Theatre*. London: Ebury Press, 1968.

GRICE, F. "The Theatre Royal at Worcester", *Theatre Notebook,* Vol. X, 1955–56.

Grove's Dictionary of Music and Musicians. 5th ed.; London: Macmillan & Co. Ltd., 1954.

GUEST, IVOR. "Parodies of 'Giselle' on the English Stage, 1841–1871", *Theatre Notebook,* Vol. IX, 1954–55.

HARDWICK, J.M.D. (ed.) *Emigrant in Motley. The Unpublished Letters of Charles and Ellen Kean*. London: Rockliff, 1954.

HARE, ARNOLD. *The Georgian Theatre in Wessex*. London: Phoenix House, 1958.

HARTNOLL, PHYLLIS (ed.) *The Oxford Companion to the Theatre*. 2nd ed.; London: Oxford University Press, 1957.

HODGKINSON, J.D., and POGSON, REX. *The Early Manchester Theatre*. London: Anthony Blond, 1960.

HUGHES, LEO. *A Century of English Farce*. Princeton, N.J.: Princeton University Press, 1956.

251

IRELAND, JOSEPH N. *Records of the New York Stage from 1750 to 1860.* New York: 1866. Reissued London: Blom, 1966.

JACKSON, ALLAN S., and MORROW, JOHN C. "Aqua-Scenes at Sadler's Wells Theatre 1804–1824", *Ohio State University Theatre Collection Bulletin,* No. 9, 1962.

JEFFERSON, JOSEPH. *The Autobiography of Joseph Jefferson.* London: T. Fisher Unwin, 1890.

LAWRENCE, W.J. *The Life of Gustavus Vaughan Brooke.* Belfast: W. and G. Baird, 1892.

LENNEP, WILLIAM VAN. "Dykwynkyn of Old Drury", *Theatre Annual.* New York: 1946.

LEWES, G.H. *Dramatic Essays. Criticisms from "The Leader".* London: Scott, 1896.

McGUIRE, PAUL, with ARNOTT, BETTY and McGUIRE, FRANCES MARGARET. *The Australian Theatre.* Melbourne: Oxford University Press, 1948.

MACLEHOSE, J. *New South Wales and Port Phillip General Post Office Directory for 1839.* Sydney: James Maclehose, 1839.

MORLEY, MALCOM. *The Old Marylebone Theatre.* London: St. Marylebone Society Publication No. 2, 1960.

———. *The Royal West London Theatre.* London: St. Marylebone Society Publication No. 6, 1962.

NAGLER, A.M. "Goethe's Ideal Spectator", *Theatre Annual.* New York: 1951.

———. "The Fürttenbach Theatre in Ulm", *Theatre Annual.* New York: 1953.

———. *A Source Book in Theatrical History.* 2nd ed.; New York: Dover Publications Inc., 1959.

NICOLL, ALLARDYCE. *A History of English Drama 1660–1900.* London: Cambridge University Press, reprinted 1955.

ODELL, G.C.D. *Annals of the New York Stage,* Vol. V. New York: Columbia University Press, 1931.

OPPENHEIM, HELEN. "The Author of 'The Hibernian Father'; An Early Colonial Playwright", *Australian Literary Studies.* Vol. II, No. 4, 1966.

REES, ABRAHAM (ed.) *Cyclopaedia, or Universal Dictionary of Arts, Sciences, and Literature.* London: J.F. and C. Rivington, 1819.

RICE, CHARLES. *The London Theatre in the Eighteen Thirties.* London: Society for Theatre Research, 1950.

RODERICK, COLIN (ed.) "Giacomo di Rosenberg" (James Tucker), *Ralph Rashleigh, or The Life of an Exile*. Sydney: Angus & Robertson, 1952.

ROWELL, GEORGE (ed.) *Nineteenth Century Plays*. The World's Classics Series. London: Oxford University Press, 1953.

———. *The Victorian Theatre*. London: Oxford University Press, 1956.

RUSSELL, W. CLARK. *Representative Actors*. London: Frederick Warne & Co. n.d. (*ca.* 1860).

SCOTT, CLEMENT. *The Drama of Yesterday and Today*. London: Macmillan and Co. Limited, 1899.

SHATTUCK, CHARLES. "A Victorian Stage Manager: George Cressall Ellis", *Theatre Notebook*, Vol. XXII, 1968.

SOUTHERN, RICHARD. *The Georgian Playhouse*. London: Pleiades Books Limited, 1948.

———. *Changeable Scenery*. London: Faber and Faber Limited, 1952.

———. *The Seven Ages of the Theatre*. London: Faber and Faber Limited, 1962.

SOUTHERN, RICHARD, and BROWN, IVOR. *The Georgian Theatre, Richmond, Yorkshire*. Yorkshire: The Theatre Trust, 1962.

SPRAGUE, ARTHUR COLBY. *Shakespeare and the Actors*. Cambridge, Mass.: Harvard University Press, 1944.

———. *Shakespeare's Histories*. London: Society for Theatre Research, 1964.

———. *The Doubling of Parts in Shakespeare's Plays*. London: Society for Theatre Research, 1966.

THOMPSON, ALAN REYNOLDS. *The Anatomy of Drama*. 2nd ed.; Berkeley, Calif.: University of California Press, 1946.

VERGE, WILL GRAVES. *John Verge, Early Australian Architect*. Sydney: Wentworth Books, 1962.

WHITE, ERIC WALTER. *The Rise of English Opera*. London: John Lehmann, 1951.

WILSON, ARTHUR H. *A History of the Philadelphia Theatre 1835 to 1855*. Philadelphia: University of Pennsylvania Press, and London: Oxford University Press, 1935.

WILSON, A.E. *East End Entertainment*. London: Barker, 1954.

WINSTANLEY, MRS. ELIZA. *Shifting Scenes in Theatrical Life*. London: Routledge, Warne & Routledge, 1859.

Year Book of Facts in Science and Art. London: David Bogue, 1855.

253

INDEX

254

seating, 105; opening prologue, 107–109; staging at, 112–26; first anniversary, 138; adverse reports, 141; new season, 145; theatre attacked, 150; why theatre has "failed", 183; lessees take over, 184; altered and repainted, 186; lessees farm out lease, 189; Levey offered management, 189; offer withdrawn, 191; Wyatt new lessee, 191; repainted, redecorated, 191; theatre criticized, 198; Levey back as proprietor, 202; changes in auditorium, 205; to be widened, and lit with gas, 209; saloon theatre to be fitted up again, 209; attack on, 214; support for, 214; theatre attacked, 219; closed, 225; desultory attempts to reopen, 226; Wyatt buys, 226; destroyed by fire, 227

Theatre Royal (1875), 232
Thorne, Charles R., 232, 234
Three Wishes, 96
Three Wives of Madrid, 178
Tippety-witchet, or Pantomimical Paroxysms, 57
Tom and Jerry, 21
Tonti, Lorenzo, 63
Town and Country, 180
Trente Ans, 143
Two Friends, 172

Underwood, James, 12, 16, 19, 22
Used Up, 177

Vale, Mr., 82, 96, 99

Venice Preserved, 86, 151, 173
Verge, John, 78, 103
Vestris, Madame, 87, 176
Victoria Theatre, vi, 105, 163, 164, 171, 191, 192, 225, 232
Victorian theatre, vi
Village Lawyer, 63, 80, 83, 86, 136
Virginius, 178

Wages, 93, 127, 144
Wallack, Lester, 177
Waller, D. Wilmarth, 232, 233
Waller, Emma, 232, 233
Walnut Theatre, 178
Ward, Mrs., 96
Wardock Kennilson, 178
Warner, Mrs., 177
Waverley, 22
Wedding Day, 172
Welder's Wedge Box, 11
Wentworth, William Charles, 8, 27, 69
Weston, Mrs., 85, 89, 90
Wheatley, Mr., 206
Wheel of Fortune, 175
White, Mr., 136, 206
Wilson, John Thomas, 192, 194
Windmill, 181
Windmill, Levey's, 50
Windsor theatricals, 181
Winstanley, Ann, 149, 168
Winstanley, Eliza, 149, 151, 163, 165–82, 185, 206, 226
Winstanley, Robert, 167, 168
Winstanley, William, 168
Winters, Mr., 206, 226
Winter's Tale, 175
Wyatt, Joseph, 100, 190, 191, 192, 195, 198, 201, 225, 226, 232